SHAKESPEARE : THE ROMAN PLAYS

Shakespeare: The Roman Plays

DEREK TRAVERSI

STANFORD UNIVERSITY PRESS
STANFORD, CALIFORNIA

PUBLISHER'S NOTE

The edition used as a basis for the act, scene
and line references printed next to the quota-
tions in the text is the Oxford University
Press *Complete Works of Shakespeare*, edited by
W. J. Craig.

Stanford University Press
Stanford, California, 94305
© 1963 by Derek Traversi
ISBN 0 8047 0182 2
Library of Congress Catalog Card Number 63–15218
Printed in Great Britain
Fifth printing 1973

Preface

IT IS strange that, since M. W. MacCullum's long study published in 1910, it is hard to find a single work exclusively devoted to Shakespeare's major plays on Roman history. Two of these at least are among his masterpieces, and the unity of theme which the subject provides would, it might have been thought, have made this the obvious subject for a book; but, though essays and passages of insight abound, it seems that apart from Maurice Charney's study of the plays (Oxford, 1961), which offers an approach different from that here attempted, a complete and comprehensive study based on a modern approach is lacking. The present volume attempts to go some way towards filling this gap. I am conscious that its method, which is that of following the text in detail, may not always make for easy reading; but there is so little superfluous matter in Shakespeare's greater plays, and so much depends upon the sequence of action and the meaningful juxtaposition of incidents and characters, that I have found it impossible to depart from the order he established.

In view of what has just been said about earlier criticism of these plays, it is not easy to say exactly how much this book owes to previous writers. Bradley's lectures on *Antony and Cleopatra* and *Coriolanus* include some of his best work; J. Middleton Murry wrote admirably on the Roman plays on more than one occasion, and I have found stimulation in the views of Mr John Danby and Professor L. C. Knights, more especially on *Antony and Cleopatra*. Once again, the most ambitious modern study of the plays is that put forward by Professor G. Wilson Knight in *The Imperial Theme* (Oxford, 1930); but, though what he has written is, as usual, full of insights which no later critic can afford to ignore and which have not always received due acknowledgement, I have found that his general view of the plays, and more particularly of *Antony and Cleopatra* – possibly the supreme test of balanced Shakespearian criticism – is too full of personal idiosyncrasies to be acceptable as a whole. Readers of my book will no doubt find other echoes, but these will have been the result of past reading not specifically undertaken for the preparation of this book.

Short studies of *Antony and Cleopatra* and *Coriolanus* were published some years ago in my book *Approach to Shakespeare* (Second edition New York, 1956: London, 1957).

DEREK TRAVERSI *Madrid, September 1962*

Contents

I
Introduction

I

Introduction

SHAKESPEARE'S MAJOR plays on Roman history span between them the supremely creative years of his dramatic career. The earliest of the three, *Julius Caesar*, was separated by no great distance in time from the two parts of *Henry IV* and *Henry V* and is concentrated, like those plays, upon the interplay of personal motives and public necessity; whilst the other two – *Antony and Cleopatra* and *Coriolanus* – belong to the dramatist's last years and combine an acute understanding of historical processes with the illuminating presence of a distinctive tragic vision. Thus variously situated in time the plays, by bringing together into a mutually enriching unity two of the principal themes of Shakespeare's mature work – those expressed respectively in the historical chronicles and in the series of great tragedies which followed them – constitute one of the undoubted peaks of his achievement.

The historical matter of all three plays is principally derived from Plutarch's *Lives of the Noble Greeks and Romans*, as translated into English from the French of Amyot by Thomas North.[1] The fact is important for an understanding of the plays themselves; for, whereas it is, generally speaking, true that Shakespeare's acknowledged masterpieces – *Hamlet*, *Macbeth*, *King Lear* – owe little more than the barest outline of their plots to the comparatively artless narratives from which they derive, in the Roman tragedies we are conscious of dealing with what might almost be called a collaboration. It is well known that long passages from North's highly workmanlike translation were almost directly versified by Shakespeare; but a comparison of the relevant passages, which has often been undertaken,[2] show that the dramatist, in following his original closely, was in fact developing his own conception, being fully himself. The material to his hand having been, so to speak, predigested, the poet was free to reserve himself for his deeper purposes, to slip in with unobtrusive mastery the transforming word or image required

---

[1] North's translation was first published in 1579, and there were further editions in 1595, 1603, and 1612.

[2] The material for such a study may be found in Kenneth Muir's *Shakespeare's Sources*, Vol. I (London, 1956).

to illuminate the dramatic presentation of motive or to bring out the full implications of his developing action. The style of these plays, far from reflecting a pedestrian process of versification, shows a unique combination of narrative lucidity, achieved through the easy, almost conversational use of spoken rhythms and vernacular phrases, with poetic intensities that flow effortlessly from this foundation whenever the state of the action so requires. This marriage of colloquial ease with the heights of emotional expression is achieved with a consistency hardly paralleled elsewhere in Shakespeare's work. By the side of these plays, even some of the effects of the great tragedies seem to have been reached with effort, to represent a sensibility strained to the utmost in the intensity of its expression of feeling, its reaction to emotional stresses; whilst the verse of the final comedies seems at times to achieve its symbolic effects through conventions of greater and more artificial complexity.

What is true of style applies equally to the handling of action. Beyond the word, the image, and the single dramatized utterance Shakespeare found in Plutarch a narrative that moved easily and consistently, the work of a writer who saw clearly the ends he had in view and disposed his material accordingly. This unclouded narrative logic he was content to incorporate into plays which are, in a very real sense, the culmination of his life-long concern with the dramatic chronicle. When we come to look at the Roman tragedies with an eye to critical exposition, we find it difficult, if not impossible, to break up their plots for discussion in any truly significant way. In both *Antony and Cleopatra* and *Coriolanus* – *Julius Caesar*, written so much earlier, stands a little apart in this respect from the two greater masterpieces – we are conscious of the smooth progress of a single narrative current, unimpeded from the beginning of the action to its logical conclusion. Events follow one another easily and without turning back upon themselves: the tragic sequence has a single trajectory, and the dominating purpose is written into the action for all to see and participate in its impact. There is in these plays nothing like the elaborate contrasts which convey the universal vision of *King Lear*: contrasts which have in the world of that tragedy their own splendid justification, leading us progressively into the depths of slavery and redemption in nature itself, but which would here be out of place. Neither is there anything – to take an example closer to the political vision with which the Roman plays are in part, if not exclusively, concerned – like the shifts of scene from court to tavern, Westminster to Eastcheap, the rhetoric of high policy to Falstaff's penetrating comment, in the two *Henry IV* plays.[1]

[1] For a study of the structure of these plays see my *Shakespeare: from 'Richard II' to 'Henry V'* (London, 1958).

Effects of equal subtlety are obtained within the development of a single narrative that is neither interrupted nor held back for comment, but which moves on continuously, assimilating all its vital contrasts, from a clearly defined beginning to an equally determined end. The admirable lucidity of *Antony and Cleopatra*, which reflects a dramatic imagination working at the height of its power, owes much of its effect to the foundation upon which it so confidently rests.

Stylistically, therefore, and in the matter of narrative exposition, Shakespeare owed much to North's gifts as a translator. More directly from Plutarch, on the other hand, and through him from the great tradition of historical moralizing which he initiated, he derived not merely a story, the presentation of a sequence of events, but a highly dramatic reading of history itself. The classical historian consistently dramatized his protagonists, providing them with set speeches to correspond to moments of decisive importance and, in more general terms, selecting the episodes he chose to describe with an eye to their dramatic possibilities; moreover, he combined with this highly selective treatment of events a firm belief in the value of history as affording moral examples useful to posterity. Shakespeare's attitude – it is necessary to repeat – was not limited to the reproduction of his source. It reflected deep personal meditation, developed through the greater part of his career as a dramatist, upon the nature and significance of public processes and upon their presentation in the theatre; but the classical tendency to endow the behaviour of the hero with an exemplary significance fitted in naturally enough with his own dramatic interests, and more particularly with his own presentation of the exalted and isolated figure of the king in the earlier chronicle plays. The Roman political leader – upon whom an almost intolerable weight of responsibility devolved from the very nature of his public vocation – could now also be considered in the light of experience gained through the presentation of successive tragic heroes; this added greatly to the depth and universality of the dramatic conception.

Following this general line of thought, it is possible to distinguish successive stages, answering to the dates of the respective plays, in Shakespeare's treatment of his Roman political themes. In *Julius Caesar*, he is presenting the most familiar and obviously dramatic of all Roman subjects, one moreover which prompted in his own time a great number of passionate and conflicting judgements.[1] The issue lay, very broadly speaking, between those who abhorred the murder of a man raised to authority, on the one hand, and those who, on the

[1] See on this subject, Professor T. J. B. Spencer's essay, 'Shakespeare and the Elizabethan Romans' published in *Shakespeare Survey 10*. (Cambridge, 1957).

other, were ready to applaud the elimination of a tyrant. Either view had universal implications, relevant to Shakespeare's own times, and rendered more weighty by the fact that Caesar's death represented a turning-point in the longest and most influential historical process, the one with the greatest exemplary validity, known to his age. Shakespeare's treatment of this situation is marked by a characteristic refusal to fall into simplification, to follow the emotional excesses almost universal around him. *Julius Caesar* is still close in spirit to the detached analysis of public behaviour which marks the English historical plays[1] and which, indeed, the removal from a contemporary or national subject made it easier to observe. As in the English sequence, he accepts the necessity of order in public affairs – this conviction had only recently prompted the reaction against the threat or reality of civil war which emerges so clearly from his later chronicle dramas – and is ready to believe that, in Rome and at the moment under consideration, this order rests in some sense upon Caesar's exercise of power; but he is also notably less than willing to suggest what form the dictator's rule might have taken or to accept at his own valuation the self-appointed keystone of this order in Rome. The result is a play in which dramatic suspense is supported by a keen and detached insight into human motives. Throughout the earlier part of the action, before Caesar's murder, there is a sense of discrepancy between the massive public projection and the human reality of the dictator. This, in turn, is balanced by a similar ambivalence in the conspirators who oppose him. Their fear of Caesar is shown to be in part, though only in part, justified; but equally, once the object of their hostility has been removed by their own action, they collapse disastrously into rivalry and self-annihilation. The play, in fact, concentrates rather upon the deed and the behaviour of those concerned in it than upon the abstract political principles involved. At the end of the play an order is indeed restored in Rome, but one which, we must surely feel, is invested with no particular institutional prestige, which is portrayed indeed with an acute and rather disillusioned detachment. In the process of being removed from England to Rome the study of personal motivation in politics achieves a greater degree of impersonality and so, by the very nature of things, a wider human relevance, a greater universality.

In *Antony and Cleopatra*, written at the other end of Shakespeare's great tragic period, the universal issues which underlie the public action are further stressed, but in a spirit of political realism which is finally similar. In no play is intelligent and scrupulous insight into the variety and complexity of personal motives more revealingly wedded

[1] Echoes from the earlier plays have often been noted in *Julius Caesar*.

to a universal public theme. Whatever else *Antony and Cleopatra* may be, it contains within itself the presentation of a world in which ripe universal intuitions of empire turn persistently towards decay. We are aware of strife between the dissolute but still strangely vital corruption associated with Egypt and the cold competence of Rome reaching out through firm self-assertion to the benefits of universal rule. The human and the political elements of the tragedy are consistently balanced one against the other. In the political order Octavius prevails, and we would not have it otherwise. In a somewhat similar way the Lancastrian ideal had prevailed in the *Henry IV* plays and had been confirmed by national triumph in *Henry V*. In neither case are we left in doubt that it must be so, that the defeat of the principle of authority and ordered rule would have meant ruin for the universal empire of Rome, just as that of Henry IV or his son by their enemies would have brought riot and misrule to England. Order is, in fact, a necessary, an indispensable good; but it is affirmed, in the political sphere, through a choice that involves the rejection, as incompatible, of certain possibilities of life. From this point of view, and without seeking to minimize the enormous differences that separate them, the rejection of Falstaff and the death of Cleopatra share a common tragic implication.

In *Coriolanus*, finally, Shakespeare produced, if not the greatest of his tragedies, the most balanced and complete of all his political conceptions. The very fact that, unlike the other two plays, Shakespeare seems to have been alone in treating this theme as material for a play, may indicate the depth and originality of the interests which attracted him to it. The strains and divisions of Rome, all hinted at in Plutarch's account, are shown as operating within a unity, the seeming contraries bound together as aspects of a whole which is greater than any of its parts; the conflicting elements in the hero's own nature, of which it is his tragedy to be imperfectly aware, stand in relation to a society divided against itself, tending fatally to its own ruin. The realism of treatment which Shakespeare largely draws from his source is gathered by him into a superior unity of vision, the various aspects of the theme bound together in a dramatic presentation which is distinctively his own.

This, however, is only the first part of the story. The political presentation of Shakespeare's Roman themes is indeed, for all its originality, a development from earlier work, and the findings of the English historical plays are still discernible in them; but, between the earlier series and the two greater tragedies there lie, not simply Plutarch's severe conception of the classical hero, but Shakespeare's own great plays of the intervening years. In the isolated and superhuman eminence of the king, indeed, as the English chronicle plays present him, the tragic conception is already foreshadowed[1]. We are required to share as spectators the difficult nature of his choices, to participate in the burden which his vocation imposes upon him. In the great tragedies this same sense of participation, of sharing in an action proceeding from the presence of a flaw in a single exalted nature, receives its highest expression, adding a new and universal dimension to individual perversity and its expiation through the ruin which it brings upon itself; and in the Roman dramas this tragic content is finally allied to the more detached public vision of the earlier chronicles. The universe of *Antony and Cleopatra*, the more narrowly concentrated world of *Coriolanus*, are not indeed those of *King Lear*. They are a universe and world less metaphysically, more politically conceived, and this difference is reflected in the type of construction we have already discussed, which turns neither upon the revealing interrelation of contrasted plots nor upon the presence of symbolic overtones, but upon the direct presentation of unfolding events; but it is equally true to say that, if *King Lear* had not been written, Shakespeare could not have exploited to the full the implications of his classical themes.

The vast extension of the poetic resources revealed in the later Roman plays is, indeed, related to the growth of a tragic vision which, in the process of giving them new meaning, a wider relevance to human experience, finally transforms their political content. Already, in the series of plays on English history, political processes are shown, as the dramatist must show them, in terms of individual motives and personal idiosyncrasies. The same feature, extended and developed, can be found in the Roman plays. At the centre of the public scene there is placed in each case the figure of a hero who is faced, in his related greatness and weakness, with a *choice* the consequences of which are of decisive importance, not only for himself, but for the world around him. This development was already implicit in the great tragedies of the preceding period. Othello, Macbeth, and Lear each, after his own fashion, *chooses*; but each choice is affected by the fact that the protagonist is a public figure and that his decision embraces not only his own well-being but that of a state, an organized society in a very real sense dependent upon its head. At this point again Shakespeare, when he turned to his Roman subjects, found congenial material in Plutarch, who regards his heroes with a varying mixture of admiration and mistrust. Fascinated by the eminent position of the hero and by the scope of the example which this confers upon him, Plutarch consistently sees this greatness in contrast to universal human frailty, the presence of weakness and –

[1] See the relevant passages in my studies of *Henry IV – Part II* and *Henry V* (op. cit.).

perhaps above all – of a lack of true self-knowledge. This last tragic quality is shared in one form or another, by all the great heroes of Shakespeare's mature tragedies. It is perhaps best exemplified, before the plays now under consideration, in Othello who, noble and generous as he is, is destroyed by failings which he is unable to understand but which – brought out as they are by certain aspects of the world in which he finds himself a stranger and by the action upon him of malevolent external forces – finally shatter his ideal consistency, make his life intolerable to himself, and lead inexorably to his ruin.

In the course of the Roman plays, this relation of the hero to his surroundings can be followed through various stages. In *Julius Caesar*, the tragic structure is divided, significantly, between two poles of interest: Caesar, the dominating political presence in the action, is not, as he would have been in a later tragedy, its hero. The dilemma, whether to kill or not to kill the dictator, is concentrated upon Brutus, who thus becomes the nearest approach to a hero, a central tragic protagonist, which this play can offer. Brutus is impelled to act as he does by imperatives which his whole being seems to confirm, but is none the less unable to accept fully the consequences to which his decision would lead him. He becomes therefore at once leader and tool, a man divided against himself who strives in vain to understand his own motives. The character is one which, reflecting certain intuitions of *Hamlet*, also has points of contact with *Macbeth*[1], but fails to realize the full possibilities of either: a character who, rendered ineffective by the divisions in his own nature and by the contradiction between his own generous instinct and the spurious nature of the arguments which impel him to action, is finally brought to ruin.

Antony, in *Antony and Cleopatra*, is much more firmly at the centre of his tragedy. He, too, is faced, against a vastly more universal background, with the necessity of making his choice. Cleopatra, representing with Egypt a combination of life and corruption, stands at one limit of his range; at the other, the figure of Octavius recalls the position he might have occupied as a public figure in the world, stands for Rome, for a cold practicality of outlook and, with it, for a dedication to his public destiny and to universal purposes. Between these two extremes, Antony makes his choice, suffers the tragedy which is involved for him in the making of it, and experiences – but in death, where alone he can do so – the exaltation it implies. Antony surrenders himself to an emotion which might have been of its nature ennobling, but which is here abstracted from the rest of life,

---

[1] This point has been well made by G. Wilson Knight in his study of the play (see *The Wheel of Fire*, Oxford, 1930).

pursued as a part at the expense of the whole. He sacrifices his imperial responsibilities, his relation to the world around him, in favour of a love which can only assert itself against a background of, and as a contrast to, the death which it finally implies. In no play, perhaps, are deep emotion and keen intelligence more marvellously combined. The contradiction which the tragedy so superbly presents is one which – from the point of view of the author's balance of understanding – can have no single and inclusive resolution. The action presents only the consequences, on either side, of a choice that brings with it at the same time a sense of passionate and living fulfilment and, as its inescapable complement, the loss, with moral integrity and public respect, of life itself.

In *Coriolanus*, written at nearly the same time, the relationship between the hero and his surroundings is more closely dovetailed than, perhaps, in any preceding play. In the notably smaller Roman world projected by this tragedy, Coriolanus is portrayed as a hero indeed, but as one whose heroism is largely the product of narrow class prejudice and defective human relationships; the situation, in fact, is one which at once imposes upon him a measure of superiority and irretrievably flaws him. The prejudices born of his situation Coriolanus exalts, too readily, into the rigid principles which finally separate him from his fellow men; and these principles at once support him in his true martial prowess and become – by virtue of this same unnatural exaltation, this isolation from the world around him – a focal point for the deep divisions in Roman society which have, in the last analysis, produced them. By a concentration of these conflicting factors upon a nature deficient in elementary self-understanding, Coriolanus is led to betray his better nature, wrecking his prized integrity and bringing his own city, whose fortunes he has, not without presumption, equated with his own, to the verge of a disaster from which only his own downfall and death can finally save it.

The significance of these great plays resolves itself, accordingly, into a question of the relationship between the whole, the complete and fully integrated experience which life, properly interpreted, in each case offers, and the partial aspects which, necessary and·valid in themselves, lead when followed with passionate exclusiveness to self-destruction. The earlier historical plays had seen the whole, politically conceived, in the relationship of loyalty which, in a united nation, binds the subject to his king; they stressed the need for unity as the foundation for society and hinted, in the study of kingship which accompanied the unfolding of the national theme, at the presence of certain stresses upon the figure of the monarch, at the sacrifice of common human qualities involved in the almost inhuman impersonality required by the royal office.[1] In the intervening years, meanwhile, the tragedies penetrated progressively deeper into the nature of personal unity and of the strains laid upon it by the promptings of obscure and imperfectly understood instinctive forces. They concentrate increasingly upon the figure of a hero – Othello, Macbeth, even Lear – in some sense divided against himself, endangering the reasonable unity of nature by the disproportionate following of some exclusive and absorbing passion of whose true perversity they are, initially at least, largely ignorant. This progress to personal disaster takes place in the great tragedies against an expanding pattern of ruin. Good and evil – if we may use these terms without any sense of preconceived moralizing conceptions – come to be seen in terms of harmony and division, the fulfilment and the frustration respectively of life itself, and the effects of evil, once introduced by the hero's wilful act of personal choice, are bound to work themselves out through disharmony and death. A tragic and remorseless determinism emerges as the result of these misplaced attempts to follow the illusion of absolute autonomy at the expense of natural and freely accepted order. 'Things bad begun make strong themselves by ill':[2] these words represent in *Macbeth*, the philosophy of illusion by which the central protagonist seeks to justify his perverse choices, and at the end of which can lie only slavery to external circumstances and annihilation. 'Nothing will come of nothing':[3] Lear speaks for himself, in the early stages of his self-inflicted passion, more truly than he yet knows, and when at the end of the course upon which his self-will has embarked him,' the great rage'[4] of his self-engendered conflict has been mortified in his ruined frame, utter exhaustion has to precede such spiritual recovery as is still open to him.

In the Roman plays a similar attitude finds expression on the somewhat different level implied by the public context of each personal tragedy. The political and the personal elements, which Shakespeare had elsewhere treated with varying degrees of emphasis but which seem always to have been associated in his maturing thought, are now brought together in a new and distinctively Roman vision for which Plutarch provided the foundation. The *whole* has become again, much as it had been in the English historical plays but on a vaster and more universal scale, an ordered society, at the head of which stands the individual hero, at once indispensable

[1] Henry IV on his death-bed, Henry V before Agincourt both express their sense of isolation and disappointment.

[2] *Macbeth*. [III. ii. 55.]

[3] *King Lear*. [I. i. 92.]

[4] *King Lear*. [IV. vii. 78.]

B

to its functioning and needing its support, confirming by the quality of his public choices its unity and purpose. He finds himself obliged to choose between reason and passion, between the elements in his personality which make for harmony and fulfilment and those which lead to his isolation and final undoing, by forcing him to follow unilaterally a self-centred impulse. It is this that confers upon the hero the tragic stature, emanating from his nature, which now illuminates the society which conditions it and so gives to these plays their distinctive and unparalleled scope. The tragedy proceeds in each case from flaws in the hero's character, which reflect themselves in his failure to discharge the public duty which his situation imposes upon him; but, it has to be added, the failure itself is one which, by its very nature, vindicates the forces of unity and integration which his choice has spurned and, in one play at least, in *Antony and Cleopatra*, the partial passion which leads the protagonists inexorably to ruin is itself shown as possessing true nobility and a measure of transforming greatness.

2
Julius Caesar

2

Julius Caesar

THE ACTION of *Julius Caesar* turns, in the tense simplicity of its narrative, upon an event of unique historical importance. Round this event, with its varied and often contrasted significances for the Elizabethan mind,[1] Shakespeare has developed a pattern of political passions which answers to a closely-knit dramatic plan. The early scenes show Caesar and his enemies converging upon the striking of a blow which has, in its inevitability, in the universal concern it focuses upon itself, the quality of a tragic sacrifice. The deed itself and the action which follows from it lead, in the central episodes of the tragedy, to the conflict of public and personal motives involved in the clash between Brutus and Antony over the dictator's dead body. Finally, in the concluding stages, the consequences of the murder are revealed through their effect upon each of the contending parties. The conspirators, brought to see their motives in the unflattering light of reality, collapse into mutual recrimination and confessed futility; whilst, against a background of practical assertion and ruthless calculation of the odds, a new Roman order rises to replace that which has been so wilfully destroyed.

To this presentation of events, as direct and self-explanatory as any to be found in his work, Shakespeare has added a study of character and motive more complex and varied than may immediately be realized. Although every thought and action is concentrated upon Caesar's assumption of unique and unlimited power and upon the doom to which this leads, the dictator's own appearances are brief and transitory. Such insight as we gain into his personality and motives emerges principally through the observations of his declared enemies; and these in turn, as they seek from one another the confirmation of their intentions, reveal the weaknesses and contradictions of their own motives. The action, in other words, turns, in what is coming to be the typical Shakespearian manner, upon an interplay of personalities in contrast. No motive or claim is accepted at its own valuation, each presented as much through the reactions it arouses in others as in itself. The key to the motivation of the tragedy,

[1] See, for an account of these significances, Professor Spencer's essay already quoted (see footnote to p. 11 above).

which lends variety to its taut dramatic structure, lies in a contrast
between what men propose and what, as political beings, they in fact
achieve.

I

The play opens with a first passing glimpse of Caesar in his isolated
and uneasy eminence. As the action proceeds, and his path
approaches that of his enemies, the strange alloy of grandeur and
frailty in his nature will be rather more intimately revealed; but,
meanwhile, with the 'holiday' mood of the citizens ominously
blended with the high-pitched, hysterical emotion of the tribunes as
they seek to stir up resentment against him, he steps for a first brief,
revealing moment into the rising clamour of expectation which
accompanies his progress. Those who surround him hang deferen-
tially, even obsequiously, upon his words and gestures; as he turns to
address Calpurnia, Casca calls for silence, and Antony's first words
convey an ingratiating gesture of submission: 'When Caesar says
"do this", it is perform'd.' Already, however, a first indication of
strain emerges as he reacts to the Soothsayer's enigmatic warning.
Surrounded by the hush that waits upon his words, Caesar offers the
gesture of one whom his position obliges to conform to the mask of
superhuman impersonality he has assumed. 'He is a dreamer: let us
leave him: pass.' For the first, but not the last time,[1] he thrusts aside
a warning which might have saved him from the fate to which the
very nature of his eminence is leading him.

Throughout these early episodes, however, the initiative in moving
forward the action lies less with Caesar than with his enemies. The
definition of the conspiracy awaits Brutus' still undeclared resolution; and Brutus, uneasily aware of this as the dictator proceeds on
his way, opens his prolonged effort to obtain the self-clarification
which his nature craves. His initial reflections are already charged
with implications of character. Lacking by his own confession the
'quick spirit' of Mark Antony, and reproached by Cassius for his
'stubborn' response to suggestion, he excuses himself by asserting his
need to

> turn the trouble of my countenance
> Merely upon myself, [I. ii. 38.]

to contemplate a weight of oppression which, although he would
scarcely admit as much, he imperfectly understands:

[1] Compare Caesar's treatment of Calpurnia's dream [II. ii.] and of Artemidorus's
warning [III. i.] just before his death.

Vexed I am
Of late with passions of some difference,
Conceptions only proper to myself,
Which give some soil perhaps to my behaviours. [I. ii. 39.]

The expression, notably reminiscent in spirit of certain utterances of
Hamlet, stresses the nature, essentially inward-looking and explora-
tory, of his dilemma. To this Stoic theorist, tied to the contemplation
of his own virtue, the 'passions' present themselves as disturbing
elements, shadowing the unity and self-control which he craves as
the key to action. It is of the nature of his conflict to be without
communication, 'proper' to himself alone; and this inwardness, the
product of his character and of his assumptions about life, affects
him, when uneasily stirred to action, as a blot upon the harmonious
personality at which he aims, a 'soil' upon the fair outward presentation of himself which he so persistently craves.

It is the function of Cassius, by playing upon this desire for communication, to mould him to ends not finally his own. The peculiar
relationship between the pair, and the method of its dramatic
presentation, are both indicated in the query which opens his attack
and in Brutus' reply:

– Tell me, good Brutus, can you see your face?
– No, Cassius; for the eye sees not itself
  But by reflection, by some other things.[1] [I. ii. 51.]

Under the guise of providing, in the shape of 'thoughts of great
value, worthy cogitations', a 'mirror' to reflect his friend's '*hidden
worthiness*', Cassius will bring him to see not a reality, an objective
vision of his strength and weakness, but the 'shadow' of the
imperfectly understood desires which will finally bring him, not to
the affirmation of his ideals, but to personal and public ruin. In so
doing, moreover, he will notably widen the scope of the dramatic
presentation by indicating a closer estimate, partial indeed, but none
the less relevant, of Caesar himself, and by revealing more fully than
he knows the hidden motives of his own determination.

Beneath his assertions of friendship and plain dealing, Cassius'

---

[1] Compare, for an elaboration of this idea, Achilles' speech in *Troilus and Cressida*:
  The beauty that is borne here in the face
  The bearer knows not, but commends itself
  To other's eyes: nor doth the eye itself,
  That most pure spirit of sense, behold itself,
  Not going from itself; but eye to eye opposed
  Salutes each other with each other's form:
  For speculation turns not to itself,
  Till it hath travell'd and is mirror'd there
  Where it may see itself. [III. iii. 103.]

approach to Brutus is fraught with calculation. Those of 'the best respect in Rome' look to him for redress; as they groan beneath 'this age's yoke', their desire is that *noble* Brutus' – the adjective initiates a line of flattery which, precisely because it contains truth, will be particularly insidious – understood his own wishes and motives, 'had his eyes'. Brutus' first reaction is honest and true to character:

> Into what dangers would you lead me, Cassius,
> That you would have me seek into myself
> *For that which is not in me?* [I. ii. 63.]

It is some time before he will speak so truly again; but, meanwhile, it is Cassius' mission to undermine this candid self-estimate, replacing it by a false confidence which carries no inner conviction. Taking up once more the image of the mirror, he turns to his own ends the need for guidance which makes his friend so pliable to his purposes:

> since you know you cannot see yourself
> So well as by reflection, I your glass,
> Will modestly discover to yourself
> That of yourself which you yet know not of. [I. ii. 67.]

This is indeed a dangerous proceeding, made the more so by the tendency, which the following exchanges reveal, for the two friends to vie with one another in setting up idealized images of themselves to minister to what is finally, beneath their poses of Roman virtue and public spirit, an intimate self-satisfaction. When Cassius denies that he is 'a common laugher', 'fawning' on men with the intention of later 'scandalling' them, he is no doubt comparing himself, not altogether unjustly, with such as Antony and pointing to some true consequences of Caesar's exorbitant power; but, beneath the implied contrast, envy, the desire to debase what he has been unable to achieve, already vitiates the judgement.

For Brutus, similarly, devotion to the public good expresses itself through assumption of that 'honour' which was, more especially at this time, so much and so variously in Shakespeare's mind:

> What is it that you would impart to me?
> If it be aught toward the general good,
> Set honour in one eye and death i' the other,
> And I will look on both indifferently. [I. ii. 84.]

Though expressed with a more 'philosophic' detachment and reflecting a more self-conscious indifference, the spirit behind these words is akin to that which prompted Hotspur to his generous but useless sacrifice;[1] and it reveals much the same tendency to replace the balance of judgement by simpler but more illusory certainties. As Brutus concludes, not without a touch of self-esteem,

> let the gods so speed me as I love
> The name of honour more than I fear death. [I. ii. 88.]

It will be, perhaps, one of the lessons of Brutus' tragedy that the 'names' of things, however noble and consoling in abstraction, are no substitute for a balanced consideration of their reality. 'Honour' is in the way of becoming a trap set for those who, like Brutus, fail to temper idealism with a proper measure of self-awareness.

This revealing introduction to the main purposes of the scene has been set against the massive reality of Caesar's progress towards his goal. Under the impression of the 'flourish and shout' which interrupts their reflections Cassius broaches his principal business by an acceptance, at once sincere and flattering, of his friend's self-estimate: 'I know that virtue to be in you, Brutus.' His account of Caesar, to which this leads, broadens further the scope of the episode; it brings a little closer the reality of the enigmatic figure whose fortunes, even in absence, dominate the stage, and it tells us more of Cassius himself. Both aims are admirably interwoven in the development of the long speech from its significant preface:

> I had as lief not be as live to be
> In awe of such a thing as I myself. [I. ii. 95.]

The implied criticism of Caesar as 'a thing', inflated beyond the proportions of common humanity, has no doubt a measure of validity. Shakespeare's concern to stress the contrast between Caesar's elevation and his weaknesses is amply confirmed by his presentation of the dictator. There is, however, another side to the picture. When Cassius asserts that he was born 'free as Caesar', the affirmation is, as far as it goes, acceptable in the light of the speaker's declared principles, but in the materialism of the comparison which backs the claim:

> We both have fed as well, and we can both
> Endure the winter's cold as well as he [I. ii. 98.]

the argument is in danger of degenerating to a level lower than that to which it lays claim. So much is indicated by the manner of Cassius' expression, rarely more individual, more a reflection of

---

[1] Compare Hotspur's outburst to Worcester:

> Send danger from the east unto the west,
> So honour cross it from the north to south,
> And let them grapple. [*Henry IV, Part One*, I. iii. 195.]

personal idiosyncrasy, than at this point. In his description of the wintry river on 'a raw and gusty day', 'troubled', 'chafing with her shores', a certain embittered crudity communicates itself to his exultation; and a similar sense of flawed, unbalanced emotion colours the emphasis on *daring* in his account of his challenge, reveals a nature which has always sought through 'controversy', through the querulous assertion of its independence, the confidence which normal human relationships have failed to give it.

By the standards which Cassius proposes Caesar is found wanting; but they are, of course, standards expressly chosen to induce a gratifying contempt. In the battle against the elements, to which Cassius' strained, nervous energy so triumphantly responded, Caesar 'tired'; and the satisfaction which this memory produces in his rival finds issue in his account of the dictator's fever:

> when the fit was on him, I did mark
> How he did shake; 'tis true, this god did shake. [I. ii. 120.]

Here, as ever, we should not simplify. Caesar's physical weaknesses are fairly contrasted with the magnitude of his claims; but in the tart, contemptuous tone, the callow and denigrating reference to the 'sick girl' and to the ailing man's 'coward lips', a tone of complacent belittlement colours the speaker's words and is related to its true cause in the revealing conclusion:

> this man
> Is now become a god, and Cassius is
> A wretched creature, and must bend his body
> If Caesar carelessly but nod on him. [I. ii. 115.]

Perhaps it is not altogether certain that Cassius might not, in his innermost heart, desire to be Caesar; at all events, his resentment is directed rather at the dictator's 'feeble temper', which has just been set against his own assertion of bold decision, than at the isolated and superhuman power which circumstance has conferred upon him.

This combination of idealism and personal resentment pervades the 'philosophy' which Cassius urges upon Brutus. When he uses it to persuade his friend to action –

> The fault, dear Brutus, is not in our stars,
> But in ourselves, that we are underlings – [I. ii. 139.]

the appeal to assert himself is one which Brutus, precisely because he feels himself in certain respects unable to respond to it, is likely to find attractive; but his words, too readily detached from their context and presented as a universal, 'philosophical' statement, are in fact uttered in character. Cassius' following words confirm that a sense of personal inferiority has played a decisive part in their conception. 'Why should that name be sounded more than yours?' The question, so opposed in spirit to that sense of necessary distinctions, of freely accepted hierarchies, which lies at the foundations of Shakespeare's political thought and which is compatible in him with the most dispassionate estimate of public realities, is driven home by an argument which, in its characteristic stressing of material processes –

> Upon what meat doth this our Caesar feed,
> That he is grown so great? – [I. ii. 148.]

once more tells its own tale. When Cassius deplores the decadence of the 'age', its loss of 'the breed of noble bloods', the statement need neither be taken at its face value nor simply equated with the devices of an envious politician. It is in part the condemnation of a genuine moral decline in Roman public life; but – we must add – there is also calculation, deliberate exploitation of idealism, in the appeal which rounds off the speech to the republicanism that has played so great a part in shaping his friend's family tradition.

Brutus, though weakening, is not yet ready to commit himself. His comment, 'What you would work me to, I have some aim', and the further plea that he should not be 'further moved', amount to a 'philosophic' putting off of the moment for decision. It is set against the implacable reality recalled by Caesar's brief return which, in the process of revealing a little more of the dictator's own nature, provides a judgement upon Cassius and, by implication, on the influence he exercises over his friend. Referring graphically to Cassius' 'lean and hungry look', Caesar ascribes it to the defect of thinking 'too much'; as he departs visibly from his Olympian pose, deploring thought as an excess, announcing his preference for the 'fat', 'sleek-headed' companions who will confirm him in his own comfortable assumptions, a sense of his own complacency is related to a deeper unease. He still declaims fear as incompatible with his position; but the suggestion that, had he been 'liable to fear', he would have been wary of this particular enemy indicates an incipient sense of insecurity. When he goes on to describe Cassius as one who 'reads much', a 'great observer' who

> looks
> Quite through the deeds of men, [I. ii. 201.]

there is an impression that this concentrated critical acumen may reveal in Caesar himself a certain weakness, a disproportion between the humanity which he shares with the rest of mankind and the exalted eminence to which his destiny is so inexorably calling him.

If Caesar, however, thus unwittingly revealed himself, he can still give us his rival in a vivid piece of portraiture:

> Seldom he smiles, and smiles in such a sort
> As if he mock'd himself, and scorn'd his spirit
> That could be moved to smile at anything. [I. ii. 204.]

Here, at least, the inhumanity of the doctrinaire is presented in the flesh. The turning into self-conscious superiority of weakness, of a lack of capacity for normal human relationships, could not be better conveyed; not for nothing is the blow shortly to strike down Caesar to be presented, apart from its political meaning, as an act of treachery, a denial of friendship and common feeling. Yet, even as he makes this valid point, Caesar's words imply a first indication of fear, a crack in the façade of imperturbable superiority to circumstance which he presents to the world. The revelation is momentary, covered at once by a return to the pedestal –

> I rather tell thee what is to be fear'd
> Than what I fear, for always I am Caesar – [I. ii. 210.]

which only just fails to ring entirely true. The introduction, at this point, of the weakening personal detail – 'Come on my right hand, for this ear is deaf'[1] – completes an effect of some complexity. 'I fear him not,' Caesar has affirmed. It is part of his position that he cannot confess himself 'liable to fear'; and yet, were he as the rest of men – and is he not perhaps more so, in these intimations of physical decline, than he can allow himself to admit? –

> I do not know the man I should avoid
> So much as that spare Cassius. [I. ii. 199.]

As always in his best work, Shakespeare's characters, as they comment relevantly on others, expose more than they realize of their true selves.

The dramatic revelation of character takes place, throughout these early episodes, against the background of a constantly developing action. After Caesar has once more left the stage, the pressure of outside events asserts itself yet again through Casca's 'sour' account of the offering of the crown on the Capitol. The entire episode, as reported, is histrionically conceived. Caesar is said to have plucked open his doublet, offered the mob his throat to cut; whilst the irresponsible spirit of those who applaud him is that of the wenches who, 'if Caesar had stabb'd their mothers', would have given him their approval. Caesar's 'falling-sickness' reinforces Cassius' previous

[1] The detail is taken from Plutarch, but its introduction in the immediate context of Caesar's declaration of fixity of purpose is surely revealing.

account of his physical infirmity, and – on the popular side – the contemptuous evocation of the 'rag-tag' people not only adds something to our understanding of revolutionary idealism and of the unconfessed cynicism which may accompany it, but draws the holiday crowds of the opening a little further into the action, initiates their transformation into the vicious and irresponsible rabblement which Antony will rouse to fury.

This, of course, is yet another partial vision of events and, as such, can claim no finality. Left alone with Cassius, Brutus refers somewhat disparagingly to Casca's 'bluntness', only to qualify the implied criticism by recalling that he had been '*quick metal* when he went to school'. Cassius, whom the phrase would fit to perfection, sees in this plain-speaking a proof of devotion to 'any noble or bold enterprise'. Nobility and boldness pushed to the extreme are, indeed, the qualities he supremely admires. They have, however, become associated in his thought with a rancid quality, a fretting of envy into petulant distaste, which is to be felt in his characteristic use of the imagery of appetite:

> This rudeness is a sauce to his good wit,
> Which gives men stomach to digest his words
> With better appetite. [I. ii. 305.]

A connection can be traced between this sharply pungent emphasis upon a digestion on edge, requiring the sauce of plain-speaking before it can be assimilated, transformed into 'good wit', and Caesar's own account of Cassius himself as 'lean and hungry', craving insatiably the satisfaction which embittered instinct imposes upon his restless nature.

Cassius' final comment on Brutus in this scene comes strangely on the heels of so much profession of friendship. It serves, of course, the familar dramatic function of alerting the audience to the dubious methods that he proposes to use in persuading Brutus to join the conspiracy; but Shakespeare generally shows himself able to turn this kind of convention to ends of his own, and in this case the result is, beyond the practical device, a notable revelation of character. Brutus, Cassius says, is 'noble', and so indisposed to enter into unworthy relationships; but this same 'nobility', to which he has so persistently made appeal, now appears to him as a sign of weakness, of incapacity for practical action. The influence of Cassius upon Brutus will henceforward be based in part upon the conviction, strangely pessimistic, opposed to the idealism he professes, that even the most 'noble' of men may be perverted to end implicitly recognized as 'base':

> Thy honourable metal may be wrought
> From that it is disposed; [I. ii. 314.]

for there is, in Cassius' candid view, 'none so firm that cannot be
seduced'. The observation amounts finally to a confession of political
cynicism. Though explicitly reflecting the fear that Brutus' friendship for Caesar may weaken his devotion to libertarian principle, and
so turn him aside from the resolution which this imposes upon him, it
colours his own approach to his friend's 'nobility'. Cassius has observed that Caesar, who 'bears him hard', loves Brutus; the observation
rouses in him, besides fear for the future of his own project, an
emotion that fluctuates between envy and contempt, creating a kind
of moral queasiness, a determination not to be imposed upon, which
he is resolved to communicate to Brutus himself:

> If I were Brutus now and he were Cassius,
> He should not humour me. [I. ii. 319.]

It is typical of Cassius that, appealing self-consciously to the love and
friendship which his nature genuinely craves, he should yet pride
himself on having seen through these attachments as illusions, im-
pediments to the high-principled and 'noble' actions upon which he
has staked his being. The true nature of the conspiracy is implied, as
the scene closes, by the device to rouse Brutus by bringing forged
messages to bear upon his indecision.

II

With the intimate motives of the leading conspirators thus revealed, the various threads of the action concentrate upon Brutus'
decision. This will lead to a reversal of the relationships which
properly bind men together in the natural bonds of society: it is therefore appropriately preceded by a scene in which his future associates
meet under the shadow of the sinister aberrations by which nature
herself is afflicted. 'The sway of earth,' in Casca's breathless words,
shakes 'like a thing unfirm'; a state of tempest, confounding the
'ambitious ocean' with the 'threatening clouds', either reflects the
existence in heaven of a 'civil strife' which answers to the state of
human affairs or, more ominously still, points to the anger of the
gods. As they seek to interpret these portents in the light of their own
impulses – tense, fevered, hysterical – the conspirators are drawn
ever further into the world of illusion to which their project belongs;
for, as Cicero puts it,

> men may construe things after their fashion,
> Clean from the purpose of the things themselves. [I. iii. 34.]

The human tendency to err, by imposing upon events the interpretation which the partialities of passion dictate, is to be a principal moving force in the developing action.

It is typical of this tendency to interpret its own delusions as certainties, its weakness as a sign of strength. To Cassius the chaos of the elements presents itself as 'a very pleasing sight to honest men'; the disorder of the skies answers to an earth 'full of faults' and, in the mood of strained exaltation which is in him the prelude to resolve, he submits to 'the aim and very flash' of the 'cross-blue lightning' as it opens 'the breast of heaven'. It is, however, a perverse, an unnatural strain that thus moves him to welcome the signs of disorder in earth and sky; and his rashness inspires in those who hear him the misgiving which Casca voices:

> It is the part of men to fear and tremble
> When the most mighty gods by tokens send
> Such dreadful heralds to astonish us. [I. iii. 54.]

Cassius, wedded to his own interpretations, reads the warnings otherwise. He sees in them a rebuke to those who lack the 'sparks of life' which should animate a Roman and in the absence of which he is – like the hesitant Brutus, dare we say? – 'dull', lifeless. Fascinated by the very 'monstrous' quality he senses in the phenomena of nature, he reads the tempest as a symbol of Caesar's rule, a sign of the overthrow of normal order in society which tyranny implies; but the very emphasis on 'monstrosity', and the complacency with which he dwells on it, indicate the perversity of his designs. The monstrosity, indeed, exists primarily in his own heart, and his determination to relate it to Caesar –

> a man
> Most like this dreadful night – [I. iii. 72.]

whilst it truly emphasizes the menace of absolute power, cannot hide the reversal of true order which his thwarted nature conceals.

These preliminaries lead Cassius to a doctrinaire contrast between modern cowardice and the constancy he ascribes to 'our fathers' minds'. Theatrical pose and true emotional tension combine in his assertion of man's power to affirm his freedom, if only through self-destruction:

> Nor stony tower, nor walls of beaten brass,
> Nor airless dungeon, nor strong links of iron,
> Can be retentive to the strength of spirit;
> But life, being weary of these worldly bars,
> Never lacks power to dismiss itself. [I. iii. 93.]

Like not a few of Shakespeare's 'moral' utterances, the precise tone
of this speech needs to be weighed carefully. We are reminded once
more of Hotspur exalting the claims of 'honour' in *Henry IV – Part I*.
In each case, genuine positive values are involved; but in each case,
too, a touch of rhetoric marks, if not the sentiment itself, its affirmation by a speaker who identifies his moralizing too readily with
the needs of his flawed nature. The assertion of man's power over
circumstance can be accepted as in some measure ennobling, but
only provided we realize that it is suicide, self-annihilation, that
is being exalted. This necessary balance of judgement will be
seen in due course to have its bearing upon the final scenes of the
play.

Meanwhile, the conspirators, thus animated, rise to the strained,
self-exasperating tension which is, for them all, the prelude to
resolution. When Casca has asserted that every Roman has the
power, through suicide, to 'cancel his captivity', Cassius takes this
up as a proof of the vanity of Caesar's tyranny. He does this, most
characteristically, by pouring denigration upon his countrymen.
Caesar is a 'lion' because the Romans who passively contemplate
his exaltation are 'hinds', 'trash', 'rubbish', 'offal' to 'illuminate' his
vileness by contrast with their dishonour. Cassius, as he exhibits his
emotion and indulges his natural tendency to belittlement, plays
rhetorically on the sentiments of those who hear him. Casca replies
by striking an attitude:

> You speak to Casca, and to such a man
> That is no fleering tell-tale [I. iii. 116.]

and by asserting that none shall exceed him in the coming action.
The final appeal is made, again by Cassius, to the 'noblest-minded
Romans' who are to be moved, once again like Percy before them, to
'honourable-dangerous' enterprises.

This rivalry in honour conceals, none the less, an obstinate sense of
weakness. As much is implied in the general anxiety to buttress the
cause with Brutus' support:

> O Cassius, if you would
> But win the noble Brutus to our party; [I. iii. 140.]

Cinna's wistful plea amounts to a confession of doubt in the justifying
motives and practical outcome of the dubious adventure upon
which he and his associates are embarked. The problem is to convert
rhetorical into true nobility where the roots of humanity and justice
are absent. In Casca's recognition that it is Brutus – and, by implication, he alone – who 'sits high' in the people's hearts, so that

that which would appear offence in us
His countenance, like richest alchemy,
Will change to virtue and to worthiness, [I. iii. 158.]

the true reason for 'our great need of him' is revealed. Fortunately, as
Cassius says, 'three parts of him' are 'ours already'; the rest will
speedily be won over by the devices he has set in motion.

To Brutus, therefore, thus placed unwillingly at the centre of
events, the action logically returns (II. i). Upon the choice he has
now to make depends the confirmation of the conspirators in their
purposes; through it, he will seek the illusion of effectiveness, of
devoted and public-spirited consistency, which his nature so
obscurely but persistently craves. The spirit of intimate contradiction
in which he approaches his decision is established by the preliminary
exchange with Lucius, which associates the presence of night and
uncertainty –

I cannot, by the progress of the stars,
Give guess how near to day – [II. i. 2.]

with the desire for that 'sound' sleep which reflects a harmonious
nature and a clear conscience. Hesitating between night and day,
good and evil, harmony and division, Brutus is disturbed by the
intimation of obscure elements of strife in his own soul; these he will
seek to resolve through a self-imposed dedication to the apparent
certainties of action.

The speech that follows is so riddled with implicit contradictions
that some students of the play[1] have judged it incomprehensible.
Once again, in point of fact, Shakespeare is using the dramatic
convention of the soliloquy, not merely to stress the unnatural
quality of the action which the speaker is urging upon himself, but
to expose the flaws in his moral make-up which make this perverse
resolution conceivable. Brutus, not himself an evil man, is about to
perform an act which will release evil impulses whose true nature
he persistently fails to grasp; the discrepancy between what he is
and what he does is reflected at this point in his recognizable effort
to persuade himself, against convictions intimately present in his
nature, that the resolve he is about to take is necessary and just. Had
Brutus been consistently the doctrinaire republican Cassius would
have him be, the admitted fact that Caesar 'would be crown'd' would
have been, for him if not for Shakespeare and most of his contempor-
aries, a sufficient reason for his elimination. Brutus, however, as the
play presents him, is no such thing, but rather a man who seeks in
decisive action the confirmation of his own virtue, whose purposes

---

[1] Coleridge gave classical expression to this point of view in his study of the play.

are imposed upon him by those who play, with varying degrees of consciousness, upon inconsistencies, weak spots in his own nature; and it is part of his tragedy that he cannot forget, much as he now desires to do so, that his intended victim is a human being and his friend. This situation bears fruit in his recognition, which a convinced republican would have found irrelevant, that he has as yet no valid *personal* reason for the deed he contemplates. 'To speak truth of Caesar,' he admits,

> I have not known when his affections sway'd
> More than his reason. [II. i. 20.]

'I know no personal cause to spurn at him': the admission is, for a man who sincerely values friendship, personal relationships, serious enough; but, since another side of Brutus' nature craves abstract consistency, the wedding of high principle to effective action, he turns this recognition into an argument for clearing himself of dubious personal motives and seeks to place the burden of justification squarely upon an appeal to the 'general' good.

The argument, inevitably, under these circumstances, is pressed home with less than complete conviction. 'How that *might* change his nature, there's the question,' Brutus urges upon himself, in a strangely tentative attitude, only to recognize in a later outburst of honesty that

> the quarrel
> Will bear no colour for the thing he is; [II. i. 28.]

but, since a contrary necessity of his nature urges him to overrule these doubts, calls upon him to assert a certainty which he is far from feeling, emphasis must be laid on a *possible*, an unproven danger:

> Fashion it thus; that what he is, augmented,
> Would run to these and these extremities. [II. i. 30.]

The vagueness, the readiness to 'fashion it thus' in accordance with preconceptions in which observed reality has little part to play, is highly symptomatic. Brutus, precisely because the vacillation which has characterized his reactions since the beginning of the play covers deep inner uncertainty, speaks to himself evasively in terms of specious 'philosophical' commonplace –

> lowliness is young ambition's ladder . . .
> The abuse of greatness is when it disjoins
> Remorse from power – [II. i. 22, 18.]

and takes refuge in an imposed ruthlessness:

think him as a serpent's egg
Which hatch'd would in his kind grow mischievous,
And kill him in the shell. [II. i. 32.]

The tendency to cover lack of intimate consistency with a show of impersonal brutality belongs to Brutus' particular brand of theoretical idealism. It is part of the presentation of human contradiction whose exposure is so close to the spirit of this play; the whole speech may be read as an early effort to follow thought in the clarifying of its uncertain ideas, and not a few of its phrases anticipate later Shakespearian presentations of the tragic implications of moral choice. When Brutus affirms that Caesar 'would be crown'd', it is as though we heard, but to another end, the voice of Lady Macbeth meditating on her husband's indecision; and when the serpent is conjured into the sunlight –

It is the bright day that brings forth the adder;
And that craves wary walking – [II. i. 14.]

or when the speaker reflects upon the temptations which accompany the exercise of authority we seem to be hearing intimations of the greater tragedy. Brutus seeks at this moment to resolve an intimate, tragic disharmony through an act of decision foreign to his nature; the confusion revealed in his own motives, and in his attitude to the world of external realities around him, is one which will follow him through the contradictions of his career to the final resolution of suicide.

The equivocal nature of his decision is immediately confirmed by the messages which Cassius has caused to be thrown in at his window. All appeal to an element of high-minded vanity in his nature. By stressing his ancestral traditions, and by insinuating that he 'sleeps' when wakeful action is required of him, they rouse his desire to 'speak, strike, redress', to do just those things which his nature, though one side of it craves for them, prevents him from wholeheartedly willing. The effect is to lead him to the spurious resolve at which the soliloquy aimed. The process of clarification, however, issues fatally on a tragic note. Between conception and act, the 'first motion' and the 'acting' of 'a dreadful thing',

all the interim is
Like a phantasma or a hideous dream. [II. i. 64.]

Once more there is something here that recalls Macbeth's hallucinatory approach to his more inhuman crime. Macbeth is more subtly conceived, belongs to a far richer world of metaphysical and psychological realities; but he too will be concerned, when his moment of choice comes, with the 'state of man' which

> Like to a little kingdom suffers then
> The nature of an insurrection.[1] [II. i. 68.]

The notion that disunity in the individual is in some sense a reflection of greater cleavages, obscure rifts in the fabric of society and even, it may be, of nature itself, is one which will lie very close to the heart of Shakespeare's greatest tragedies.

Having arrived at his decision, Brutus is ready to meet his fellow-conspirators. Their secretive entry prompts him to a comment strangely opposed in spirit to his recently declared resolution. Conspiracy, he remarks, is afraid to reveal its 'dangerous brow' even by night, 'when evils are most free'. As in Macbeth, the impulse to evil flees the light and clarity of day, seeks

> a cavern dark enough
> To mask [its] monstrous visage. [II. i. 80.]

The 'cavern', perhaps, is not without relation to obscure places in his own soul. Treachery works under a mask, covering in 'smiles and affability' a 'native semblance' which, if openly adopted, would lead to 'prevention'.[2] The characteristic qualities of Shakespearian evil make themselves felt in Brutus' effort to overcome an inner conflict between reverence for a necessary order and the growing conception of his crime.

In presenting his associates Cassius stresses one of Brutus' chief weaknesses, his need to live up to the conception of himself which his ancestors and his 'philosophy' have laid upon him. He suggests that, unlike these ancestors, Brutus is weak, indecisive; public opinion demands of him that 'opinion' of himself which every true Roman shares. It is primarily his desire to live up to this picture of his own nobility that has led Brutus to his decision. It now inspires him to a typically high-minded utterance in which, urging his new associates to confirm their dedication, he seeks confidence in a rhetorical declaration of his own. The occasion is Cassius' call for an oath:

[1] Compare Macbeth's reflection after the revelation of the Witches:

> My thought, whose murder yet is but fantastical,
> Shakes so my single state of man that function
> Is smother'd in surmise, and nothing is
> But what is not. [Macbeth, I. iii. 139.]

[2] For the idea compare, once more, Macbeth:

> To beguile the time,
> Look like the time; bear welcome in your eye,
> Your hand, your tongue: look like the innocent flower,
> But be the serpent under't. [I. v. 64.]

> do not stain
> The even virtue of our enterprise,
> Nor the insuppressive mettle of our spirits,
> To think that or our cause or our performance
> Did need an oath: when every drop of blood
> That every Roman bears, and nobly bears,
> Is guilty of a several bastardy
> If he do break the smallest particle
> Of any promise that hath pass'd from him. [II. i. 132.]

The best comment on this earnest, but slightly self-conscious harangue is provided by the return, which at once follows, to practical considerations. Cassius and his friends wish to enrol the support of Cicero, whose reputation will 'purchase us' – the verb is appropriately chosen – 'a good opinion',

> And buy men's voice to commend our deeds. [II. i. 146.]

Since, however, it is Brutus' adhesion that all desire, it is enough for him to reject Cicero as incapable of 'following' for all to agree that he should not be approached.

The basic weakness of the plot is more closely touched upon when Cassius urges that Mark Antony, 'a shrewd contriver' whose survival may be of the greatest danger, should die. Brutus' rejection of this advice is of very considerable interest as a further revelation of the kind of man he is. It combines an effort to be practical, revealed in the opening concession to expediency ('Our course will *seem* too bloody'), with failure to be so. It is finally the pose, the elevation of himself into a figure of magnanimous principle, that engages his emotions. The expression is not without a touch of the grotesque. 'Let us be sacrificers, but not butchers, Cassius,' he urges, and follows up the plea with an unreal distinction between 'the spirit of men' and their material 'blood' which must so regrettably be shed:

> We all stand up against the spirit of Caesar,
> And in the spirit of men there is no blood!
> O, that we then could come by Caesar's spirit,
> And not dismember Caesar! [II. i. 167.]

The distinction no doubt answers in part to the desire to make credible Brutus' nobility, in the absence of which there would be no tragedy, in the face of the nature of the deed on which he has set himself. Once more, however, the difficulty is turned into an asset, a revelation of character. Brutus the idealist is seen as one more example of that typical Shakespearian creation, the man who, willing an end, is ready to deceive himself concerning the means necessary to gain it. 'Caesar must bleed for't', he recognizes, but covers the admission with futile and self-conscious posing:

> gentle friends,
> Let's kill him boldly, but not wrathfully:
> Let's carve him as a dish fit for the gods,
> Not hew him as a carcass fit for hounds:
> And let our hearts as subtle masters do,
> Stir up their servants to an act of rage,
> And after seem to chide 'em. [II. i. 171]

The speech points to the presence of a variety of motives in the process of decorating brutality with strained emotional expression. Addressing his future accomplices as 'gentle friends' Brutus, in admitting the fact of bloody death ('a carcass fit for hounds'), embroiders it with the far-fetched and finally absurd evocation of 'a dish fit for the gods'. The odd mixture of unpracticality and a certain unconscious cynicism is brought home forcibly in the description of the conspirators' hearts as *'subtle* masters' who, in rousing their 'servant' feelings to a simulation, an 'act of rage', *seem* after, for the purpose of obtaining public approval, 'to chide them'. In this way, their project will be made necessary, not appear 'envious'. 'We shall be call'd purgers, not murderers': the reality, as so often occurs with men of Brutus' type, is disguised by a change of name, and this becomes the justification of a decision politically unwise, if humanly comprehensible, which will finally bring the conspiracy to ruin.

Brutus rounds off his harangue with a gesture of generosity, characteristically delivered as a sneer, towards Antony. If the latter truly loves his master, the best he can do

> Is to himself take thought, and die for Caesar;
> And that were much he should, for he is given
> To sports, to wildness, and much company. [II. i. 187.]

No doubt there is truth in this belittling comment; but in the tone of Brutus' dismissal there is, besides unwisdom, a touch of complacency. A similar excess of confidence, allied to more than a little cynicism, now takes possession of his hearers. It can be heard in Trebonius' rejoinder that Antony may be spared because 'there is no fear in him' and because, moreover, 'he will live and laugh at this here-after.'

In the light of this agreement, the discussion turns to Caesar's forthcoming visit to the Capitol. Caesar himself is now revealed a little more intimately to our understanding. The impression of a man in some sense declined from his former stature[1] confirms what

---

[1] This reading of Caesar's character has been suggested by J. I. M. Stewart in his *Character and Motive in Shakespeare* (London, 1949).

we have already been shown. Caesar is 'superstitious grown of late', a new trait which differs notably from the 'main opinion' he once held of 'fantasy, of dreams, and ceremonies'; Cassius fears he may be induced to stay at home, thus destroying the plot hatched against him. More revealing still is Decius' rejoinder, expressing his confidence of being able to 'sway' the dictator: and most notable of all is the hint that he may be influenced by playing up to the impression he has created of himself for his own esteem:

> But when I tell him he hates flatterers,
> He says he does, being then most flattered. [II. i. 207.]

With their confidence thus restored, the exchange between the conspirators ends with a theatrical assumption of their collective role, as Brutus calls upon his followers to 'look fresh and merrily', like 'Roman actors',

> With untired spirits and formal constancy. [II. i. 227.]

As always with Brutus, true nobility and its deliberate assumption are blended in the presentation of the character.

Before the end of this remarkably rich and varied scene, something of the cost of Brutus' strained and artificial resolve emerges with the entry of Portia. The preceding reflection upon Lucius' speech, coming immediately after the exhortation to 'look fresh and merrily', shows that he is bearing a burden he can scarcely contemplate; and Portia confirms this when she expresses wifely concern at his distracted state. Brutus, indeed, confesses that he is not 'well in health', prompting Portia to relate the thought of sickness shrewdly to its true cause; for she sees it not as a physical malady but rather as the sign of 'some sick offence within your mind'.[1] There follows her appeal to know the truth, to give their proper value to the human relations supremely incarnated in marriage:

> Dwell I but in the suburbs
> Of your good pleasure? [II. i. 285.]

In this query the sense of what Brutus will lose by following the lead of his idealistic egoism is strongly stressed. The impression of theatrical abstraction as an ingredient of their common Stoic 'philosophy' is confirmed, moreover, by Portia herself when she refers to her origins as 'Cato's daughter' and discloses, surely a trifle grotesquely, the 'voluntary wound' she has inflicted on herself. Without overstressing the point, there is a sense of strain beneath the true emotion of the entire exchange, as though both parties to

---

[1] Compare the Doctor in *Macbeth*: 'More needs she the divine than the physician.' [V. i. 81.]

this marriage were limited, beyond their real and impressive capacity for tenderness, by their devotion to abstract principle and to their common origins. That Brutus' love is genuine and deep is confirmed, were confirmation needed, by the tone of his declaration:

> You are my true and honourable wife,
> As dear to me as are the ruddy drops
> That visit my sad heart; [II. i. 288.]

but, for all the compensations which this relationship brings with it, the speaker's heart remains 'sad', torn by contradictions and tied to the elements of theory and self-deception which accompany him to the field of public action.

Sickness, indeed, overshadows the entire conspiracy. This is confirmed by the entry of Ligarius, heralded as a 'sick man', the possessor of 'a feeble tongue'. Once again physical frailty, and the sense of standing strained at the limits of normality, go together with eager exaltation. Promised the revelation of Brutus' aims, Ligarius rhetorically 'discards' his sickness, asserts the revival of life in his 'mortified spirit'. He even affirms that he will 'strive with things impossible'[1] and get the better of them. The scene, thus raised once more to a hollow pitch of declamation, ends on a quibble:

> – What's to do?
> – A piece of work that will make sick men whole.
> – But are not some whole that we must make sick? [II. i. 326.]

where the jest covers a sense of fundamental irresponsibility when decisions affecting life and death are at stake. Not for nothing is Ligarius ready to follow in doing 'I know not what',

> but it sufficeth
> That Brutus leads me on. [II. i. 333.]

In this abandonment of reason we can sense, not merely the irrational basis on which the entire enterprise rests, but the un-founded quality of the idealism which makes Brutus ready to assume responsibility for resolutions so frivolously accepted by those whose decision hangs upon his own.

With the conspirators thus finally united in purpose, the time has come for Caesar to face his moment of decision. In his person the grandeur of the Roman state is supremely gathered; all that we have so far seen stands in some relation to this central reality. Its human

---

[1] Compare Northumberland's fevered reaction to the news of defeat at Shrewsbury [*Henry IV – Part II*, I. i.].

manifestation, however, is oddly and significantly faltering. Reflecting on the prevailing portents Caesar is ill at ease, seeks the confirmation of his purposes in the 'opinions' delivered by the oracles. As Calpurnia presses him to stay at home, he clings obstinately, and indeed unreasonably, but with a determination which strikes him as necessary, to the pose which his situation has forced upon him. 'Caesar shall go forth': the dangers that threaten are always *behind* him, indefinitely out of sight, waiting to assert themselves against a man whom his position obliges to outface them:

> when they shall see
> The face of Caesar, they are vanished. [II. ii. 11.]

Upon this illusion of constancy, the dictator's position, and with it the fortunes of the Roman world, depend.

Calpurnia's dream answers to the elemental disturbances already described at length.[1] It forms an extension of the play's emotional climate, and each individual reacts to it in accordance with his own nature. Caesar responds to portents 'beyond all use', threats to human conceptions of order and purpose, with what is, as so often with him, at once the striking of an attitude and a touch of sincerity:

> What can be avoided
> Whose end is purposed by the mighty gods? [II. ii. 26.]

In the light of this implicit fatalism the renewed affirmation which follows – 'Caesar shall go forth' – must seem strangely obstinate. It is followed by a further insistence upon the pose which we have come to associate with his dignity, and which is now fused with a genuine sense of fatality:

> Cowards die many times before their death;
> The valiant never taste of death but once. [II. ii. 32.]

The speech opens with a noble affirmation of consistency, but, as it proceeds, we are made aware of a notable change, a stressing of self-consciousness which ends by insinuating the presence of the weakness it seeks to deny:

> Of all the wonders that I yet have heard,
> It seems to me most strange that men should fear;
> Seeing that death, a necessary end,
> Will come when it will come. [II. ii. 34.]

The lines answer to that sense of fatality, of subjection to the temporal process, which is present as a factor limiting human choices and

[1] In I. iii.

decisions in all Shakespeare's plays of this period. Against this pervasive influence, Caesar is engaged in building up an impression of
consistency which began no doubt as a real reflection of greatness,
but which his situation, and the destiny which covers all human
actions, now imposes.

Caesar is revealed, in fact, less as brave and consistent, than as
talking himself into consistency. The exchange which follows the
report of the adverse augury reveals, moreover, a reaction incompatible with his show of personal decision. Having taken the initiative in consulting the augurs, he realizes that he cannot accept the
warning they have conveyed:

> Caesar should be a beast without a heart,
> If he should stay at home to-day for fear; [II. ii. 42.]

and he goes on to assert an inflexibility of purpose in which the sense
of strain, however comprehensible, borders on the absurd:

> danger knows full well
> That Caesar is more dangerous than he:
> We are two lions litter'd in one day,
> And I the elder and more terrible:
> And Caesar shall go forth. [II. ii. 44.]

The conclusion, so strangely disjointed from the effort at dignified
self-affirmation that has gone before, tells its own tale. 'Caesar shall
go forth': not so much perhaps because this is the right, the natural
thing for him to do, but because to hesitate would be to convict him
of cowardice both in his own esteem and in the public eye.

Beneath this determination, however, weakness once more asserts
itself. Calpurnia persuades him to a course which his own instincts
have already insinuated; he acquiesces ('Mark Antony shall say I
am not well'), even while clinging to the excuse that it is the frailty
of others that has imposed this change of plan: 'for thy humour, I
will stay at home'. The arrival of Decius Brutus to escort him to the
Senate brings to the surface the contradictions by which he is torn.
Decius is to tell the senators that he 'will not come to-day'; since it is
false that he 'cannot', and that he 'dare not, falser', only the bare
affirmation of his will can meet the case. When Calpurnia tries to
soften the refusal by suggesting sickness as an excuse, his self-respect
prompts the question 'Shall Caesar send a lie?' and drives him to
insist again that the decision lies in his will alone. Here Decius sees
his chance. 'Most mighty Caesar' he pleads, with a flattery to which,
as he has already told us,[1] the dictator is particularly susceptible:

[1] In II. i. See p. 39 above.

> let me know some cause,
> Lest I be laughed at when I tell them so, [II. ii. 69.]

and receives a reply that in reality evades the issue, escapes into the emphatic affirmation that conceals an awareness of inconsistency:

> The cause is in my will: I will not come;
> That is enough to satisfy the senate. [II. ii. 71.]

The retort reveals, as in passing, the arbitrary nature of the consistency which circumstance imposes upon Caesar. It also covers an inner uncertainty; the pose has taken possession of the man, and will from now on lead him to his fate.

After Caesar's account of Calpurnia's dream and Decius' ingenious exercise in interpretation – both expressed in the heightened, almost hysterical language which surrounds conspiracy throughout, and both destined to be dreadfully confirmed – Decius drives home his point by a highly effective combination of flattery with an appeal to the dictator's unavowed love of power. The Senate have decided to confer a crown upon 'mighty Caesar', and if he does not attend the session, 'their minds may change'. More dangerously still, because close to his easily-wounded self-esteem, Decius emphasizes the mockery which may follow if the truth were known:

> It were a mock
> Apt to be rendered, for some one to say
> 'Break up the senate till another time,
> When Caesar's wife shall meet with better dreams.' [II. ii. 96.]

The appeal to vanity supports that to ambition, and indifference to Calpurnia – reflected in an attitude towards her that surely stands in significant contrast to Brutus' tender treatment of Portia[1] – is present in both. Above all – and here Decius is careful to cover his daring with a profession of love – it will be whispered that the master of Rome is 'afraid': a hint than which none is better calculated to play upon the strange complex of conflicting emotions at the dictator's heart.

With this last speech, Decius achieves his aim. As he finishes, his followers enter to bring Caesar to the Senate. The victim brushes aside all misgivings – 'How foolish do your fears seem now, Calpurnia' – jokes with his enemies, and greets Antony with a manly jest:

> Antony, that revels long o' nights,
> Is notwithstanding up. [II. ii. 116.]

[1]See p. 40 above.

Throughout we feel a recovery of confidence, a readiness to accept willingly what has now become his fate. The emphasis on 'friend-ship', on taking wine together, underlines by contrast the monstrous treachery afoot; only Brutus, standing aside from the main stream, 'yearns' to think that appearances are 'false', that 'every like is not the same'. From this moment, Caesar's history marches together with that of his enemies to converge at the base of Pompey's effigy.

III

Caesar's last words and attitudes, spoken in the immediate shadow of his fall, contribute outstandingly to the impression of fatality which has from the first overshadowed the play. It is apparent in his reaction to the warnings which seek to deflect him from his declared purpose. 'The Ides of March,' he says, with illusory confidence, 'are come'; they are not, however, as the Soothsayer ominously retorts, 'yet gone'. Artemidorus, in turn, is similarly brushed aside with a regal declaration of disinterest: 'What touches us ourself shall last be served.' Henceforward to the moment of his death Caesar is engaged in elaborating his assimilation to the exigencies of his exalted office; and, as he does so, a striking contrast is for the last time insinuated between the grandeur of his claim and the frailty, the sense of tension and uneasy strain, which marks the individual who so precariously advances it.

Around this stressed impersonality, the whispered misgivings of the conspirators are built to striking effect. Popilius' greeting inspires in them a fear of discovery, and leads to Cassius' dramatic declaration of his readiness to kill himself. All eyes turn towards Caesar, soon to be reassured by what they see: 'He smiles, and Caesar doth not change'. Mark Antony is drawn aside in preparation for what is to follow, and Metellus Cimber kneels to present the offering of 'a humble heart'. As the successive stages of his plea come home to him, Caesar once more reaffirms the superhuman exaltation which his position imposes upon him. Metellus' first approach is countered by an arrogant assertion of control over the Senate:

> What is now amiss
> That Caesar and *his* senate must redress? [III. i. 31.]

and this, in turn, produces from the suppliant an appeal, now more consciously flattering, to 'Most high, most mighty, and most puissant Caesar'. The result of this plea is to lead the dictator to stress yet further his superiority to the motives which cause 'the blood of ordinary men' to be fired by 'couchings' and 'low courtesies', thus inverting to the 'law of children' the natural claims of authority, 'predominance and first decree'. The assertion is presented in familiar Shakespearian terms, connecting the revolt of 'rebel blood' with melting sweetness and cloying flattery:

> Be not fond,
> To think that Caesar bears such rebel blood
> That will be thaw'd from the true quality
> With that which melteth fools, I mean, sweet words,
> Low crooked court'sies and base spaniel-fawning. [III. i. 39.]

Yet even this repudiation is not allowed to stand alone. The rejection of the arts of the courtier, whom his master spurns 'like a cur' out of his way, leads to a typically theatrical climax:

> Know, Caesar doth not wrong, nor without cause
> Will he be satisfied. [III. i. 47.]

The combination of dignity with the weight of underlying tension could hardly be more effectively presented than at this moment, when time hangs, dramatically speaking, suspended in expectation of the coming blow.

To this refusal Brutus and Cassius respond with more pressing appeals (but not in 'flattery', Brutus clarifies, while Cassius does violence to his principles by kneeling 'so low as to the foot') in favour of Metellus' suit. These interventions lead Caesar to the last and most theatrical of all his assertions of fixity. To be 'moved' would be to share in the frailty around him; against this possibility he reaffirms once more his detachment, relating it to the constancy of the 'northern star', a necessary fixed point conferring order upon the otherwise random movements of the firmament. His claim has personal as well as public implications. Just as his fall is about to stress the common humanity which binds him to other men, he accentuates unnaturally the distance which separates him from them:

> men are flesh and blood, and apprehensive;
> Yet in the number I do know but one
> That unassailable holds on his rank,
> Unshaked of motion. [III. i. 67.]

That this claim, in which the historical imagination resounds, covers a measure of reality will be confirmed by the events which follow Caesar's fall; but, already, his own unsuspecting words –

> and that I am he
> Let me a little show it, even in this – [III. i. 70.]

amount to a plea, an appeal to the world to support him in this self-estimate. From this moment of unintended self-revelation, the last short exchanges rise with splendid dramatic economy to the fall which takes place – and here we may recall the tribune's speech in the opening scene[1] – at the foot of the effigy of Pompey, whom the dictator himself formerly overthrew.

The fall is followed by a tense moment of silence, set against the gathering climax which has so splendidly preceded it. Immediately after this, the emotions so far held in check, concentrated upon Caesar's overpowering presence, break out, cover the stage with the rising hysteria of libertarian sentiment. 'Liberty! freedom! tyranny is dead!' cries Cinna, and calls upon his words to echo through the streets; Cassius moves to the 'common pulpits', and only Brutus, firm in abstract self-control, calls on those around him to maintain their calm: 'Fly not; stand still; ambition's debt is paid'. In this, however, he stands alone, helpless to impose his will upon the flood which he has let loose. His gesture of reassurance to Publius – 'There is no harm intended to your person' – and his grimly prophetic assumption of responsibility –

> let no man abide this deed
> But we the doers – [III. i. 94]

represent the last echoes of a sanity already being carried away in the chaos to which Caesar's fall will lead. Antony, taken by surprise (or perhaps to take stock of his position?), has fled to his house 'amazed' and

> Men, wives, and children stare, cry out and run
> As it were doomsday. [III. i. 97.]

Only Brutus, still self-consciously serene in his doctrinaire fatalism, stands out against the course of events, asserting his self-command against 'doomsday' and rallying his associates, albeit with a growing touch of hysteria, around his person:

> That we shall die, we know; 'tis but the time,
> And drawing days out, that men stand upon. [III. i 99.]

The reflection draws from Cassius a rejoinder grotesque, even absurd in its caricature of reasoning:

> Why, he that cuts off twenty years of life
> Cuts off so many years of fearing death, [III. i. 101.]

---

[1]   ... do you now cull out a holiday?
And do you now strew flowers in his way
That comes in triumph over Pompey's blood? [I. i. 53.]

where self-deception leads Caesar's murderers logically, as Brutus
points out, to conceive themselves as the benefactors of their victim.

That these efforts to assert control over the course of events cover a
sense of distraught unreality is proved when Brutus himself turns to a
more emotional line of appeal. He transforms, in effect, the dreadful
reality before them into a ghastly and incongruous mixture of blood-
stained emotionalism and doctrinaire exaltation:

> Stoop, Romans, stoop,
> And let us bathe our hands in Caesar's blood
> Up to the elbows, and besmear our swords;
> Then walk we forth, even to the market-place,
> And waving our red weapons o'er our heads,
> Let's all cry, 'Peace, freedom, and liberty!' [III. i. 105.]

Here, if anywhere, and in the self-congratulatory exchanges that
follow, a final comment on the true nature of conspiracy is unerringly
made. The gap between profession and reality, the aspiration to
freedom and the deed on which it so perversely rests, is remorselessly
asserted in the insistence upon spilt blood: blood not, as in *Macbeth*,
horrifyingly sticking to the murderer's hands, but lavish, free-
flowing, answering to the strained emotions with which the assassins
have from the first sought to disguise, even from themselves, the true
nature of their crime.

Against this reality, and its inevitable issue in the reversal of
natural order, the conspirators stress with unconscious irony the
universal reverberations of their deed. Cassius refers to the future
occasions in which this murder will be 'acted over',

> In states unborn and accents yet unknown; [III. i. 113.]

he goes on, combining high theatricality with a further irony, to say
that, as often as this scene of death is re-enacted 'in sport',

> So often shall the knot of us be call'd
> The men that gave their country liberty. [III. i. 117.]

'Liberty', indeed, in its various possible connotations, is a key-
word of the entire episode. It is, as events will show, a double-
headed concept which will lead finally to civil strife and enslavement; but meanwhile the conspirators, following Brutus' lead, shore
up their illusion of self-assurance by conceiving themselves to be –
still in the words of Cassius – 'the most boldest and best hearts of
Rome'.

The entry of Antony's messenger marks the beginning of a recall
to reality. In his very readiness to prostrate himself before Caesar's
murderer, we can sense political realism feeling its way cautiously to

a true estimate of the forces which have been let loose. At this stage,
still uncommitted, Antony evades any open expression of judgement. Brutus is 'noble, wise, valiant, and honest', but Caesar too was
'mighty, bold, royal, and loving'; Brutus he loves and honours, but
Caesar in addition he 'fear'd'. The condemnation of murder, if
already implied, is not ripe for expression. Antony senses that time is
on his side; but, meanwhile, he asks only to be informed – and the
question is big with implied menace – why Caesar 'deserv'd' to die.
If Brutus can satisfy him, Antony will be ready to follow the new
leader's 'fortune and affairs':

> Mark Antony shall not love Caesar dead
> So well as Brutus living. [III. i. 133.]

But this hypothetical pledge of 'true faith' combines oddly with
references to the 'hazards' of an 'untried state', producing a most
immediate impression of the uncertain times from which a resolution as yet unrevealed will in due course be brought to birth.

Confronted by this new development, Brutus clings to an un-
realistic confidence in the rectitude which inspires his cause. He
recognizes Antony to be 'a wise and valiant Roman', who will only
need to be 'satisfied' by the justice of the arguments he is ready to put
before him; Cassius' shrewder 'misgiving' is allowed no influence on
the course of events. With the stage thus set for his return, Antony
himself enters. To Brutus' welcome he responds not directly, but by
turning his eyes and emotions to the dead Caesar. The spectacle
impels him to reflect upon the passage of worldly glory –

> Are all thy conquests, glories, triumphs, spoils,
> Shrunk to this little measure? – [III. i. 149.]

and then to turn, with an irony that only gradually reveals its full
implications of menace, upon the murderers. A scarcely veiled
accusation underlies his opening demand for a declaration of
intention:

> I know not, gentlemen, what you intend,
> Who else must be let blood, who else is rank. [III. i. 151.]

This is followed by the emotional exaltation of Caesar, slain by those
whose swords have been

> made rich
> With the most noble blood of all this world. [III. i. 155.]

In this play, and not least in the mouth of Antony, emotion flows
easily and attaches itself most typically, as it considers Caesar's fall,
to images of spilt and gushing blood; so now the victim's blood,

which has for the speaker almost the value of a religious relic, generating round itself emotion at once sincere and dangerous, genuine and liable to perversion, 'reeks and smokes' on the 'purpled' hands of his murderers. The devotion of a friend and the beginnings of a denunciation of those who are called in irony 'the choice and master spirits of this age' are typically combined.

Brutus' reply, reaffirming the purity of motive which has animated himself and his followers, is oddly strained, even, beneath the declaration of high principle, shame-faced. The act just committed must appear 'bloody and cruel', as the evidence of their blood-stained hands confirms. The effect is to combine abstract high-mindedness with insensibility to butchery, to the 'bleeding business' so recently dispatched. 'As fire drives out fire, so pity pity': there is something facile about the assertion, as well as about the too-ready contrast between the 'sincere' heart and the external appearance of things, which the closing gesture of calculated conciliation further emphasizes:

> Our arms in strength of malice, and our hearts
> Of brothers' temper, do receive you in
> With all kind love, good thoughts and reverence. [III. i. 174.]

We may feel something too easy, finally insensitive, in this convenient readiness to ignore the blood that must separate the assassin from the victim's friend; and indeed Cassius hastens to add a note of more practical inducement:

> Your voice shall be as strong as any man's
> In the disposing of new dignities. [III. i. 177.]

This, uttered by the very man who so recently advocated Antony's elimination, combines with the uneasy tone of Brutus' admission – 'I, that did love Caesar when I struck him' – to point to a necessary duplicity which the development of the action will amply confirm.

By the end of this exchange, Antony knows that his position is stronger then he can have dared to hope. His next speech brings him nearer to the centre of the action, rises to a barely disguised denunciation. His first phrase – 'I doubt not of your wisdom' – is ironic and finally contemptuous; immediately after it, he returns to the persistent evocation of blood – 'Let each man render me his bloody hand' – and proceeds to a grotesque parody of the reconciliation which Brutus has so impossibly proposed. The handshaking, in turn, leads to an observation, pregnant now with calculated irony, in which Antony, under the guise of reflecting upon the 'slippery ground' upon which his own credit stands in the eyes of the world, condemns Caesar's enemies by implication for being so foolish as to believe him

D

either 'a coward or a flatterer'. This becomes the opening for an emotional exaltation of the dead man and – indirectly – an exposure of the enemies whose 'bloody fingers' he is so unnaturally engaged in shaking. As the speech rises to its elaborate climax, feeling replaces, or reinforces, calculation. The copious shedding of blood is associated with the generous flow of tears; eyes and open wounds pour out together their respective floods –

> Had I as many eyes as thou hast wounds,
> Weeping as fast as they stream forth thy blood – [III. i. 200.]

and the memory of betrayal leads up to the last elaborate image of Caesar's fall, in which true emotion finds almost undisguised expression:

> Here wast thou bay'd, brave hart,
> Here didst thou fall, and here thy hunters stand,
> Sign'd in thy spoil, and crimson'd in thy lethe. [III. i. 204.]

Taking up the flow of rhetorical emotion and the prevailing association of blood and tears, Antony is, by the end of this speech, consciously moving towards a dominant position over his enemies.

Cassius, who realizes this, attempts to interrupt the rising tide of emotion. Antony reassures him by ascribing his words to natural friendship, and Cassius requests in reply a definite statement of where he stands:

> Will you be prick'd in number of our friends,
> Or shall we on, and not depend on you? [III. i. 216.]

Antony's reply is again fraught with an irony –

> Therefore I took your hands, but was indeed
> Sway'd from the point by looking down on Caesar. [III. i. 218.]

(where otherwise is the 'point', if not in the presence of the dead body before them?) – which casts its shadow over the following declaration: 'Friends am I with you all and love you all'; to which again is added the ominous proviso:

> Upon this hope that you shall give me reasons
> Why and wherein Caesar was dangerous. [III. i. 221.]

'Reasons', indeed, of the kind that he himself finds convincing, Brutus – who recognizes that this is at first sight 'a savage spectacle' – is always ready to give; they shall be so 'full of good regard' as to satisfy Caesar's own son that his father was justly murdered. Antony is content for the moment to accept what is offered, and goes on to insinuate his request to present his tribute, as a mere 'friend', at

Caesar's funeral. Blinded as ever by his own conviction of right, Brutus brushes aside Cassius' realistic 'You know not what you do' with the over-confident assertion that it will be enough for him to enter the pulpit first and show 'the reasons' for Caesar's death; Antony will be seen to speak by permission of Caesar's enemies and this, he blandly asserts, 'shall advantage more than do us wrong'. Finally, he offers Antony his conditions and receives in return his enemy's brief agreement: 'I do desire no more.'

Left alone with his thoughts, Antony's last speech is a further revelation of character. Couched in the facile rhetoric which comes so readily to him, it apostrophizes the dead Caesar as 'thou bleeding piece of earth' and goes on to speak of 'costly blood' and to characterize his wounds as 'dumb mouths' and 'ruby lips'. In a world so fluent in feeling, where emotion swells in accordance with the forms of rhetoric, intensely rather than deeply, like the blood which issues from the wounds it contemplates, Antony's oratory is perfectly at home. It issues, however, in a vision of chaos. The spectacle of

Domestic fury and fierce civil strife, [III. i. 263.]

the familiarity asserted with 'dreadful objects', 'blood and destruction', the assertion that

mothers shall but smile when they behold
Their infants quarter'd with the hands of war, [III. i. 267.]

all lead up to a vision of consuming anarchy. 'All pity' shall be 'chok'd' with 'custom of fell deeds',

And Caesar's spirit ranging for revenge,
With Ate at his side come hot from hell,
Shall in these confines with a monarch's voice
Cry 'Havoc!', and let slip the dogs of war;
That this foul deed shall smell above the earth
With carrion men, groaning for burial. [III. i. 270.]

This conclusion to the first open revelation of his pent-up feelings carries with it an estimate of Antony's limitations as a moral being. His rhetoric pays itself with its own expression, represents emotional irresponsibility in one who can also calculate and use his oratorical gifts for ends deliberately and cunningly conceived. The vision of chaos, far from appalling Antony, finally attracts him, answers to a necessity of his nature; and that is why his type of loyalty, not less than Brutus' frigid assertions of principle, is to be seen less in its own right than as a fragment, a partial aspect of the unity which Caesar's death has destroyed in Rome. The end of this political process is 'carrion', self-destruction, death; that Antony, carried on the flow of words which reflects his emotional nature, can dwell with complacency on these dreadful realities is, by implication, an exposure of his most intimate motives.

Antony, however, for all his emotionalism is capable of sober calculation. When Octavius' servant enters to catch sight of Caesar's body, he is careful to seize the chance to establish common feeling in the surrender to tears:

> Passion, I see, is catching, for mine eyes,
> Seeing these beads of sorrow stand in thine,
> Begin to water; [III. i. 283.]

this is the first slight use of a device that the funeral oration will carry to its highest expression. Beneath the emotionalism lies a sharp eye for the main chance. Octavius is warned against entering 'a dangerous Rome', and Antony rounds off the scene with a declaration of his intention to 'try'

> how the people take
> The cruel issue of these bloody men. [III. i. 293.]

As he leaves with Caesar's body, the stage is set for retribution and the release of chaos.

The famous oration scene (III. ii) is perhaps too familiar to call for analysis in detail. It shows a Brutus caught in the consequences of his own act, deprived – now that the mood of exaltation which accompanied him to it has passed – of the impulse to go further, exposed in his inadequate estimate of himself and his situation. Against it is set an Antony who, in the act of appearing as the adventurer and theatrical orator he is, is also the instrument by which the *truth* about murder, which Brutus' idealism cannot cover, emerges to the light of day. This clash of aims and temperaments takes place before a background provided by a new element in the action: the Roman populace. The crowd has not hitherto played a decisive part in events, though its fickleness has been indicated more than once in the early scenes.[1] It now makes the voice of its appetites heard in a more sinister fashion, thereby showing from still another point of view the nature of the forces which Brutus and Cassius have so irresponsibly released from their normal restraints.

There is, indeed, a sense as though of hunger in the insistent clamour with which the scene opens: 'We will be satisfied: let us be satisfied.' A collective will, primitive and irresponsible, but none the less exacting in its demands, has entered the action. The drama to be enacted over Caesar's corpse will take place in the presence of this force, which could well end by devouring both the contending

[1] Most notably by Casca in I. ii. See p. 28 above.

parties. When the Second Citizen announces his intention of 'comparing' the reasons offered by the speakers, a new if unconscious factor of judgement is asserting itself.

Brutus' oration, as has often been noted, is cold in its balanced abstraction, the utterance of one whose devotion to 'nobility' leads him to the illusion that his 'reasons' need only to be stated clearly and with dignity to command the assent of all right-minded and public-spirited men:

> As Caesar loved me, I weep for him: as he was fortunate, I rejoice at it; as he was valiant, I honour him; but as he was ambitious, I slew him. [III. ii. 26.]

The balanced periods aim, not at emotional appeal, which has no place in the speaker's 'philosophy', but at the statement of propositions demanding assent; and the conclusion – 'I slew him' – covers a certain self-sufficiency in its readiness to assume the responsibility for murder. The man who speaks thus is undeniably noble, but his nobility is dangerously close to self-ignorance. 'I have done no more to Caesar than you shall do to Brutus': a note of unconscious irony again asserts itself, together with the incongruous touch of attempted demagogic appeal in the offer of 'a place in the commonwealth' to Mark Antony and his friends: 'as which of you shall not'. Brutus is still unaware of the complexity of his own motives, and this unawareness makes itself felt in the ominous shadow of his conclusion: 'as I slew my best lover for the good of Rome, I have the same dagger for myself, when it shall please my country to need my death.' [III. ii. 49.]

As Brutus brings this speech of self-justification to a close, the crowd begins to play its part. The acclamation of the republican idealist culminates, with a bitter and appropriate irony, in the suggestion that he, the liberator, should be elevated to replace the dictator he has killed. 'Let him be Caesar': the anonymous acclamation is, in effect, a death-blow to all Brutus' idealistic hopes, and it is evidence of the short-sightedness with which he meets it that his last words, urging his hearers to remain with Antony, though in fact an attempt to turn to his own favour the concession offered, to his rival, amount to a connivance at his own doom. Strong in the illusion of self-confidence which his nature demands, Brutus leaves the field to an enemy who is particularly equipped to destroy him.

Faced by the initial hostility of the mob, Antony proceeds with caution. He has come, he says, not to 'praise' Caesar, but merely to bury him. As he warms to his task, however, doubt is cast upon Caesar's alleged 'ambition' –

> The noble Brutus
> Hath told you Caesar was ambitious:
> *If it were so*, it was a grievous fault – [III. ii. 83.]

more particularly by comparison with the tangible horror of his
end: 'And grievously hath Caesar answer'd it'. As the doubt begins
to come home to his audience, Antony feels strong enough to cast a
shadow upon the alleged 'honour' of his enemies, to recall the dead
man's generosity and to point to his refusal of the crown. By the end
of this process the recognition of Brutus as 'honourable' has turned
to the implied doubt of 'And *sure*, he is an honourable man'. It may
be, indeed, that the certainty is false, though the moment has not
yet come to say so openly:

> I speak not to disprove what Brutus spoke,
> But here I am to speak what I do know. [III. ii. 106.]

All his hearers once loved Caesar, 'not without cause': all therefore
have a right, even a human duty, to mourn his passing. It is typical
that Antony, who – unlike Brutus – appeals consciously to the
emotions and finally rouses an element in man not far removed
from the bestial, should claim to speak in the name of reason:

> O judgement! thou art fled to brutish beasts,
> And men have lost their reason. [III. ii. 110.]

Having reached the opening point in his campaign to assert his
control over his hearers, Antony pauses to allow the effect of his
insinuations to sink home.

Each stage in the change of dramatic mood is marked by the
comments of his hearers. They first greet him with doubt and
resentment – ' 'Twere best he speak no harm of Brutus here' – and
to this mood the speaker has been careful to defer. 'For Brutus'
sake, I am beholding to you' is the ingratiating preface with which
he mounts the rostrum: but gradually, as he feels his way to mastery,
he rises to the bolder questioning of 'What cause witholds you then
to mourn for him?' and ends with the effective gesture of feeling
overcoming the power to speak:

> My heart is in the coffin there with Caesar,
> And I must pause till it come back to me. [III. ii. 112.]

The response is just what the orator intended. There is 'much
reason' in what he says; the death of Caesar may open the way for a
'worse' to take his place. The ambition so recently condemned in the
murdered man has now become 'certainly' no part of his nature; the

eyes of the speaker, moreover, by a most telling piece of sentiment, are seen to be 'red as fire with weeping'.

All this implies, beyond insight into the nature of demagogy, something perhaps even more important: the assertion of realities which the conspirators have neglected at their peril and which are already gathering to overwhelm them. The change of emotional climate has become such that Antony can now proceed to a new stage in his manœuvre. This consists in open play upon the fickleness of popular emotion. Caesar's authority of 'yesterday' is contrasted with his solitude in death: none is now 'so poor to do him reverence'. As always with Antony, genuine emotion is mingled with its conscious exploitation in others. The orator, in the act of disclaiming his intention 'to do Brutus wrong and Cassius wrong', proceeds to stir up his hearers 'to mutiny and rage'. Rather than do them wrong, he will 'wrong the dead', 'wrong myself and you'; and the final reference to 'honourable men' comes, now openly ironic, to point his intention. The culminating moment in this part of the speech is an appeal to the interest of the mob in the reference to the will, which however – following the normal tactic of seeming to withdraw what he offers – he says that he does not 'mean to read'. The height of emotional tension at which he aims has, indeed, still to be reached, and Antony procedes to stimulate it by a sensational use of imagery which unites the evocation of wounds and blood with the 'religious' associations to which his audience most readily responds:

> they would go and kiss dead Caesar's wounds
> And dip their napkins in his sacred blood,
> Yea, beg a hair of him for memory. [III. ii. 138.]

The feeling here typifies the play in its combination of violent external colour and inner emotion. The idea of sacred and bloody relics both heightens the value ascribed to the dead Caesar and points to a deliberate manipulation of popular sentiment.

The appeal to emotion produces the desired effect. The crowd demand to hear the will. Antony, still pretending to refuse, hints ever more definitely at its importance – 'It is not meet you know how Caesar loved you' – and rouses the very passions he ostensibly condemns. 'It will enflame you, it will make you mad': the words, seemingly designed to restore calm, create the very excess which they deprecate. The determination of the mob makes itself felt in repeated calls for 'the will'; it is the irony of the situation that the people affirm their power to obtain their desire – 'You shall read us the will, Caesar's will' – as they are in fact being moulded to Antony's purpose. One more reference to the 'honourable men' whose daggers 'have stabb'd Caesar', and Antony judges that the time is ripe; but,

before acceding to read the will, he makes a last show of unwillingness – 'You will *compel* me then to read the will' – and prepares for
his disclosure by calling upon his hearers to form a ring about the
corpse. In full sight of the wounds, and as Antony descends to still
closer contact with his audience, the emotional content of the
situation will effectively reinforce the appeal so variously made to
simple gratitude, base cupidity, and blind ignorance.

The third long part of the oration is devised to bring the crowd to
join in the speaker's own brilliant, colourful flow of emotion: 'If you
have tears, prepare to shed them now.' Once more, the emphasis is
on wounds and on the blood which, spilt by traitors, flows with an
ease which answers to the emotion now being expressed. Brutus was
'Caesar's angel', so that the dead man's blood, when it followed the
withdrawn dagger, was, as it were,

> rushing out of doors, to be resolved
> If Brutus so unkindly knocked, or no. [III. ii. 184.]

Here and in the following re-creation of Caesar's fall, Antony's
appeal to sentiment, his calculated release in others of the emotions
which it is his own nature easily to feel, reaches its culminating point.
He is now able to appeal to the natural pieties –

> O now you weep, and I perceive you feel
> The dint of pity: these are gracious drops – [III. ii. 198.]

before he makes his last and supremely effective gesture by turning
from 'Caesar's vesture wounded' to the body of the victim, 'marr'd,
as you see, with traitors'.

It is, indeed, now a religious relic that is being displayed to call for
its own intensity of responding feeling. The response comes in broken
exclamations, which stand out against the wonderfully facile flow of
what has gone before, and leads finally to the sinister call for death
and revenge: 'Revenge! About! Sack! Burn! Fire! Kill! Slay!' To
the last Antony follows his method of inciting his hearers by disclaiming the very ends he has in mind. He begs them not to be
stirred up to 'such a sudden flow of mutiny'. Caesar's assassins are
still 'honourable', though the reasons for their deed are beyond the
understanding of one who is, like those who hear him, 'a plain blunt
man',

> That love my friend: and that they know full well
> That gave me public leave to speak of him. [III. ii. 223.]

It is essential to the irony which prevails at this point that this, in
part, is precisely what Antony is: though it is equally true that the

conscious orator in him, in asserting this 'plainness', is using it for
calculated ends. His self-assumed part is that of one who has

> neither, wit, nor words, nor worth,
> Action, nor utterance, nor the power of speech,
> To stir men's blood, [III. ii. 225.]

one who can 'only speak right on'; and, having said so much, he
returns by contrast to the rhetorical devices which are the secret of
his success:

> I tell you that which you yourselves do know;
> Show you sweet Caesar's wounds, poor poor dumb mouths,
> And bid them speak for me: but were I Brutus,
> And Brutus Antony, there were an Antony
> Would ruffle up your spirits, and put a tongue
> In every wound of Caesar, that should move
> The stones of Rome to rise and mutiny. [III. ii. 228.]

It is the familiar mixture for the last time: the disclaimer of the
oratorical gifts and graces he is using, the personification of Caesar's
wounds, the rousing of his hearers to mutiny through the mention of
'the stones of Rome'.

The effect is immediately gained. The mob, moving off to burn the
houses of Brutus and his followers, forget to listen to the terms of the
very will which they so passionately demanded to hear; Antony's
reminder – 'You have forgot the will I told you of' – is one of the
most effective strokes of the scene. As they go off, his last comment is
a revealing disclaimer of responsibility. 'Now let it work': the orator,
resting on his laurels, looks with satisfaction on his achievement,
dwells with a certain pleasure on the chaos he has let loose:

> Mischief, thou art afoot,
> Take thou what course thou wilt. [III. ii. 265.]

The final effect is a revelation of irresponsibility accompanied by
sinister pleasure:

> Fortune is merry,
> And in this mood will give us anything. [III. ii. 271.]

That, later on, she will assume other moods, ultimately less congenial
to the speaker, remains to be seen. Meanwhile, the sinister little
episode (III. iii) of the destruction of Cinna the poet for a chance
coincidence of name, comes effectively to announce the brutality
which will from now on so frequently preside over the course of
events.

IV

By the end of the forum scene the central episode of *Julius Caesar* has been concluded, and the clash between Brutus and Antony resolved. The last part of the tragedy exhibits the consequences of Caesar's murder. It shows a Rome divided by covert rivalries which can only end in the elimination of all but one of its contending factions and, after that elimination, in the restoration of unity under Octavius. Apart from this resolution, which the end of the play foreshadows with notable detachment, the personal tragedy of Brutus is rounded off in the self-inflicted death which is its logical conclusion.

The first scene (IV. i) reflects the political spirit which, in one form or another, will from this time forth dominate the action. The triumvirs are engaged in bargaining, in a spirit of cold calculation, for human lives. Death is contemplated without illusion and without feeling. The opening words of Antony, who has so recently exhibited himself in the forum as a man of sensibility, are 'These many then shall die'; Octavius, passing typically from the general statement to its particular application, adds (turning to Lepidus) 'Your brother too must die', and obtains his companion's assent:

> Upon condition Publius shall not live,
> Who is your sister's son, Mark Antony. [IV. i. 4.]

The callousness of the exchange, the readiness to write off human lives by marks on paper, is rounded off by Antony's complacent: 'He shall not live; look, with a spot I damn him.' The final suggestion that the will, which Antony has so recently used to stir up mob emotion in the name of generosity, should be studied to determine 'How to cut off some charge in legacies' adds a revealing touch of parsimony to the display of cynicism in action.

The world which is to replace that formerly dominated by Caesar is indeed mean, petty, and dangerous. The triumvirs are already engaged in the first stages of a ruthless struggle for supremacy. As soon as Lepidus has been dispatched for the will, Antony refers disparagingly to him ('a slight unmeritable man': 'meet to be sent on errands') and proposes his elimination:

> is it fit,
> The three-fold world divided, he should stand
> One of the three to share it? [IV. i. 13.]

Octavius, whose moment has still to come, bides his time, pointing out only that Antony has himself accepted Lepidus ('So you thought

him') as an equal in the conduct of affairs. Antony's reply is the
cynic's appeal to experience ('Octavius, I have seen more days
than you'): an experience which leads him to dismiss Lepidus as
'an ass', bearing gold 'to groan and sweat[1] under the business',
before being finally turned off

> to shake his ears
> And graze in commons. [IV. i. 26.]

The continued reserve of Octavius ('he is a tried and valiant soldier')
Antony meets with a further display of cynicism. 'So is my horse,
Octavius,' he rejoins, and goes on to dismiss Lepidus as a 'creature'
under direction:

> A barren-spirited fellow: one that feeds
> On abjects, orts, and imitations,
> Which, out of use, and staled by other men,
> Begin his fashion, [IV. i. 36.]

and ends by setting him contemptuously aside as a mere 'property'.
With Lepidus thus removed from consideration, the two leaders
return to discussion of the 'great things' in which their own future is
involved. The last words of the scene, spoken by Octavius, stress the
insecurity that surrounds the entire political future:

> some that smile have in their hearts, I fear,
> Millions of mischiefs. [IV. i. 50.]

Such is the world which has survived Caesar, and in which his
avengers are fated to move.

The circumstances of Caesar's enemies, revealed in the next two
scenes (IV. ii, iii), answer to a conception which is, in its accepted
pessimism, finally similar. In them, division and self-doubt replace
the cynical manœuvres of their foes. Brutus complains that Cassius

> Hath given me some worthy cause to wish
> Things done undone; [IV. ii. 8.]

but, in spite of the air of invincible rightness which these words
suggest, he is ready to believe that his friend may yet be 'full of regard and honour'. The abstract idealist, who has lived in the world
of his own concepts of duty and honour until a combination of
external circumstance and intrigue forced uncongenial action upon
him, is now in the process of being brought into disillusioning

---

[1] The verbal coincidence with *Hamlet* –

> who would fardels bear,
> To *grunt* and *sweat* under a weary life – [III. i. 76.]

may be just worth noting.

contact with the realities of Roman politics: these are now realistically shown, and tragically considered, through the eyes of an
idealist enmeshed in the web of action he has chosen for himself.
The process of decline is seen as fatal, inevitable. Cassius, no longer
the ardent friend of the early scenes, whom the prospect of action
united (perhaps, in the last analysis, spuriously) to a colleague whom
interest also demanded as his associate, now salutes that associate
with distant correctness, no longer shows

> such free and friendly conference,
> As he hath used of old. [IV. ii. 17.]

Brutus' reaction is heavy with the sense of fatality. Lucilius has
described 'a hot friend cooling', and the process by which 'love
begins to sicken and decay' has its symptoms in 'an enforced ceremony':

> There are no tricks in plain and simple faith;
> But hollow men, like horses hot at hand,
> Make gallant show and promise of their mettle;
> But when they should endure the bloody spur,
> They fall their crests and like deceitful jades
> Sink in the trial. [IV. ii. 22.]

The wish of Brutus to maintain 'plain and simple faith' is at once
moving and strangely inadequate. It springs from his most deeply
held theoretical conception of life, in the absence of which his
integrity, his belief in himself and in the purity of his motives, must
founder; but it runs against the nature of things as determined by
the course of action in which he has compromised his honesty. The
result is the sense of 'hollowness' which dominates the speech,
and from now on imposes itself on the entire action. Against the
background of advancing armies ('Comes his army on?') we feel
already the 'sinking at the trial' which, proceeding from adverse
external realities, mirrors inner dejection.

The approach of Cassius, indeed, is accompanied by the traditional signs of tragedy. A 'low march' is heard, Brutus and his
followers go 'gently' to meet him. Against this muted background,
punctuated by the respective challenges on either side, Cassius'
blunt accusation breaks with double force: 'Most noble brother, you
have done me wrong.' The appeal to 'nobility', recalling the ideal
basis of their past association, emphasizes by contrast the present
reality; and Brutus meets the accusation with a familiar mixture of
idealistic protest and self-conscious virtue:

> Judge me, you gods! wrong I mine enemies?
> And if not so, how should I wrong a brother? [IV. ii. 38.]

Against this fixity of principle, this abstract affirmation of a brother-hood for the reality of which, however, Brutus deeply craves, Cassius' emotional sense of wrong breaks in headlong form: 'Brutus, this sober form of yours hides wrongs'; and though Brutus is sufficiently master of himself to see that the quarrel is concealed from the public eye, it is immediately brought to a head in the private discussion which follows.

The motives behind this discussion are, from the first, of some complexity. Cassius, rushing typically into the void which opens before him, initiates it with the blunt accusation that he has been 'wrong'd'; but it is clear from his explanation that the wrong has been inflicted in a dubious context. Brutus has accused Lucius Pella of accepting bribes, and Cassius' protest, far from denying this, confines itself to the fact that he has pleaded, in vain, because he 'knew the man', and because further, 'in such a time as this',

> it is not meet
> That every nice offence should bear his comment. [IV. iii. 7.]

To this mixture of fellowship and expediency, Brutus is no doubt in his right to reply 'You wrong'd yourself to write in such a case'; but there is about the moral tone of his retort an implication of superiority that cannot fail to rankle in the mind of his associate.

Brutus, indeed, cannot refrain from rubbing salt into the wound. By accusing Cassius of 'an itching palm', he rouses the impetuous self-respect of his friend to violent protest:

> You know that you are Brutus that speaks this,
> Or, by the gods, this speech were else your last; [IV. iii. 13.]

and there is surely a touch of insensitivity in the responding reference to 'chastisement' which leaves Cassius speechless in its implication of lofty superiority. The two characters, so precariously united against Caesar, are now seen to be perfectly designed to exasperate one another to the limits of endurance.

As the gap between them widens, Brutus, in a mood at once self-righteous and nostalgic for the lost simplicities of his original con-ception, recalls the moral integrity which inspired their actions: 'Did not great Caesar bleed for justice' sake?'. This thought, contrasted with the sad reality of the present, leads him to back his reproof with a further gesture towards the idealism of the past:

> What, shall one of us,
> That struck the foremost man of all this world
> But for supporting robbers, shall we now

> Contaminate our fingers with base bribes,
> And sell the mighty space of our large honours
> For so much trash as may be grasped thus? [IV. iii. 21.]

The gesture is ample, noble, and yet it covers weakness. So much can be felt in the rhetorical tone in which 'the mighty space of our large honours' is recalled, 'honours' which circumstance and the very fact of the present quarrel are revealing as compromised. As always, Brutus is taking refuge in a satisfactory picture of himself as one who has dared, for 'honour' alone, to lead and inspire a conspiracy that overthrew 'the foremost man of all this world'; but where disinterest ends and egoism, the need to live up to an ennobling vision of his own motives, begins, we might be hard put to decide.

Whatever the truth about Brutus' purity of motive (and no simple judgement would be appropriate) his attitude could not be more precisely calculated to rub the raw edges of Cassius' sense of inferiority. As Brutus ceases, he describes what he has just heard, most bitterly, as a 'baiting' of himself and utters the ominous warning: 'I'll not endure it.' His touchy self-respect has been offended, and now responds by appealing to his superior experience, in which he feels on stronger ground than when moral judgements are in question:

> I am a soldier, I,
> Older in practice, abler than yourself
> To make conditions. [IV. iii. 30.]

The repetition of 'I' itself indicates the nature of the wound inflicted upon Cassius' own type of egoism. That of Brutus, though more complex, is not less strong. It impels him, where tact would have passed over the burning issue, to exasperate his companion further by contemptuous denial. 'You are not, Cassius.' 'I am.' 'I say you are not': the result is to create an ugly wrangle in which the last shreds of self-respect seem likely to be swallowed up. At the culminating moment, Cassius' threatening 'tempt me no further', uttered on the brink of an open explosion, is matched by the infuriating superiority of 'Away, slight man!' and by the final insult:

> Hear me, for I will speak.
> Must I give way and room to your rash choler?
> Shall I be frightened when a madman stares? [IV. iii. 38.]

At this moment, the realities of character which underlie the previous affirmations of constancy and devotion to principle are revealed for what they are. The rest of the scene will be devoted to working them out fully, and to an attempt to cover them up in the interests of a cause already lost.

At first, however, it is not a matter of covering up, but of adding further irritation to Cassius' open wound. In this Brutus, by a trait which links curiously with his self-conscious idealism, but which is not on reflection incompatible with it, is a master. 'Must I endure all this?' Cassius cries, as though demanding clemency, and receives in return the bitter exasperation of the insult – 'All this! ay more! Fret till your proud heart break' – and the contemptuous dismissal which follows it:

> Go show your slaves how choleric you are,
> And make your bondmen tremble! [IV. iii. 43.]

The rest of the speech, so true to life in the frigid egoism of the man 'armed strong in honesty', rises through the self-centred rhetorical question 'Must I budge?' and the impatience of

> Must I observe you? must I stand and crouch
> Under your testy humour? [IV. iii. 45.]

to a final, almost sadistic determination to inflict humiliation

> By the gods,
> You shall digest the venom of your spleen,
> Though it do split you; for, from this day forth,
> I'll use you for my mirth, yea, for my laughter,
> When you are waspish. [IV. iii. 46.]

The lines are rich in inflection, in the varied revelation of character. There is pleasure in inflicting humiliation ('You shall digest the venom of your spleen'), moral callousness born of self-sufficiency – 'Though it do split you' – and contempt – 'I'll use you for my mirth' – together with a bitter pleasure in true characterization in the final description of Cassius as 'waspish'. The fact is that the element of egoism present from the first beneath Brutus' noble façade is coming to the surface under the stress of his growing awareness of standing intolerably in a false situation. In any case, the effect of this outburst, though palliated, can never be undone; and Cassius' broken reply 'Is it come to this?' clearly involves a glance back to the idealistic unity of purpose in which Caesar's murder was carried out and which is now being revealed in so unflattering a light.

Brutus, his sense of superiority roused, loses no opportunity for turning the screw further. In so doing, he is moved, at least in part by indignation at Cassius' claim to be a 'better' soldier. He challenges him to make this 'vaunting' true, adding ironically that this will 'please' him well, and takes refuge in the superiority of

> for mine own part,
> I shall be glad to learn of *noble* men. [IV. iii. 53.]

The reproof moves Cassius to excuse himself:

> I said, an elder soldier, not a better:
> Did I say, better? [IV. iii. 56.]

A glance back will show that Cassius, in making his original remark, at least implied 'better', in the sense of more experienced; but the excuse, and the rather pathetic query which follows it, must strike us as in some redeeming sense human.

Brutus, however, is not yet ready to see it so. When he dismisses Cassius' excuse with the frigid comment 'If you did, I care not', he rouses his friend to say that Caesar himself 'durst' not so have provoked him and receives, most woundingly, the retort: 'Prithee, peace! you durst not so have tempted him'. The effect is to provoke Cassius to the limit, until he threatens dangers unspecified: 'I may do that I shall be sorry for,' only to prompt the impossibly irritating rejoinder: 'You have done that you should be sorry for.' This part of the exchange concludes in Brutus taking up once more his own peculiar pose of self-admiring superiority:

> There is no terror, Cassius, in your threats;
> For I am armed so strong in honesty,
> That they pass by me as the idle wind
> Which I respect not: [IV. iii. 66.]

where the moral integrity of the 'philosopher' is combined with the striking of an attitude, an assumption of superior virtue that corresponds to the maintenance of a necessary self-idealization. The pose thus adopted, there is a revealing return to the theme of the original dispute. Brutus accuses Cassius of having denied him 'certain sums of gold', and goes on to say:

> I can raise no money by vile means:
> By heaven, I had rather coin my heart,
> And drop my blood for drachmas, than to wring
> From the hard hearts of peasants their vile trash
> By any indirection. [IV. iii. 71.]

The dismissal as so much 'vile trash' of the very means he was so anxious for Cassius to provide is as revealing as the disclaimer of 'indirection' in obtaining it. One finds oneself asking whether this attitude is calculated to win wars and, indeed, whether Brutus' reliance on his friend to provide the means which will enable him to avoid a course of action morally repugnant to himself is not more than a little disingenuous. The final accusation of 'covetousness' leads to the snarl and counter-snarl of

- I denied you not.

- You did.

- I did not, [IV. iii. 83.]

and to what appears to be a complete deadlock.

The healing of this breach and the return to at least the appearance of unity are accomplished with no small tact. The conspirators, seeing the abyss opening at their feet, draw back in horror. Cassius excuses himself on the grounds that it was a 'fool' who conveyed his answer. He goes on to express himself in the pathos of 'Brutus hath rived my heart' and to appeal to true friendship with the plea that 'A friend should bear his friend's infirmities'. Perhaps, as in much of this play, the expression of emotion contains a touch of exhibitionism; but true feeling is present too, and the recrimination which follows is cast in a quieter key, contains hints of repentance:

CASSIUS You love me not.
BRUTUS I do not like your faults.
CASSIUS A friendly eye could never see such faults.
BRUTUS A flatterer's would not. [IV. iii. 87.]

Both, we may feel, are moved beneath the surface of their reproaches by a sense that things have gone too far, that it is their own past, their capacity for continued belief in their moral dignity, which they are in reality abjuring; and when Cassius breaks into further reproach, self-exhibition is subtly combined with a true sense of personal betrayal. 'Cassius is a-weary of the world': here it may seem that a conscious appeal to emotion prevails, but the following phrases surely strike a valid note in their criticism of Brutus' frigid moralizing:

Hated by one he loves; braved by his brother!
Check'd like a bondman; all his faults observed,
Set in a note-book, learn'd and conn'd by rote,
To cast into my teeth. [IV. iii. 95.]

Truth and the striking of an attitude are here most subtly combined, as they are in the flow of hitherto pent-up emotion to which these considerations lead:

O, I could weep
My spirit from mine eyes! [IV. iii. 98.]

Once more, at the end of the speech, true feeling turns into the assumption of a pose, the sense of weakness is covered by the striking of a 'Roman' attitude:

E

> There is my dagger,
> And here my naked breast; within, a heart
> Dearer than Plutus' mine, richer than gold;
> If that thou be'st a Roman, take it forth;
> I, that denied thee gold, will give my heart;
> Strike, as thou didst at Caesar; for I know,
> When thou didst hate him worst, thou lovedst him better
> Than ever thou lovedst Cassius. [IV. iii. 99.]

Once more, it is necessary to distinguish carefully between the pose and the presence of true emotion. The offer of the dagger contains an attempt to cover failure, but corresponds also to the tragic sense of an illusion shattered, a relationship, potentially precious, destroyed; and it is worth noting that the gesture is made in the shadow of the original crime against Caesar, by which indeed the whole exchange is truly dominated.

Brutus, realizing no doubt that he has said too much, meets this outburst with a genuine attempt to reduce the tension. He is, however, characteristically clumsy in his effort to adjust his words to a new mood. His phrase 'Be angry when you will, it shall have scope' still sounds stiffly, rather like the humouring of a self-willed child; men such as Brutus do not easily descend from the pedestal on which their lives are based. Beneath the clumsiness, however, there is now revealed a deep unhappiness, the immediate cause of which is still being held back from us:

> O Cassius, you are yoked with a lamb,
> That carries anger as the flint bears fire,
> Who, much enforced, shows a hasty spark,
> And straight is cold again. [IV. iii. 109.]

The reference to feeling hardly struck as from a flinty surface, an innate coldness, reveals tellingly the diffidence, the emotional clumsiness, which is part of the character; and the sincerity of the revelation opens the way to a rueful, disillusioned reconciliation. Cassius, reproaching Brutus – but now less urgently – for reducing him to an object of 'mirth and laughter', proffers tentatively the excuse of 'grief and blood ill-temper'd', and receives in reply the admission 'When I spoke that I was ill-temper'd too'. The confession leads to a gesture of reconciliation, in which 'hands' and 'hearts' are again given in amity, and the depth of the feelings now being brought safely back to control is indicated in Cassius' simple apostrophe: 'O Brutus!' His confession to 'that rash humour which my mother gave me' is balanced by Brutus' typically clumsy effort to bind reconciliation to a jest:

from henceforth,
When you are over-earnest with your Brutus,
He'll think your mother chides, and leave you so, [IV. iii. 120.]

where, as it were, the muted echo of his earlier superiority is turned to
an insecure, but genuine gesture of humanity. The impression left by
the whole exchange is one of the cooling embers of a passion doomed
to extinction, but surviving, at least for the moment, the death of the
original flame.

The intervention of the poet, enjoining the need for unity, interrupts for a moment the gathered tension of the exchange. His
rhymes are absurd, but the sentiment itself is reasonable, and we
may feel that Brutus' contemptuous reference to 'these jigging fools'
is less than kind. The reason for his state, however, and for much
which has gone before has so far been held back by an admirable
stroke of dramatic tact. It is now revealed. After calling for a bowl of
wine, symbol – as it were – of harmony between friends, he meets
Cassius' wondering comment 'I did not think you could have been
so angry' and the reproof of 'Of your philosophy you make no use',
with the tone, still self-justifying, answering to his need to conform
to the prevailing picture of himself, but now also deeply human, of
his simple revelation: 'No man bears sorrow better: Portia is dead.'
The disclosure, followed by an admirably brief and tense exchange
of phrases –

BRUTUS   Portia is dead.
CASSIUS Ha, Portia!
BRUTUS   She is dead – [IV. iii. 146.]

gives a centre of stillness to the bitter exchanges that have gone
before. From this heart of silence, Cassius' emotion speaks in a new,
transformed tone: 'How 'scaped I killing when I cross'd you so?',
and backs it with the almost choric quality of his following exclamation: 'O insupportable and touching loss!' The use of verse
rhythms to compass deep dramatic effect is never better illustrated
in this play.

The revelation is rounded off with the recovery by Brutus of his
Stoic mask: 'Speak no more of her!' If the 'philosopher' in him
dictates this assertion of emotional control, the husband's affection
warns him not to give voice to a feeling which, once expressed,
might shatter all containing limits. In this sense the revelation of
Portia's death confirms what we have learnt of their relationship,
and of the effect upon it of Brutus' project, earlier in the play.[1] The
hidden cause of emotional stress having thus been revealed, the

[1] In II. i. See p. 39 above.

bowl of wine is brought in, and in it Brutus pledges himself to 'bury all unkindness', receiving in return the emotional fullness of Cassius' answering pledge:

> My heart is thirsty for that noble pledge.
> Fill, Lucius, till the wine o'erswell the cup;
> I cannot drink too much of Brutus' love. [IV. iii. 159.]

The reconciliation takes place under the shadow of tragedy; it cannot be a restoration of the original relationship, now irretrievably flawed by past choices; but, in spite of this, the human content is there, beyond all the purposes of political realism, and it rounds off suitably the issues so dramatically represented in what is, in some respects, the most interesting scene of the play.

The personal conflict thus covered, the action moves in the dim light of a 'taper' to a consideration of tactics. Cassius, still struck with awe by what he has just heard, muses once more 'Portia, art thou gone?', addressing, as it were, himself; but with Brutus' quiet 'No more, I pray you', that particular issue is cleared and the discussion turns to the gathering clouds without. Octavius and Mark Antony have assembled 'a mighty power', and in Rome the grim climate of 'proscription and bills of outlawry' gains daily in menace. Cicero is reported dead, and his death is linked by Portia's passing to the need for a spirit of Stoic acceptance; for, in Brutus' words,

> We must die, Messala;
> With meditating that she must die once,
> I have the patience to endure it now. [IV. iii. 189.]

The second report of Portia's death, and Brutus' passing over of it, is likely to reflect an imperfect text;[1] but it would also be in character for Brutus to remain tensely silent where the public discussion of his loss was concerned. His 'philosophy', thus tempered by experience, is at this point attuned to reality in a way which Cassius finds it hard to share –

> I have as much of this in art as you,
> But yet my nature would not bear it so – [IV. iii. 193.]

but which enables Brutus to urge, by contrast, a return 'to our work alive'.

The following argument reveals further dissension among the leaders. Both are aware of weakness, to which, however, they react differently and – finally – in vain. Cassius prefers to see the enemy taking the initiative and so 'doing himself offence'; but Brutus admits the lack of local support –

[1] Most editors of the play have so considered it.

> The people 'twixt Philippi and this ground
> Do stand but in a forced affection – [IV. iii. 203.]

and calls for action precisely because he senses that the logic of
events is moving against him. The argument, pressed with the rather
irritating self-sufficiency usual with him – 'Good reasons must of
force give place to better'; 'Under your pardon. You must note
beside . . .' – rests finally on an admission that circumstances are
moving along paths beyond all personal control:

> There is a tide in the affairs of men
> Which taken at the flood leads on to fortune;
> Omitted, all the voyage of their life
> Is bound in shallows and in miseries. [IV. iii. 217.]

The last word is, characteristically, a recognition of man's limited
capacity to impose his will upon the course of reality. Afloat on the
'full sea' of events, his freedom is limited to 'taking the current when
it serves'. It is not in any way certain that to do so will lead to victory,
but to allow things to take their course is 'to lose our ventures', to
court certain failure. The end of the exchange is heavy with a sense
of descending darkness – 'The deep of night is crept upon our talk' –
and of subjection to fate: 'nature must obey necessity'. In Brutus'
farewell to 'noble, noble Cassius', and in the nostalgic wish for
'good repose', balanced by his friend's glance back to the 'ill beginnings of the night' and his prayer that the quarrel between them
may never be repeated –

> Never come such division 'tween our souls!
> Let it not, Brutus – [IV. iii. 234.]

there is some glimpse of the strain through which both have passed.

The approach of sleep for Brutus, surrounded with intimations of
harmony that at once attract and elude him, but which lead in any
case deathward, is accompanied by solicitude for Lucius and by the
broken disconnected nature of his instructions. 'Bear with me, good
boy, I am much forgetful,' he says, and calls upon Lucius to 'hold
up' his 'heavy' eyes long enough to play a sleep-inducing melody.
The youthful innocence of the boy has had throughout a nostalgic
value by contrast with his own overladen experience; but the background is now one of approaching dissolution –

> I will not hold thee long; if I do live,
> I will be good to thee – [IV. iii. 264.]

and sleep itself is 'murderous', lays its 'leaden mace' upon the page
even as he plays his instrument. With the appearance of Caesar's

ghost, there enters into the fabric of uneasy dreams a premonition of
all that the conspirators have failed to kill, of all that now awaits at
Philippi to overwhelm them. It is to be noted that Lucius, at this
same moment, refers in his sleep to the strings of his instrument as
'false'.

v

After this presentation of dissension, the two approaching armies
come together for the final resolution. At first sight, Shakespeare
may seem less deeply engaged than usual in these closing episodes.
There are, perhaps, too many lines like 'Alas, thou hast misconstrued
everything', flat in tone and oddly perfunctory in expression. Yet we
should not simplify unduly the effect at which these scenes would
appear to be aiming. Various plays of this period – *Henry IV*, *Henry
V*, and *Troilus and Cressida*[1] perhaps most notably – coincide in
presenting martial action with a notable detachment. It would
seem unlikely that the dramatist who, at this time, developed the
complex attitude to 'honour' in his great series of English historical
plays should be ready to accept at its face value the conventional
attitude to Roman suicide. The seeds of self-destruction have, in
fact, been present from the first in the minds of Caesar's enemies,
sometimes rhetorically declared,[2] sometimes contemplated with a
certain perverse nostalgia : and now, in the moment of decision, they
bea: fruit in the reality of suicide. The combination of a detached
irony of presentation with the resolution of Brutus' personal tragedy
is perhaps more subtle, calls for a more perceptive interpretation,
than we might at first be inclined to allow.

The opening of this last stage in the action is marked, at all events,
by a notable realism in the presentation of contrary attitudes.
Octavius, cool and dispassionate, stresses the wrong decision of the
enemy ('our hopes are answer'd') and is supported by Antony who
remarks that Brutus and his forces

> come down
> With fearful bravery, thinking by this face
> To fasten in our thoughts that they have courage;
> But 'tis not so. [V. i. 9.]

The comment on the tactical discussion between Brutus and Cassius
is terse, accurate, and final. On the other hand, the relations between

---

[1] For *Henry IV* and *Henry V*, see my book quoted above. I have discussed *Troilus
and Cressida* in my *Approach to Shakespeare* (London, 1957).

[2] As in Cassius' speech in I. iii., quoted on p. 31 above.

Octavius and Antony, the one ascending against the other's foreseen decline, are also briefly indicated in a clash of purposes:

ANTONY Octavius, lead your battle softly on,
    Upon the left hand of the even field.
OCTAVIUS Upon the right hand I; keep thou the left.
ANTONY Why do you cross me in this exigent?
OCTAVIUS I do not cross you; but I will do so. [V. i. 16.]

Certainly, this opening indicates the presence of a full dose of realism in the spirit in which these final scenes are conceived.

When the rival leaders are confronted, the tone of their dispute confirms the prevailing mood. Antony has no difficulty in exposing the moral contradiction between Brutus' idealism and the actions to which he stands committed. 'In your bad strokes, Brutus, you give good words'; but Brutus is able, not less truly, to reply by stressing the gap that in Antony separates the profession from the deed:

> The posture of your blows are yet unknown;
> But for your words, they rob the Hybla bees,
> And leave them honeyless. [V. i. 33.]

If it is true that Antony 'threatens' before he stings, it is equally certain – as he retorts – that Caesar's murder was an act of treachery, in which the conspirators, at the very moment of bowing like 'bondmen', 'fawning like hounds' in the act of kissing his feet, 'show'd their teeth like apes' and finally struck down their unsuspecting victim from behind. A sense of vain recrimination prevails to the end of the exchange. Cassius, roused by Antony's contemptuous reference to 'flatterers', recalls the unwisdom of Brutus' decision to allow him to live; whilst Octavius, standing aside from these bitter exchanges to concentrate upon the present, prefers to leave words for the issue of battle. Possibly his attitude, coldly practical and self-contained, approaches most nearly to the truth; but he too appears to Cassius, who judges him with envious bitterness, as a 'peevish schoolboy' joined in his youth and inexperience with 'a masker and a reveller'.

On the side of the conspirators, at all events, divided purpose is clearly a prelude to the defeat which they have already accepted in their hearts. Cassius confesses to Messala his distrust of the tactics which Brutus has imposed upon him;

> against my will,
> As Pompey was, am I compell'd to set
> Upon one battle all our liberties. [V. i. 74.]

The reference to Pompey, by defeat of whom Caesar himself rose to power, confirms the presence of a continuing fatality, which is supported by the account of the unfavourable omens which at once follows. Cassius' vacillation, however, is stressed, paradoxically, in the partial withdrawal of what he has just said:

> I but believe it partly,
> For I am full of spirit and resolved
> To meet all perils very constantly. [V. i 90.]

Reacting thus against the elements of uncertainty in human affairs, he tries to induce Brutus to consistency by the use of reason; but his arguments are steeped, in spite of his assertion of 'spirit' and resolution, in an unmistakable pessimism. He urges his friend so far to consider the likelihood of defeat as to 'arm himself with patience' and to determine, though suicide before the final resolution is still held to be 'cowardly and vile', not to go 'bound' to Rome.

Suicide, indeed, is by now the end to which all these activities, essentially self-destructive, are tending. Brutus, on his side, is overshadowed by a more explicit sense of fatality –

> this same day
> Must end that work the ides of March begun – [V. i. 113.]

which provides the background for what he already feels to be his 'everlasting farewell'. His attitude is, as far as it goes, genuinely tragic; but most of the effect derives from passivity, reflects the sense of subjection to fate which now dominates his thoughts:

> O, that a man might know
> The end of this day's business ere it come!
> But it sufficeth that the day will end,
> And then the end is known. [V. i. 123.]

If this expression of fatalism strikes us as oddly jejune, even broken-backed, it corresponds appropriately to the speaker's situation. The stoicism of Brutus, now contrasted with the active confidence required for the blow against Caesar which was to end tyranny and inaugurate a more happy future, amounts to a confession of the illusion which that apparent certainty implied. Against the background of this bitter awakening to truth, life has become a matter of making the best of an unhappy situation, with the accompanying show of dignity, and no more.

The battle itself is presented almost entirely with reference to the conspirators, who fight it under the signs of error and misunderstanding. Cassius, feeling the approach of the defeat he has long foreseen, faces it 'thicksightedly'; Brutus, 'too eager' to push home his initial success, compromises the general cause by his impetuous advance. At the end of these engagements Cassius, meeting death with a sense, typical of the play's 'philosophy', that

> time is come round,
> And where I did begin, there I shall end, [V. iii. 23.]

falls upon the sword 'that ran through Caesar's bowels'. His death is at once followed, with appropriate irony, by Titinius' report of Brutus' compensating success, and by the newcomer's observation, even as he pronounces Cassius' rhetorical epitaph, that 'Mistrust of my success hath done this deed'. To the last, the nobility which they assert is contrasted with a sense of fallibility –

> O hateful error, melancholy's child,
> Why dost thou show to the apt thoughts of men
> The things that are not – [V. iii. 67.]

whilst Titinius' final flat comment on Cassius' error – 'Alas, thou hast misconstrued everything' – shades from fatality to something very like personal irony, to which his own suicide lends an almost sardonic effect.

Thus surrounded on all sides by fallibility and death, Brutus proceeds to the resolution which his own choices have imposed upon him. He relates the deaths which surround him to the continued vitality of Caesar's spirit and stresses the element of retribution in the orgy of self-destruction now taking place:

> O Julius Caesar, thou art mighty yet!
> Thy spirit walks abroad, and turns our swords
> In our own proper entrails. [V. iii. 94.]

This too is an appropriate comment upon the exhibition of Roman virtue, an admission of the failure which it implies. Brutus himself has recently, by implication, repudiated the spirit which exalts suicide as an act of heroic resolution.[1] If his followers now die as Roman convention requires, and seek consolation in their declared resolve, they have in fact little alternative before them. The rhetoric with which they brace themselves in the face of doom rests finally, in part at least, on their continued need to seek comfort in illusion; self-destruction is, after all, the logical end of the process by themselves initiated when they murdered Caesar.

The short scene which follows (V. iv) shows the conspirators, as darkness gathers upon their isolation, engaged in a final parody of vain self-assertion. Cato announces that he will 'proclaim his name

[1] I do find it cowardly and vile,
For fear of what might fall, so to prevent
The time of life. [V. i. 104.]

about the field' – 'I am the son of Marcus Cato, ho!' – and even
Brutus is moved to echo him: 'And I am Brutus, Marcus Brutus, I!'
If they advertise the virtues which they ascribed to themselves when
they murdered Caesar – 'A foe to tyrants and my country's friend' –
it may be, indeed, that little else remains for them to advertise.
Thus heralded, the final scene (V. v) opens with only Brutus' own
tragedy awaiting resolution. He enters shattered, accompanied by
'poor remains of friends' – the idea of friendship has haunted him
throughout, and this is its last expression – and surrounded by the
darkness which answers to his state of soul and fortune. 'Slaying',
death, is now the word in fashion, and Brutus is left with no alternative but to die; but even now – we must add– the devotion he inspires in those whom he approaches with the plea to kill him is a
sign that, almost alone in this play, he exhibits a tragic stature
which transcends the end he has brought upon himself. The obsessive presence in his mind of Caesar's ghost confirms him in his mood
of fatality: 'Thou seest the world, Volumnius, how it goes'. There is
now no alternative to death, and only in suicide a show of resolution:

> Our enemies have beat us to the pit:
> It is more worthy to leap in ourselves
> Than tarry till they push us. [V. v. 23.]

The stress laid on worthiness can now be little more than an effort to
dignify the inevitable; so, from another standpoint, is the emphasis
on past friendship and personal devotion ('we two went to school
together') as the last remaining positives in a life otherwise empty of
meaning and value. The presence, amid the rhetoric, of lines
strangely lacking in poetic resonance – 'Strato, thou hast been all
this while asleep' – perhaps answers fittingly to the sense of flatness,
of empty exhaustion, in which these last episodes are steeped.

Brutus' last farewell, however, rises once more to the dignity of
tragic assertion. 'Countrymen', he says, addressing through his
remaining followers Rome and posterity:

> My heart doth joy that yet in all my life
> I found no man but he was true to me.
> I shall have glory by this losing day,
> More than Octavius and Mark Antony
> By this vile conquest shall attain unto. [V. v. 34.]

It is important to avoid any simple reaction to the mood so expressed.
The speech is truly noble, and yet also an effort made by the speaker,
in the absence of more solid ground for satisfaction, to encourage
himself on the threshold of the annihilation which he has, after all,
brought upon himself, and perhaps even obscurely come to desire.

The mood is, in any case, neither false nor triumphant, implies rather an acceptance of the end Brutus has come to see as inevitable, involved in the entire logic of his own past, and which he now approaches with a certain nostalgic craving for the dark:

> Night hangs upon mine eyes; my bones would rest,
> That have but labour'd to attain this hour. [V. v. 41.]

In this mood of self-awareness, and snatching some crumb of comfort from the fact that Strato, the instrument of his release, is 'a fellow of a good report', he dies in a mood akin to expiation:

> Caesar, now be still;
> I kill'd not thee with half so good a will. [V. v. 50.]

In this admission, the whole contradictory nature of the enterprise to which Brutus so perversely forced himself in the name of humanity is gathered up in the prelude to a last act of self-annihilating resolve.

When Octavius enters to wind up the action with Antony, Strato is able to turn on Messala, now a bondman to the conqueror, with an assertion of the freedom that Brutus has found in death:

> Brutus only overcame himself,
> And no man else hath honour by his death. [V. v. 56.][1]

For all his devotion, however, he is ready to follow Messala by joining the conqueror; the world of rhetorical aspiration and that of practical reality rarely run parallel. The contrast between personal integrity and the way of a world from which, we have good reason to believe, it will be increasingly exiled, is implicit in Antony's famous epitaph, in which he justifiably glorifies Brutus' personal qualities –

> This was the noblest Roman of them all – [V. v. 68.]

without concealing the 'envy' which surrounded this nobility and used its inherent flaws for ends of its own. Octavius, having made the victor's appropriate gesture of generosity, now that generosity can no longer endanger his triumph, turns away with his companion 'To part the glory of this happy day'. The results to which this sharing of the fruits of victory will lead are to be the theme for another play.

---

[1] Compare Antony's dying words to Cleopatra:

> Not Caesar's valour hath o'erthrown Antony,
> But Antony's hath triumph'd on itself.
>
> (*Antony and Cleopatra* [IV. xiii. 14.])

3

Antony and Cleopatra

PUBLISHER'S NOTE

It should be noted that in *Antony and Cleopatra* Act III the three scenes (viii, ix and x) set on the Plain near Actium are in the Oxford University Press edition referred to collectively as Scene viii; thus there are eleven, not thirteen, scenes in Act III. Similarly in Act IV the three scenes (x, xi and xii) set on Ground Between the Two Camps are referred to collectively as Scene x; there are thirteen, not fifteen, scenes in Act IV.

3

Antony and Cleopatra

THE STUDENT of *Antony and Cleopatra* has, in offering an account of this great tragedy, to resolve a problem of approach, of the interpretation of the author's intention. Sooner or later, he finds himself faced by two possible readings of the play, whose only difficulty is that they seem to be mutually exclusive. Is *Antony and Cleopatra*, to put the matter in other terms, a tragedy of lyrical inspiration, presenting the relationship of its central figures as triumphant over adverse circumstance, or is it rather a pitiless exposure of human frailties, of the dissipation of spiritual energies through wilful surrender to passion? Although the terms of the dilemma are perhaps inadequately stated, too romantic on the one hand and excessively moralizing on the other, either interpretation can be defended by reference to what Shakespeare has written; but to give each its due, to see them less as contradictory than as complementary aspects of a unified artistic creation which neither, taken in isolation, can exhaust, is as difficult as it proves, in the long run, necessary for a proper understanding of the play.

Both readings, considered exclusively, depend in some measure upon a partial and incomplete reaction to the play's theme. It should never be forgotten that *Antony and Cleopatra* is, whatever else it may also be, a play about the fortunes of a universal empire. Individual fortunes are throughout related to a sequence of public events as undeviatingly pursued to its conclusion as any in Shakespeare. To this closely-knit succession of incidents, the contrast between Rome and Egypt, two worlds embodying contrary attitudes to life and bound to seek one another's destruction, gives variety and a kind of structural unity; and to see the tragedy of the central protagonists as embedded in this presentation of a world in conflict is to maintain the balance which Shakespeare's conception requires. For *Antony and Cleopatra* is at once the last, and greatest, of his chronicle plays[1] and – with the exception of *Coriolanus* which stands, as we shall see, in a unique position in his work – his final exercise in tragedy. As a chronicle play, the marvellously fluent

[1] *Henry VIII* is, of course, later, but it is at least doubtful whether this was entirely Shakespeare's play.

presentation of historical events carries with it a balanced estimate of
the hero's political stature; as a tragedy, it relates the story of his
downfall to the desire, at least as old as some of the Sonnets, to see in
the ecstasies of love a manifestation of spiritual value. The rich and
revealing interplay of these two themes, political and 'metaphysical'[1]
respectively, constitutes the glory of the play and makes it one of the
culminating achievements of Shakespeare's genius. Antony, and
Cleopatra with him, are led to a public disaster which reflects the
degradation which their perverse choices have imposed; but, once
freed from this degradation by the very completeness of the ruin
which they have brought upon themselves, they achieve by contrast
with death a measure of fulfilment which, illusory though it be on
the plane of daily living, implies while it lasts some measure of
spiritual value.

I

   Philo's opening speech, introducing us with characteristic fluency
and ease into a world of active comment, initiates a brief exposition
of the themes which are to be developed by relationship and contrast. It leaves no doubt as to the adverse estimate which we are
bound, on a dispassionate view, to form of Antony's conduct. His
love is described as a manifestation of 'dotage', which has reached
the point at which it can no longer be tolerated; his former martial
virtues, through which he maintained his position as 'a triple pillar
of the world', have been shamefully abandoned, have become, in the
eyes of that world,

the bellows and the fan
To cool a gipsy's lust. [I. i. 9.]

Nothing in the coming tragedy, no poetic exaltation of the passion
that animates the main protagonists, can make this first estimate
irrelevant; it is, as far as it goes, the truth, and no later development
can affect its validity.
   Even of this first speech, however, there is something more to be
said, something which, without contradicting the impression it so
irrevocably makes, modifies the verdict of common sense and incorporates the soldier's blunt comment into a poetic expression greater,
more complex, than itself. Poetry in this play flows in abundant
plenty, transforming the rhythms of common speech and asserting
itself in the most improbable places. Thus it is that Antony's shame,

---

[1] Needless to say, I use the word 'metaphysical' in the literary sense coined by
Dr. Johnson and most commonly applied to the poetry of Donne.

the 'dotage' which Philo ascribes to him, is expressed by his very critic through an image of abounding generosity, 'o'erflows the measure'; and thus too the degradation of his present behaviour is contrasted with the martial splendours of a past in which his 'goodly' eyes 'glowed' before his devoted troops 'like plated Mars', whilst his 'captain's heart', now reduced to the most unworthy of servitudes, thrust aside all restraint, 'burst' the buckles which protected it. The fall from martial grace in the present is great indeed, but the memory of the past lives in the poetry which can take up a common man's sense of betrayal and raise it, through an effortless display of far-ranging imagery, to the level of an ardent devotion to heroic splendour.

The entry of Antony and Cleopatra, immediately after this indignant comment, at once confirms it and introduces fresh themes for consideration. Their first exchanges are couched in a form which will become familiar in the passionate personal passages of this play; emotion responds to emotion in a mutual heightening, a progressive accumulation of intensities. The effect at this point is a cunning combination of lyricism with artifice, passionate dedication with the conscious exhibition of feeling. To Cleopatra's calculated expression of doubt, 'If there be love indeed, tell me how much,' Antony replies 'There's beggary in the love that can be reckon'd'; and to her statement, made as it were to dare him, to provoke further and more far-reaching expressions of devotion, that she will 'set a bourn how far to be belov'd' he responds with a gesture that implies infinity, transcendence in emotion: 'Then must thou needs find out new heaven, new earth'. This assertion, like so many of Antony's utterances to come, should neither be ignored nor accepted at its face value. The sense of a superhuman content apprehended through love is one that the play will repeat and develop, in relation to a superb emotional expansiveness, even in the process of passing judgement upon it. Its final relationship will be to the experience of death imposed, as a consequence of their 'political' failure, upon both characters at the end of the tragedy; but meanwhile the emotional force of this first exchange must not blind us to its irrelevance in terms of common realism.

That the pair who can thus address one another in mutual ecstasy are themselves subdued to the course of external events is stressed by the entry of a messenger from Rome. Antony's gesture in thrusting aside the intrusion to turn again to the mistress who has enslaved him –

> – News, my good lord, from Rome.
> – Grates me: the sum – [I. i. 18.]

indicates rather petulant self-indulgence than the noble generosity to which he lays claim; and Cleopatra, playing upon his dependency, is not slow to taunt him with his wife's imagined anger or with that inferiority to the 'scarce-bearded Caesar' which already rankles in his conscience. Antony has always been a man to whom the generous pose, the fluent and effective gesture, have come easily: and now the contrast with Cleopatra's realism is admirably effective. To his accumulating determination to anchor his being to the object of his passion and his smouldering reaction to the sense that he is being turned into an object of ridicule – 'How, my love!' – Cleopatra responds with a high-pitched mixture of irony and scolding: 'Where's Fulvia's process? Caesar's, I would say? both': the quick succession of eager, mocking questions hesitates on the brink of absurdity and issues finally in the contradiction of Antony's decision: 'Call in the messengers.' The final effect is one of characteristic complexity:

> As I am Egypt's queen,
> Thou blushest, Antony, and that blood of thine
> Is Caesar's homager: else so thy cheek pays shame
> When shrill-tongued Fulvia scolds. The messengers! [I. i. 29.]

Much of the play's essential contrast is contained in these lines. There is nobility in the reference to 'Egypt's queen', but nobility engaged in making an effort to maintain itself in a situation finally void of dignity. There is a true hint of shame beneath the raillery which sees Antony blushing in a reaction which is 'Caesar's homager'; and there is irony in the transfer to Fulvia of Cleopatra's own capacity for 'shrill-tongued' reproach.

The entire situation is, in short, perilously false. The messengers whom Cleopatra is determined to force upon her unwilling lover are indeed – and, as she speaks, she knows it – the representatives of the real world undistorted by the specious transformations of passion. By relating the political action to emotion poetically expressed, and by expressing that emotion in a most subtle variety of ways, the scene calls for a balance of judgement which will have to be maintained throughout. On the one hand, Antony's readiness to turn away from outside events is given a certain weight by his first opulent gesture of triumphant love; on the other, that gesture is itself subjected to criticism, seen in its double nature as splendid and yet finally mean, a product of personal degradation. To bear *both* judgements in mind, refusing to neglect one in order to exalt the other, is to respond truly to the intention of the play.

This intention emerges further from Antony's full declaration of the emotion which moves him:

> Let Rome in Tiber melt, and the wide arch
> Of the ranged empire fall! Here is my space.
> Kingdoms are clay: our dungy earth alike
> Feeds beast as man: the nobleness of life
> Is to do thus; when such a mutual pair
> And such a twain can do't, in which I bind,
> On pain of punishment, the world to weet
> We stand up peerless. [I. i. 33.]

The expression, considered with due care, introduces a number of elements which the later action will develop. The vast spaciousness of the political background, the sense that a world order, a universal structure of society, rests on the individuals whose tragedy is to be presented, is conveyed by reference to the 'wide arch' of the 'ranged empire'; and the fact that Antony is ready to turn aside from issues so endowed with universality gives a presumption of value to his emotion. By contrast with his assertions of devotion, the material nature of the outside world is stressed. Kingdoms become 'clay' and, in a phrase as splendid as it is relevant, the earth itself is 'dungy', at once contemptible and yet, when brought to life by the transforming presence of passion, potentially fertile. Against this background, both vast and petty, equally related to 'beast and 'man', the presence of intense personal emotion emphasizes 'the nobleness of life', a nobility which has often concerned Shakespeare in his earlier tragedies,[1] which he has variously considered in its related glory and pretension, and which is here presented, for exaltation and criticism, in the story of his pair of lovers.

To what extent these will be able to justify this arrogant exaltation of themselves as 'a mutual pair', fit each for the other and ready to assert their 'peerless' quality before the world, time will show. Already there is a clear element of shame and indulgence, which the splendour of his rhetoric cannot conceal, in Antony's readiness to contemplate – publicly and with satisfaction – the crumbling into ruin of the arch of empire; and his display of emotion is not left at its own estimate. Having been largely produced in reaction to Cleopatra's calculated ironies, it is followed immediately by the realism of her comment:

[1] The preoccupation with 'nobility' of Shakespeare's tragic heroes can be taken at least as far back as Hamlet, who asked himself

> Whether 'tis *nobler* in the mind to suffer
> The slings and arrows of outrageous fortune,
> Or to take arms against a sea of troubles,
> And by opposing end them. (*Hamlet*, [III. i. 57.])

> Excellent falsehood!
> Why did he marry Fulvia, and not love her?
> I'll seem the fool I am not: Antony
> Will be himself. [I. i. 40.]

Grandiloquent folly on his side, and knowing acceptance of unreality on hers: it would be hard to conceive a more fragile basis for the relationship between the pair now posed, so exaltedly and self-consciously, before us.

Antony's own following words confirm the validity of Cleopatra's judgement. From the high-flown expression of 'nobility' we pass at one stroke to the cloying sensuality which is equally a part of his nature. He exhorts her 'for the love of love and her *soft* hours' to set aside the reality of the outer world, which he dismisses in terms of 'conference *harsh*':

> There's not a minute of our lives should stretch
> Without some *pleasure* now. What *sport* to-night? [I. i. 46.]

The desire to fill every moment of life with its utmost content of sensation belongs, perhaps, to a certain vital element in Antony's apprehension of passion; but this vitality is qualified at once by the nature of the content which he foresees. *Sport* and *pleasure*: these turn out, when we pass from the universally lyrical to concrete reality, to be the true ends of Antony's devotion. The *sport* is obtained by neglecting the speaker's public duty in hearing the ambassadors; the seizing of the *pleasure* of the moment, and the desire to endow it with a spurious eternity by thrusting aside all other responsibilities (even those upon attention to which his own life and self-respect depend), represent the real content of Antony's generalized expressions of emotional nobility. The working out of the contrast so presented until, through a fusion of poetic and dramatic resources as comprehensive as any in Shakespeare, its diverse elements are shown to belong to a single range of emotion is the true theme of *Antony and Cleopatra*.

II

Among the distinctive features of this tragedy is an appropriate amplitude in development. The decisions of the principal contendents concern not themselves alone, but the world whose fate hangs upon their fortunes. A principal effect of the action lies in the contrast between the sensuous luxury of Egypt, in which Cleopatra is at home and to which Antony has surrendered, and the severe, practical

genius of Rome. The first part of the play deals largely with Antony's
effort to free himself from his captivity, to move away from Alexandria and in the direction of the public responsibilities which await
him at Rome. This effort will be balanced, in the later part of the
play, by a compensating reaction, a contrary swing of the pendulum
which will reveal Antony's determination as essentially baseless,
false. The turning-point will be the battle of Actium, which is placed
at the centre of the entire action. Meanwhile, however, the development of the play is concentrated upon the nature and quality of
Antony's 'decisions' and upon the subtle and varied evocation of the
world of political affirmation to which they lead him.

It is fitting that the opening statement of Antony's devotion should
be followed by a presentation of its Egyptian background, in which,
besides the play's characteristic realism, we may detect some of the
first signs of its poetic transformation. This is approached through
the badinage of Cleopatra's maids-in-waiting, who will finally share
the ruin and exaltation of their mistress. The fertility of Egypt,
balancing vitality and corruption, is presented through the obsession
of two girls with the prospect of sexual fulfilment. When Iras says, in
jest, that her 'palm presages chastity', the comment of her companion – 'Even as the overflowing Nile presageth famine' – and the
following reference to the 'fruitful prognostication' of 'an oily palm'
steep the scene in a typically Egyptian obsession with fertility. The
same can be said of Charmian's expression, a few moments earlier,
of her intimate fantasies:

> Let me be married to three kings in a forenoon, and widow them
> all: let me have a child at fifty, to whom Herod of Jewry may do
> homage: find me to marry with Octavius Caesar, and com-
> panion me with my mistress. [I. ii. 28.]

This is the world of Cleopatra, expressed in the day-dreams which
her amatory triumphs have inspired in those who wait on her: the
world of Alexandria, in which the sensual imagination expands,
loses itself in the gratifying imagination of boundless fulfilment.

It is, nonetheless, the surrender to an illusion that is thus expressed.
Connected though it is with the overflowing bounty of the Nile, the
sensuality of these dreams is shadowed by a sense of barrenness and
vanity. 'O, that I knew this husband which, you say, must charge his
horn with garlands!'; in Charmian's first wheedling persuasion of
the eunuch Alexas – whose physical deficiency represents the
element of frustration which in Egypt so strangely accompanies the
unlimited expression of desire – the craving for fulfilment is characteristically intertwined with cynicism. Against the background of
'wine' and banqueting announced by Enobarbus, the atmosphere is

one of obsessive sensuality coupled with an awareness, jested at but fundamentally serious,[1] of age and inevitable decay:

> SOOTHSAYER You shall be yet far fairer than you are.
> CHARMIAN He means in flesh.
> IRAS No, you shall paint when you are old.
> CHARMIAN Wrinkles forbid! [I. ii. 18.]

The unnatural mingling of youth with experience, illusion with cynicism, runs through the episode to reflect a society in which the desire for natural satisfaction is at each turn countered by sterility. The emphasis on marriage and abundant issue, expressed in Charmian's question 'Prithee, how many boys and wenches must I have?', and in the Soothsayer's evasive reply:

> If every of your wishes had a womb,
> And fertile every wish, a million, [I. ii. 40.]

is balanced by knowledge that hers are wishes not realities, and that their normal consummation will not in fact be forthcoming. Alexas is there to stand in his impotence for one aspect of the Egyptian attitude to love and to serve as a butt for the young women who have no more solid outlet than these fantasies for desires which express themselves so forcibly precisely because they are condemned to lack natural satisfaction. The ultimate cynicism behind these exchanges finds expression in jests at the expense of the gods –

> Dear goddess, hear that prayer of the people! for, as it is a heart-breaking to see a handsome man loose-wived, so it is a deadly sorrow to behold a foul knave uncuckolded: therefore, dear Isis, keep decorum, and fortune him accordingly! – [I. ii. 75.]

upon which Alexas comments wryly: 'Lo, now, if it lay in their hands to make me a cuckold, they would make themselves whores, but they'ld do't'.

The presence of the Soothsayer confers upon this badinage a sense of obscure fatality. It is true that Enobarbus, in his realism, makes light of 'prognostication': 'Mine, and most of our fortunes tonight shall be – drunk to bed'. By so doing, he stresses another aspect of the Egyptian scene, the dissolution to which its sensuality so readily and so ignominuously tends; but in spite of this, the Soothsayer's interventions point, definitely if enigmatically, to the final tragedy. To Charmian and Iras, in their careless mixture of youth and cynicism, the statement that he can to some degree interpret 'nature's infinite

[1] A comparison with the prose scenes of *Measure for Measure* would not be entirely out of place here. See, more especially, II. i. and the interventions of Lucio throughout.

book of secrecy' comes as mere superstition; but the element of foreboding in his prophecies will finally be justified:

> You shall be more beloving than beloved. [I. ii. 24.]

> You have seen and proved a fairer former fortune
> Than that which is to approach. [I. ii. 35.]

The effect of the whole episode is not only to develop the play's
Egyptian background, but to begin the process by which that background will be bound to its total development.

Against this setting, the return of Cleopatra – typically involved in
a flurry of intrigue – brings us back to the main action. Antony's
brittle and inconstant mood has changed once more. 'A Roman
thought has struck him,' and Cleopatra meets the threat of his departure with calculated evasiveness: 'We will not look upon him.'
Antony, indeed, when he enters, is occupied with those very Roman
realities that he has so recently and ostentatiously thrust aside.
Fulvia and her late enemy Lucius (who is none other than his
brother) have joined against Caesar, who has, however, following
his ascending star, had 'better issue in the war'; whilst worse news,
which the messenger hesitates to divulge, awaits the telling. Antony,
driven by the onward movement of events beyond his control, is
ready – for the moment – to think of assuming once more the
responsibilities of his public life. To prepare himself to do so, he
proceeds to strike an attitude, embarking for his own satisfaction upon
the self-conscious building up of resolve. 'Things that are past are
done with me,' he affirms, in the belief that he can now face reality:

> Who tells me true, though in his tale lie death,
> I hear him as he flatter'd. [I. ii. 106.]

It is throughout typical of Antony, an essential part of his weakness,
that his moments of resolution have to be stimulated in him by
reaction against the thought of his degradation; the one acts as an
irritant upon the other, stirring him to a show of resolve. The rapid
Parthian advance is now associated in his mind with Roman criticism of his behaviour; he relives his shame in the imagined comment
of those who 'taunt' his faults

> With such full licence as both truth and malice
> Have power to utter, [I. ii. 117.]

and finally associates it, by an image which will recur repeatedly,
with stagnation, with the decay of that intellectual energy which is
the distinctive and justifying feature of human life when it results in
action:

> O, then we bring forth weeds
> When our quick minds lie still, and our ills told us
> Is as our earing. [I. ii. 118.]

Here at least Antony, momentarily freed from the spell which Cleopatra has imposed upon him, sees his situation in its true light,
laments the corruption of that unity of purpose in action upon which
his self-respect, both as a man and as a public figure, depends.
The result is a moment of resolution in which Antony echoes the
opening judgement of Philo upon his decline:

> These strong Egyptian fetters I must break,
> Or lose myself in *dotage*. [I. ii. 125.]

At this point the foundations of his political tragedy are being most
realistically laid. The news of Fulvia's death, relayed by a second
messenger, further brings home the contradictions in which he is
caught. He confesses that he has desired her disappearance, but
adds, with an effort at moral realism rare in him, habitually overlaid
by surrender to the feeling of the moment:

> What our contempts do often hurl from us,
> We wish it ours again; the present pleasure,
> By revolution lowering, does become
> The opposite of itself: she's good, being gone. [I. ii. 132.]

Caught in this web of contradictions, which his own 'idleness' has
contrived, Antony sees his salvation in a break with Cleopatra. 'I
must from this enchanting queen break off': but the force of the
adjective he uses to describe her, stressing the irresistible nature of
the spell she has cast upon him, more than balances the uncertain
resolution of his declaration.
The entry of Enobarbus, with his characteristic note of astringent
realism, serves to comment in more ways than one on this new determination. To leave Egypt is to 'kill all our women'; but, 'though
it were pity to cast them away for nothing', Enobarbus doubts less
the justice of Antony's resolve than his ability to maintain it. He has
seen all this before:

> Cleopatra, catching but the least noise of this, dies instantly: I
> have seen her die twenty times upon far poorer moment; I do
> think there is mettle in death, which commits some loving act
> upon her, she hath such a celerity in dying. [I. ii. 149.]

Cynical though it is, the expression achieves the end, so typical of
this play, of conferring a certain beauty upon the reality it condemns. Cleopatra's 'deaths' are so much trickery to gain ends in

themselves cloying, destructive of male integrity and self-respect: but the power which sees death in terms of the 'loving act', and confers a touch of beauty even upon the cynicism of 'such a celerity in dying', is one in which life and its opposite are strangely blended in a fusion of tenderness and moral realism. This is, indeed, a first faint anticipation of the mingled failure and triumph of Cleopatra's end.

Something of the same effect is conveyed by the discussion, which follows, of her character and complexity of motive. Antony, in a mixture of bewilderment and unwilling admiration, describes her as 'cunning past man's thought', and Enobarbus, in the very act of using this admission to confirm his own estimate, adds to it a distinctive note of poetry:

> her passions are made of nothing but the finest part of pure love: we cannot call her winds and waters sighs and tears; they are greater storms and tempests than almanacs can report: this cannot be cunning in her; if it be, she makes a shower of rain as well as Jove. [I. ii. 156.]

A cynical and realistic evaluation is clearly maintained in this estimate. 'This cannot be cunning in her', Enobarbus says, meaning precisely the opposite, and her weeping is an artifice, the 'making' of a 'shower of rain', albeit under the most convincing circumstances. Yet, almost in the speaker's despite, the transforming touch of poetry asserts itself. Cleopatra's passions are in a sense pure, 'made of nothing but the *finest* part of *pure* love'. Theirs is a quality which allies them to 'winds and waters', 'storms and tempests'; artificial and calculated beyond those reported by the 'almanacs', they have yet their own resemblance to the elemental processes of nature. Even her 'cunning' – for 'cunning', crafty she is beyond measure – has about it a touch of divinity, makes her emulous, in the skill with which she displays it, of Jove. At the end of this exchange, when Antony declares that he wishes he had never set eyes upon her, Enobarbus' reply combines irony with true appreciation: 'you had then left unseen a wonderful piece of work; which not to have been blest withal would have discredited your travel.' The 'wonderful piece of work' carries with it, if we will, a sense of artifice, of a creation remote from nature, which will, in due course, find its consummation in Enobarbus' account of Cleopatra on her barge;[1] but artifice does not exclude admiration, the true appreciation of a unique creation. The balance of cynicism with what we may call unwilling poetry is most typical of the emotional range which this play so triumphantly, and apparently so effortlessly, spans.

[1] II. ii. See p. 115 below.

Antony's announcement of Fulvia's death, and Enobarbus' comment – 'Why, sir, give the gods a thankful sacrifice' – restore us once more, as always when Cleopatra is not directly in question, to open cynicism. This is the price, in terms of elementary human decency, of Antony's infatuation. The final reference is to the mutually incompatible nature of his compulsions. If, as he says, the business 'broached' by Fulvia cannot endure her absence, Enobarbus' reply that 'the business you have broached here cannot be without you; especially that of Cleopatra's, which wholly depends on your abode', is beyond question true. Antony is bound to choose, and, in choosing, to renounce; and it is finally because renunciation is beyond him that he fails to make the choice which his human stature demands of him and is ruined. It is noteworthy indeed, that even in announcing to Enobarbus his determination to take up his political responsibilities, he already weakens to the extent of declaring that he will approach Cleopatra for leave to part. The resolution of his contrary impulses will not be so easily obtained.

As the scene closes on this note of dubious decision, the presence of outside events imposes itself in the concentrated urgency of the impressions that constitute Antony's closing speech. The expression, free and easy-flowing in its movement, is packed with an effortless intensity. The considerations which drive him back to Rome crowd in upon him with haste and power; 'not alone' the death of Fulvia, but other, more *urgent* touches' speak 'strongly' to his conscience, and are backed by the letters of '*contriving* friends' petitioning his return. The political situation hangs by a slender thread and awaits the resolution of no individual destiny. Sextus Pompeius, bold in the pursuit of his ambitions, has 'given the dare to Caesar' and obtained 'the empire of the sea'. The people are 'slippery', their loyalty

> never link'd to the deserver
> Till his deserts are past. [I. ii. 199.]

The rival contendent,

> high in name and power,
> Higher than both in blood and life. [I. ii. 202.]

'stands up' in daring self-assertion 'for the main soldier'; and, as he does so, the quality of his actions is such that it, 'going on',

> The sides o' the world may endanger.

To be noted, too, is the intense, ominous quality of the image with which Antony rounds off his recital of the growing pressure of events –

> Much is breeding,
> Which, like the courser's hair, hath yet but life
> And not a serpent's poison – [I. ii. 205.]

and the quick, keen compression of his final phrase of resolution:

> Say, our pleasure,
> To such whose place is under us, requires
> Our quick remove from hence. [I. ii. 207.]

By the end of the scene, Antony is being carried back to his public duty, but rather as a creature of circumstance than as a willing agent devoted to the responsibilities he has assumed.

The scene just considered calls, as its necessary balance, for a return to Cleopatra (I. iii), in whom at least half of Antony's nature is inextricably compromised. Fully aware of the danger that he will leave her, Cleopatra prepares to meet the situation by a typically perilous balance of calculation and feeling. If Charmian finds him 'sad', 'say I am dancing', if 'happy', she is to report her 'sudden' sickness; all this, moreover, is to be done with speed, 'quick', and the speaker, even as she dispatches her messenger, anticipates her return. In all this, she is true to her own volatile nature, blends sincerity with calculation; but Charmian's warning –

> In time we hate that which we often fear – [I. iii. 12.]

once again stresses the subjection of passion itself to the action of time and forecasts approaching danger.

As Antony enters, Cleopatra's stratagem, her greeting of him with the deliberately provoking 'I am sick and sullen', combines calculation with the show of intense emotion to produce the trick of 'fainting'. A trick it undoubtedly is, but in the culminating moment –

> It cannot be thus long, the sides of nature
> Will not sustain it – [I. iii. 16.]

truth and device are cunningly united. To combine artifice with sincerity, realism with a self-deluding concentration upon the object of her passion, is of the essence of Cleopatra's nature. The first stage in her effort to maintain her slipping ascendancy is to forbid Antony's approach, and, in so doing, to stress his dependence upon the wife whom she still believes alive: 'What says the married woman? you may go.' The emotional initiative is hers and, as she develops it against an Antony whose tongue-tied reception of her tricks contrasts so significantly with his recent show of resolution, a true estimate of her situation underlies the unfolding of her stratagem:

> Why should I think you can be mine and true,
> Though you in swearing shake the throned gods,
> Who have been false to Fulvia? [I. iii. 27.]

The elements of truth and falsity, so intertwined that only in the shadow of death will they be separated, combine in a complexity of expression that is, in its balance of the opposites simultaneously present in a single situation, superbly characteristic:

> Riotous madness,
> To be entangled with those mouth-made vows,
> Which break themselves in swearing. [I. iii. 29.]

With emotion thus 'entangled' in its own intricacy, conscious of itself as 'riotous madness' and yet unwilling or unable to draw the liberating conclusion, intensely engaged in 'swearing' vows that are known to be 'mouth-made', to 'break themselves' even as they express an emotion without which life would seem to be worthless, the heart of the tragic situation which awaits its resolution in the coming action is revealed.

Complexity and the awareness of falsehood are not the only or the last words in this relationship. As Antony interposes his short but rising efforts to justify himself – 'Cleopatra', 'Most sweet queen' – her emotion responds to his own and soars finally into what is, while it lasts (and only while it lasts), an intuition of permanent value:

> Nay, pray you, seek no colour for your going,
> But bid farewell, and go: when you sued staying,
> Then was the time for words; no going then;
> Eternity was in our lips and eyes,
> Bliss in our brows bent, none our parts so poor
> But was a race of heaven. [I. iii. 32.]

The supreme statement of mutual dedication is made to rest, for its force and poignancy, upon a foundation of accepted parting. Like Antony, though after her own fashion, Cleopatra needs to have her emotions stimulated, brought to a pitch by what is, in the last analysis, a contemplation of their lack of solid foundation. 'Bid farewell, and go,' she says, and we know that she means the opposite; and yet the power of what follows forbids us to see in her gesture merely a stratagem, obliges us to regard it as a trick indeed, but as a trick based finally on a measure of truth. In the world of time parting is the order of the day; but there has been for the lovers a time when 'eternity' at least *seemed* at their command, 'was in our lips and eyes', and when the 'bliss' reflected in their mutual gaze had a transforming quality, appeared to raise ordinary human attraction to an intuition of superhuman perfection:

> none our parts so poor
> But was a race of heaven. [I. iii. 36.]

Belief in Antony's integrity, so dubious to the dispassionate eye of common sense, is made to rest on the validity of an experience which can only be held in a moment of emotional intensity and in reaction against what Cleopatra knows, even as she speaks, to be reality. While it lasts, and so far alone, the 'parts' of the lovers, the attributes of their physical presence, are transformed, rendered heavenly, and to maintain that vision is the aim, impossible but now necessary (because for it all else has been sacrificed), of life:

> they are so still,
> Or thou, the greatest soldier of the world,
> Art turn'd the greatest liar. [I. iii. 37.]

Antony has chosen this life with Cleopatra, and by the constancy of his devotion to it he can fairly, if not exclusively, be judged. This constancy may be, is, indeed, incommensurate with his other, public responsibilities; but the choice has been made and cannot now, without an acute sense of loss, be renounced.

It should be noted, however, as testifying to the compensating realism of the dramatic vision, that the rise to its height of Cleopatra's feeling is followed immediately by a drop in the tension. Once again the emotional see-saw which typifies the action at every stage makes itself felt by a descent, almost sickening in its effect, into the real. Antony, who, while she was embarked upon the tide of emotion, followed her with his broken exclamations, is roused by the final word 'liar', which strikes so dangerously close to the truth, to a blunt reproof: 'How now, lady!' His gesture of outraged self-respect prompts her to an almost ridiculous piece of scolding:

> I would I had thy inches: thou shouldst know
> There were a heart in Egypt. [I. iii. 40.]

This ability to pass from the bliss of 'heaven' to the exchanges between an outraged public figure and the scold who is engaged in undoing him is striking proof of the presence of the compensating realism which will throughout balance the transcendent lyricism which belongs to, but in no sense exhausts, the personal tragedy. It leads in Antony's following speech, so superbly expressed but in an entirely different tone, to a reaffirmation of the presence of the external world. 'The strong necessity of time' asserts itself in a call to parting, and though Antony can still say

my full heart
Remains in use with you, [I. iii. 43.]

the expression of what follows points to the existence of a contrasted
reality ineluctably strong in its own right.

The outside world of the triumvirs is, indeed, beneath its opulent
appearances, already shot through with threats of dissolution.
Antony's presentation of it is full of touches which recall the spirit of
the earlier historical plays: and his political folly (the reverse side of
his devotion to Cleopatra) is not exempt from a note of hard calculation, which his failure to calculate successfully cannot render more
attractive. His account of the state of Rome lays stress upon teachery
mingled with corruption:

> Our Italy
> Shines o'er with civil swords; Sextus Pompeius
> Makes his approaches to the port of Rome;
> Equality of two domestic powers
> Breeds scrupulous faction: the hated, grown to strength,
> Are newly grown to love: the condemn'd Pompey,
> Rich in his father's honour, creeps apace
> Into the hearts of such as have not thrived
> Upon the present state, whose numbers threaten;
> And quietness, grown sick of rest, would purge
> By any desperate change. [I. iii. 44.]

It would be hard to find a better example of the way in which a
seemingly straightforward piece of exposition is charged with an
expressive energy that relates it variously to the deeper issues of the
play. Rome is in a dangerous state of 'equality', poised between
contrary powers which, uncertain of the future and unable to trust
one another in the present, 'breed' (the verb, with its sense of
organic growth, has a quality of its own) a 'scrupulous', calculating
'faction'. Pompey, the common enemy of Caesar and Antony, is
'rich' principally in his father's reputation. Thus endowed, he
'creeps' like a stealthy traitor into the hearts of those who have not
made their fortunes, 'thrived' in the 'present state' of deceptive
peace. The factions so initiated grow (through the 'breeding' process
already indicated, we might say) into a threatening condition, and
the result of the whole development is summed up in one of those
images of dislocated organic function by which Shakespeare habitually expresses the implications of civil strife. The discontented
elements in Italy are 'sick'; sick in themselves, because domestic
war is a symptom of public disorder, and 'sick' too of the false state
of 'rest', or stagnation, by which rival interests prosper. The end of

this sickness here, as ever, is a 'purge', but one scarcely less uncertain, 'desperate' in its consequences, than the malady it comes to cure.

If Antony is now to return to this dubious reality, it is less as a free agent than as one whom 'the strong necessity of time' constrains to leave what he has made the centre of his being. He offers, indeed, a most unworthy surety for his going in Fulvia's death. This Cleopatra receives with justifiable irony:

> Though age from folly could not give me freedom,
> It does from childishness: can Fulvia die?; [I. iii. 57.]

to which Antony, plunging deeper into unworthiness, replies with an unseemly expression of pleasure – 'at the last, best' – only to meet the withering realism of Cleopatra's reply:

> Now I see, I see,
> In Fulvia's death, how mine received shall be. [I. iii. 64.]

Throughout the exchange, Cleopatra combines her deliberate playing upon Antony's emotions (and, surely, it is a weak nature that needs to be thus titillated) with a clear vision of her own situation.

Antony, in reply, can only beg her to 'quarrel no more', plead that he is ready, in the last resort, to bow to her will:

> be prepared to know
> The purposes I bear, which are, or cease,
> As you shall give the advice. [I. iii. 66.]

This readiness to subject his manhood, the capacity to act decisively which he has so recently been affirming, to the demands of passion is Antony's fatal weakness. It expresses itself, at last, in the spirit of his self-dedication to her, the poetry of which is variously related to what are beginning to emerge as the ruling themes of the play:

> By the fire
> That quickens Nilus' slime, I go from hence
> Thy soldier, servant, making peace or war
> As thou affect'st. [I. iii. 68.]

Upon the imagery of fire, and of its 'quickening' effect upon the 'slime' of Nile, the spirit of the culminating scenes of the tragedy will be largely built;[1] but the effect is far from simple in kind. The contrast is between life, 'fire', and the slime which is at once its opposite and its foundation; the same passion which can give fresh vitality to the earthly stuff of experience can also be the source and sign of

[1] Such imagery is particularly evident in Cleopatra's death, V. ii, and pp. 199–201 below.

corruption. When Antony announces his readiness to be Cleopatra's 'soldier, servant', he is confounding the order of soldiership, in which a man should be independent, dedicated to the action of his choice, with that of passion, which has its own transforming magnificence, but which, when it seeks to impose itself unilaterally upon life, can lead only to disaster and degradation.

This Cleopatra knows; but, since her life is built upon the encouragement of this subjection, her reaction combines calculated play-acting ('Cut my lace, Charmian') and true emotion:

> I am quickly ill and well,
> So Antony loves. [I. iii. 72.]

Antony, lost and clumsy in the face of a versatility which continually astounds him, takes him unaware, can only plead with her to 'forbear': to forbear, at least by implication, from leading his bewildered reactions into so complex a dance. Almost ridiculously, he begs to be accepted at his own valuation, praying Cleopatra to

> give true evidence to his love, which stands
> An honourable trial; [I. iii. 74.]

he receives, however, only the devastating reply 'So Fulvia told me', and the equally damaging accusation of play-acting, delivered by one who is herself supremely acting a part to keep control over his emotions:

> bid adieu to me, and say the tears
> Belong to Egypt: good now, play one scene
> Of excellent dissembling, and let it look
> Like perfect honour. [I. iii. 77.]

The whole exchange amounts to an exposure of the 'honour' by which Antony feels that he must live, and by the subjection of which to the deliberate exploitation of passion Cleopatra has to maintain her hold over him. Out of his depth in this world of passionate artifice mingled with true feeling, Antony can only plead – almost incoherently – against the rousing of his emotions ('You'll heat my blood: no more') and clutch feebly at the sword ('Now by my sword –') which he feels to be the symbol of his endangered manliness. Even this gesture she turns to the debased and the theatrical, calling upon Charmian to behold 'this Herculean Roman' – and we must remember that Antony considers Hercules to be his ancestor – in the act of living up to this semblance of heroic passion, exhibiting in absurd self-consciousness 'the carriage of his chafe'.

Thus deprived of his bearings, Antony can only offer to leave; for, though his self-respect impels him to think that his mind is made up, the reality is far otherwise. His offer provokes in Cleopatra yet another change of mood, a retreat into emotional directness which is also part of the inexhaustible richness of her nature:

> Sir, you and I must part, but that's not it:
> Sir, you and I have lov'd, but there's not it:
> That you know well: [I. iii. 87.]

a sincerity, however, which calculation can still use for its own ends:

> something it is I would, –
> O, my oblivion is a very Antony,
> And I am all forgotten. [I. iii. 89.]

The tongue-tied Antony, in reply to this, can only lapse into a poetry which finally glorifies the very 'idleness' he is accusing, and which goes on to point most immediately to the depths of his entanglement:

> But that your royalty
> Holds idleness your subject, I should take you
> For idleness itself, [I. iii. 91.]

This bringing together of 'idleness' and 'royalty' provokes from Cleopatra, in turn, a phrase which, carefully calculated though it is, transcends calculation to touch the heart of feeling:

> 'Tis sweating labour
> To bear such idleness so near the heart
> As Cleopatra this. [I. iii. 93.]

The splendour of the phrase, so various in its reflection of the speaker's emotional state, so impossible to tie down to any single set of impressions, is further backed by an assertion of humble dependency. Having drawn her emotional net round Antony, Cleopatra leaves him with a sense of her own simple deference –

> my becomings kill me when they do not
> Eye well to you – [I. iii. 96.]

of her dependence (which is genuine) and of a gesture to that 'honour' which she at once loves and is impelled by the nature of her passion to undermine:

> Your honour calls you hence.
> Therefore be deaf to my unpitied folly,
> And all the gods go with you! [I. iii. 97.]

Accepting the separation which she sees to be inevitable, though far

G

from final, and exploiting for her own ends the sorrow and desolation which she really feels, she so turns this acceptance as to make it yet another claim to bind her departing lover to her. Antony, now ready to leave, confirms the continued fact of his dependence in his final words:

> Our separation so abides and flies,
> That thou residing here go'st yet with me,
> And I hence fleeing here remain with thee. [I. iii. 102.]

No better comment could be imagined upon Antony's preceding statements of resolution than these backward-gazing confirmations of what is intended to show as decisiveness, firm resolve. The phrase, expressing the various contradictory elements present in the emotions of a pair whose sense of being united is here kept alive, intensified, by being set against the impending fact of separation, is a premonition of ruin. Antony can only survive as a warrior by freeing himself from the bonds of love; but so to free himself would be to do violence, not only to Cleopatra, as Enobarbus has already said, but to his own being. That is why his tragedy is already assured.

III

With Antony's thoughts definitely fixed upon Rome, the field of action widens to embrace the onward movement of public events. The approaching reconciliation between himself and Caesar will bring to its conclusion the first of the successive and compensating swings of the pendulum which constitute the tragedy. Before this takes place, Octavius is introduced at Rome (I. iv), providing in his person and by his comments not only a counterpart to the spirit of the preceding Egyptian episodes, but a ruthless estimate of the character of his rival and, we may add, unconsciously of his own. A further expansion takes in the figure of Pompey (II. i), fear of whom has brought together the triumvirs in the hollow semblance of unity which is consummated immediately after (II. ii). Throughout these developments the influence of Cleopatra must be kept in mind as a determining factor which will assert itself as soon as the Romeward swing of Antony's impulse exhausts itself; accordingly, a short scene (I. v) shows her separated from Antony and living for his return. As always, the forward movement of events provides the foundation for a closely-knit construction of significant dramatic contrasts.

Whilst Antony has been striving to break free from Cleopatra, the affairs of the great world have been carried on under the watchful and dispassionate eye of Octavius. The presentation of Caesar at this point serves a double purpose. It establishes, by contrast, the practical weakness of his rival and stresses, in so doing, the importance of the public duties which he has so light-heartedly thrust aside; and at the same time, it indicates certain deficiencies in character and human sympathy in the successful politician, limitations in his outlook which will be relevant to a complete and balanced judgement. Both aspects of Octavius begin to project themselves from the moment of his first appearance.

Octavius Caesar is, throughout the play, a public personality, devoted to the political vocation he has taken upon himself. It is fitting, therefore, that his first words should display a self-conscious magnanimity:

> It is not Caesar's natural vice to hate
> Our great competitor. [I. iv. 2.]

As, however, he turns from this generalized pose to the particular consideration of his rival's conduct, the points he makes are at once valid and, in their expression, a revelation of his own nature:

> he fishes, drinks, and wastes
> The lamps of night in revel. [I. iv. 4.]

The exposure of Antony's vices is too forceful, too closely related to the note of over-ripeness which prevails in the Egyptian episodes, to be neglected. Everything he says of Antony is true. We have already been shown him as not 'more manlike' than Cleopatra, and as dismissed, in the comments of those who follow him, as

> the abstract of all faults
> That all men follow; [I. iv. 9.]

and yet the tone of thin-lipped disdain in which these comments are delivered tells its own tale. The moral condemnation is, in fact, not altogether devoid of a sense of resentment at what Octavius feels to be his rival's indifference to himself, the fact that he hardly 'vouchsafed to think he had partners'; and the result is a judgement which, demonstrably true as it is, suffers – like others which Caesar will make – from being too easily made.

The garrulous and ineffective Lepidus, indeed, insinuates that there may be behind Antony's weaknesses a certain compensating nobility:

> His faults in him seem as the spots of heaven
> More fiery by night's blackness [I. iv. 12.]

He receives in reply an expression of disdain more self-sufficient, more ultimately complacent, than those which have gone before.

Caesar contemplates, with a disgust as valid as it is revealing, the incomprehensible weakness which has allowed Antony 'to tumble on the bed of Ptolemy' and 'to keep the turn of tippling with a slave'. As always, he is right; and yet we cannot but feel the dedicated politician's disdain for the common humanity he regards as base material for his manœuvres in the contemptuous reference to 'knaves that smell of sweat'. There is more here than the one-sided antipathy to the mob which has been so often, and in the face of so much qualifying evidence, ascribed to Shakespeare. Octavius' disgust implies, besides moral repudiation, a sense of resentment that his colleague has let him down, that

> we do bear
> So great weight in his lightness. [I. iv. 24.]

It is, in other words, a political rather than a human judgement, uttered by one for whom success in worldly affairs is the substance of life. This is far from making it negligible. Upon the maintenance of Caesar's purposes rest peace, order, and social concord, all indispensable necessities of civilized existence; and yet, we must also be aware that the exclusive following of these purposes may be accompanied by loss, and response to the justice of the denunciation should not render us deaf to the tone of complacent superiority which rounds it off:

> to confound such time
> That draws him from his sport and speaks as loud
> As his own state and ours, 'tis to be chid
> As we rate boys who, being mature in knowledge,
> Pawn their experience to their present pleasure,
> And so rebel to judgement. [I. iv. 28.]

In the mind of Octavius, the 'judgement' which Antony so conspicuously lacks is coldly, effortlessly supreme. He has in fact never been aware of any temptation to abandon it, and that is why his success is assured; but behind Antony's failure, the breakdown and waste of human possibilities which his tragedy implies, there is a certain vitality – corrupted though it be, and perverted from worthy ends – which Octavius may be the poorer for finding incomprehensible.

Whether, and to what extent, this is true only the later development will show. Meanwhile, Caesar is present and vigilant at the centre of the web of world affairs, from which Antony has so conspicuously absented himself. Messengers come in to this centre 'every hour'; they bring news of an order threatened with dissolution, of 'discontents' who, having only 'fear'd' Caesar in his lifetime, are now rallying to the cause of Pompey. To Octavius the news comes to confirm the politician's necessary pessimism:

> It hath been taught us from the primal state,
> That he which is was wish'd until he were;
> And the ebb'd man, ne'er loved till ne'er worth love,
> Comes dear by being lack'd. [I. iv. 41.]

The reflection comes fittingly as a pendant to the preceding discussion of Antony. If Octavius, in excluding human sympathy with human weakness, has achieved consistency in the public sphere, this has been done at a cost perhaps scarcely less than, though widely differing from, that implied in Antony's own choice. It is the sense of this cost that here finds issue in an expression of inevitable pessimism, in the politician's awareness that it is his fatality to repose, beneath his apparent domination of events, upon a fundamental instability.

Caesar's reflections, indeed, as they pass from the contemplation of his own situation to a kind of disillusioned universality, find issue in an image which will run in various forms like a thread through the future action:

> This common body,
> Like to a vagabond flag upon the stream,
> Goes to and back, lackeying the varying tide,
> To rot itself with motion. [I. iv. 44.]

Shakespeare's mature experience seems to have moved him in this play to present his characters in a world in which imperial pretensions, themselves laden with falsity, are associated with over-ripeness and luxury in individual experience. The lines just quoted have their own function in the play, point to a tightening in poetic terms of the bond which is to unite the political action to the fortunes of the tragic protagonists. The passion of Antony for Cleopatra, whatever may be said further of it, shares the corruption of the world in which it grows to expression. One scarcely needs, in establishing this point, to feel the Elizabethan association of 'common' with sexual promiscuity; the link which binds 'rot' to the images of decay more than once associated with Cleopatra is enough to show how Shakespeare, through the continual stressing of disorder and physical corruption, connects the universal situation of his play with the particular tragedy of mature love for which it serves as the appropriate background.

The sense of rottenness and disorder issuing in disruptive action is amply confirmed by the messenger's following report. The pirates, with rare immediacy of phrase, are said to 'ear and wound' the sea with their keels; their inroads are 'hot' and 'flush youth revolt',

relating imperial disorder further to bodily intemperance and un-
leashed appetite. Faced by this hostile pressure, the once loyal
borders of the empire 'lack blood' as they shrink from these incur-
sions, and the vessels which timidly 'peep forth' in anticipation of
their ruin fall prey to the enemy. All this is, as Octavius points out,
an added reason to reprove Antony for his 'luxurious wassails',
which the moralist balances bitterly – and justifiably – against
memories of his former endurance and devotion to the soldier's
calling.

The contemplation of his colleague's behaviour does not, however,
distract Octavius from his practical concentration upon the present.
Pompey, as he puts it, 'thrives in our idleness', and, whatever his
future relations with Antony may bring, the moment is one for
unity and decisive action:

> 'tis time we twain
> Did show ourselves i' the field. [I. iv. 73.]

His decision contrasts with the less founded readiness of Lepidus to
bear his share; only 'tomorrow' will this lay figure know what he can
contribute to the common cause. Lepidus' last words are a plea to be
allowed to participate in any news that may reach his greater companion, a plea to which Caesar accedes –

> Doubt not, sir;
> I knew it for my bond – [I. iv. 83.]

with the brevity of one whose course is fixed, and who knows
precisely how much he may expect from those with whom he
ostensibly shares the conduct of affairs.

Although this part of the play is primarily concerned with
Antony's return to Rome, we are not to forget what he has left
behind. The next scene (I. v) shows a Cleopatra deprived of his
presence and already mobilizing the emotional resources which
will finally return him to her arms. After Caesar's bare emotional
sufficiency, the spectacle of Cleopatra luxuriating in her emotions,
evoking 'mandragora' and determined to

> sleep out this great gap of time
> My Antony is away, [I. v. 5.]

comes with double effect. With the eunuch Mardian as her sole male
companion she is cooped up, imprisoned in the intensity of her own
desire.

> I take no pleasure
> In aught an eunuch has, [I. v. 9.]

she affirms impatiently, but goes on to find compensation in a dream, which anticipates those of later scenes, of exaltation of her absent lover:

> The demi-Atlas of this earth, the arm
> And burgonet of men. [I. v. 23.]

To the beauty of this dream of the absent warrior carried in martial splendour on his horse we cannot fail to respond, even while we recognize it for what it is, a product of fancy and frustrated sexuality. Antony is raised, but only in an imagination which contrasts with the preceding realism of Caesar's condemnation, to the status of a demigod, decisive in action and supreme in his physical attributes; but the intimate foundations of this day-dream are revealed, by what follows, to lie in a more complacent search for emotional compensation.

So much emerges clearly when Cleopatra, having thus transformed Antony in her mind, envisages him as reflecting on her:

> He's speaking now,
> Or murmuring 'Where's my serpent of old Nile?'
> For so he calls me: now I feed myself
> With most delicious poison. [I. v. 24.]

As the speaker's fancy, in the physical absence of her lover, dwells upon his imaginative re-creation, passion expresses itself in images characteristically ambiguous. In recalling Antony's playful addressing of her as the 'serpent' that emerges from the 'old', the overwhelmingly fertile Nile, she anticipates the asp by whose bite she will at the last die; and the thought of these equivocal endearments, mingling nature with poison, life with death, is converted, as she speaks, into a sensuous source of nourishment ('I feed myself') in which the 'delicious' elements of fulfilment are strangely mingled with the 'poison' of his absence. It is in fact in her own sensuous nature, her manifold experience of passion, that Cleopatra is here glorying, raising it by the intense reliving of it to the heights of poetry:

> Think on me,
> That am with Phoebus' amorous pinches black
> And wrinkled deep in time! [I. v. 27.]

As we respond to this, the speaker's very weaknesses, her subjection to age and the realities of her past, are turned, at least for the moment, to something that may strike us as a triumphant assertion of life. That, however, is not the whole picture. Cleopatra, after all, can only achieve this effect through a day-dream, the evocation of a

past at least as dubious as it is splendid. That past she has transformed through the intensity of her desire for Antony, but – as the
speech concludes – we must feel that there is an element of illusion
in the transformation that is taking place:

> Broad-fronted Caesar,
> When thou wast here above the ground, I was
> A morsel for a monarch; and great Pompey
> Would stand and make his eyes grow in my brow;
> There would he anchor his aspect, and die
> With looking on his life. [I. v. 29.]

That we are intended to respond to the emotion thus expressed is as
evident as the fact that a note of realism, of stressed and finally
inglorious promiscuity, also underlies the dream. Pompey is recorded
as being brought to a state akin to death by 'looking on his life';
and to what degree this compensatory exaltation of the past can be
said to evoke life in the present is a principal problem in interpreting
the play.

At this point, however, news of Antony restores Cleopatra to the
present. She greets it with a contrast between the eunuch Alexas –
so 'unlike' Mark Antony – and himself:

> Yet, coming from him, that great medicine hath
> With his tinct gilded thee. [I. v. 36.]

To her evocation, so splendidly and imaginatively intense, of 'my
brave Mark Antony', corresponds – fittingly, for Antony, whatever
his defects, is always the master of the appropriate gesture – his
present of 'this orient pearl'. The gift, opulent in itself and doubly so
after the strict parsimony of Octavius' emotions, is backed with
words that aim at, and nearly achieve, conviction through sheer
poetic power:

> Say, the firm Roman to great Egypt sends
> This treasure of an oyster; at whose foot,
> To mend the petty present, I will piece
> Her opulent throne with kingdoms; all the east,
> Say thou, shall call her mistress. [I. v. 43.]

As always, the speech needs to be followed with discrimination. The
thought of Egypt is once more accompanied with intimations of
supreme material wealth, converted, however, while the poetic
effect lasts, to something more. Cleopatra is 'great Egypt', fit to
receive the 'treasure' which merely anticipates a greater offering,
being in itself 'a petty present'. Her throne, 'opulent' already, will be
'pieced with kingdoms' by Antony's coming victory, so that she shall

be the 'mistress' not – be it noted – of Octavius' severe Rome, which Antony has renounced, but of 'the east'. Behind the beauty, however, is the conscious gesture, the sense of a speaker for whom deeds and words are too easily identified. When Antony describes himself as 'the firm Roman', we have already seen – and heard from those around him – enough to suggest that the claim covers an element of the spurious, the rhetorical; and the entire speech, though it contributes as poetry to the exaltation of his passion, is yet, realistically considered, his contribution to the day-dream which his mistress has so effectively woven round his decline and her sense of loss.

Cleopatra, indeed, show signs of being less easily convinced. She responds to Alexas' martial picture of the warrior mounting his 'arm-gaunt'[1] steed; but when she anxiously seeks to confirm the reality of his reported mood, to discover whether he was 'sad or merry', the reply that he was decisively neither is pounced upon, a little too eagerly, as proof of his continued constancy:

> He was not sad, for he would shine on those
> That make their looks by his; he was not merry,
> Which seemed to tell them his remembrance lay
> In Egypt with his joy; but between both.
> O heavenly mingle! [I. v. 55.]

It is of the nature of Cleopatra's love, a sign at once of its reality and its limitation, to ignore her lover's situation in the world, to see him only in relation to her need of him; and it is because he responds to the demand thus made upon him, ignoring the responsibilities which the world imposes upon him, that Antony finally falls. Meanwhile, as the episode draws to a close, Cleopatra's heightened emotions, so splendidly and so dangerously poised, begin to collapse into something like absurdity. When she tells Alexas that who is born the day she forgets to write to Antony 'shall die a beggar', we can sense desire overreaching itself, falling into the unreality which has from the first shadowed it. The self-conscious recalling to Charmian of her conquest of Caesar implies a judgement on what has gone before; and her own indignation confirms the effect:

> By Isis, I will give thee bloody teeth,
> If thou with Caesar paragon again
> My man of men. [I. v. 70.]

Here, at least, Charmian's retort – 'I say but after you' – admits no answer, and the attempted rejoinder –

[1] The Folio text, which produces this adjective, has been questioned here; but the alternatives suggested scarcely carry conviction.

> My salad days,
> When I was green in judgement: cold in blood,
> To say as I said then! – [I. v. 73.]

for all its return to the favourite theme of Cleopatra's experience'
recognizes as much. To 'unpeople Egypt', should this be needed if she
is to send daily messengers to Antony, is clearly as impossible as it
would be irresponsible; the extravagance reflects the unreality upon
which the poetic splendours of this scene are founded. The effect of
the entire episode is at once to initiate the poetic exaltation of passion
(for the poetry, after all, compels by its own power) and to confirm
the limits of that exaltation in the judgement simultaneously
passed on it by the outside world.

With Cleopatra in the background, the way is open for the triumvirs to be brought together in precarious unity. As a prelude to their
meeting, the scope of the action is extended (II. i) to present Pompey,
whom they are united in opposing. His opening exchange with
Menecrates stresses the sense of relativity, of the inscrutable purposes
of the gods, which throughout this play conditions human actions in
the field of politics. As Menecrates puts it, commenting with native
realism on Pompey's questionable assertion that 'the great gods'
should, by 'assisting' his cause, advance the fortunes of 'justest
men':

> We, ignorant of ourselves,
> Beg often our own harms, which the wise powers
> Deny us for our good; [II. i. 5.]

Ignorance of his own true advantage characterizes man, as a
political being, throughout this play and serves as a background to
the choices of passion which, inadequate and perverse though they
often are, may yet be in some sense more significant than themselves.

Against this background of inscrutability, Pompey sums up with
accurate economy the defects of his rivals. Antony, the libertine, 'in
Egypt sits at dinner'; Caesar parsimoniously

> gets money where
> He loses hearts, [II. i. 13.]

and the negligible Lepidus

> flatters both,
> Of both is flatter'd, but he neither loves,
> Nor either cares for him. [II. i. 14.]

The picture is one of human inadequacy issuing in general mistrust,
and Pompey draws it with remorseless truth. He is not, however,

himself beyond weakness, for the news that his rivals are already in
the field is met with a denial - 'tis false' – in which the will to believe
only what is convenient replaces the dispassionate consideration of
fact.

Pompey's ultimate trust is in the dalliance of Antony, which he
describes in terms that stress the subjection of the libertine:

> all the charms of love,
> Salt Cleopatra, soften thy waned lip!
> Let witchcraft join with beauty, lust with both!
> Tie up the libertine in a field of feasts,
> Keep his brain fuming; Epicurean cooks
> Sharpen with cloyless sauce his appetite;
> That sleep and feeding may prorogue his honour
> Even till a Lethe'd dullness. [II. i. 20.]

To respond to the poetry here is to approach some of the sources of
this play's inspiration. It is poetry compatible with, and expressive
of, a pitiless realism. The 'charms of love' in Cleopatra, real as they
are, are balanced by a sense of incongruous age, can only soften
what is, after all, her 'waned lip'. True beauty and the false appeal of
'witchcraft' combine with 'lust' to produce their effect upon Antony,
tying up the 'libertine' in a web of sensual delights and reducing the
operation of reason in him to the physical lethargy which 'sleep and
feeding' produce at the end of prolonged physical indulgence: 'keep
his brain fuming'. Yet, unwillingly, contrary to the speaker's intention, there is life, of a kind, in the passage too. The keen relishing
of the sensuous processes, the 'sharpening' of the 'appetite' by the
operations of 'Epicurean' cooks, whose handiwork, however impossibly, appears in the moment of enjoyment as though its effects
cannot 'cloy'; all these balanced sensations, setting the keenness of
the senses against surfeit and corruption, are invoked to lead only,
through the animal surrender implied in 'sleep and feeding', to the
denial of that 'honour' devotion to which in action distinguishes
man from the brute, and to the victory of an impenetrable, a death-
like 'dullness'. The criticism, uttered by an enemy, marks in part an
exposure of lust and irresponsibility and, in part and more distantly,
the transformation of these things into a relevant poetic intensity.

The news brought by Varrius confirms, meanwhile, Antony's
temporary return to responsibility. Pompey seeks at first to dismiss
him as an 'amorous surfeiter'; but in the depreciation the wish is at
least in part father to the thought, and he himself goes on to admit
that Antony's martial capacities, however diminished, are still
'twice the other twain'; though the final references to 'Egypt's
widow' and the 'ne'er-lust-wearied Antony' confirms a note of

contempt which the speaker needs to maintain his own confidence. More practical in his grasp of realities, Menas refers to the seeds of future strife:

> I cannot hope
> Caesar and Antony shall well greet together. [II. i. 38.]

The memory of past rivalry should, indeed, effectively prevent them from so doing; but Pompey, where his own self-estimate is not concerned, is a realist who knows

> How lesser enmities may give way to greater.

All political judgements are indeed insecure in the world here depicted, and it is certain that necessity will make strange bedfellows:

> how the fear of us
> May cement their divisions and bind up
> The petty difference, we yet not know. [II. i. 47.]

'Be't as the gods will have it!': political issues are finally in the hands of an inscrutable fate, and it only remains for men to trust in their own resources and to hope for the best:

> It only stands
> Our lives upon to use our strongest hands. [II. i. 50.]

The fatalism implied in this philosophy makes a suitable introduction to the magnificent exercise in political realism which follows.

The portrayal (II. ii) of the 'reconciliation' between Octavius and Antony is possibly Shakespeare's masterpiece in this kind. As it opens, Lepidus timidly urges upon Enobarbus the need to persuade his master to 'soft and gentle speech', only to receive the reply of one who is realist enough to know that Antony's case is far from strong, that his best card is likely to be the decisive assertion of his manliness:

> if Caesar move him,
> Let Antony look over Caesar's head
> And speak as loud as Mars. [II. ii. 4.]

To this brusque declaration of male assertiveness Lepidus replies, unexceptionably, that the time is not for 'private stomaching'; but the character of the speaker is such as to leave no small doubt whether this advice will carry weight in the conflict of wills and interests which is clearly approaching.

The entry of the two protagonists confirms this impression. Each is accompanied by his chosen followers, each wrapped up in his private projects; for Antony, agreement in Italy is no more than the prelude to a campaign to restore his position eastward in Parthia, whilst Caesar, involved in his own train of thought, tells Maecenas to 'ask Agrippa' for information on the theme, unspecified, of their conversation. Lepidus, coming forward to greet them, is clearly anxious of the outcome, pleads the urgency of public affairs and the need for moderation in face of the external threat to their common prosperity:

> That which combined us was most just, and let not
> A leaner action rend us. [II. ii. 18.]

This is Pompey's prophecy caught in the process of assuming visible shape. Urgency and insecurity – and not least that which Lepidus senses in his own situation – are the background to these words, making present differences 'trivial' in comparison, not to be so debated as to

>   commit
>   Murder in healing wounds. [II. ii. 21.]

External necessity combines with common sense, prompting Lepidus to beg his 'noble partners' to 'touch the sourest points with sweetest terms'. We are made aware both of the speaker's realisation that he is treading dangerous ground and, by implication, of the actual intricacy of issues that must be skated over with the utmost delicacy by those who feel the presence beneath them of the thinnest possible ice. Antony greets Lepidus' appeal with one of those gestures of careless generosity that come only too readily to him –

>   'Tis spoken well.
>   Were we before our armies and to fight,
>   I should do thus – [II. ii. 25.]

and Caesar remains rigidly silent.

The initial approaches of the two leaders are laden with implied mistrust. These are two hard-faced gamesters, opposed indeed in character (and in all else), and eyeing one another in mutual wariness, each jealous of what he is pleased to regard as his reputation and each expecting the trick which he feels his fellow 'pillar of the world' may have up his sleeve. To Caesar's frigid greeting 'Welcome to Rome', Antony replies with an equally distant 'Thank you', and to his further laconic invitation to be seated with the corresponding show of wary courtesy: 'Sit, sir.' These preliminaries over, Antony, as though conscious of the justice behind Caesar's resentment, opens the discussion in a tone not far removed from deliberate churlishness, as one determined to anticipate his rival in taking offence:

> I learn you take things ill which are not so,
> Or being, concern you not. [II. ii. 33.]

This, not unnaturally, is the signal for an exchange of mutual reproaches, in which Caesar's disdain (so strangely like that displayed
by Brutus in his quarrel with Cassius)[1] and Antony's carelessness
both display themselves to the worst possible advantage. Caesar's
immediate retort is, at bottom, slighting. It would be laughable in
him to declare himself offended 'for nothing or a little'; above all, it
would be ridiculous to name Antony 'derogately' when he had no
cause to name him at all:

> when to sound your name
> It not concern'd me. [II. ii. 38.]

Caesar's approach is marked from the first by a frigid concentration
upon the ends he has in view which stands in most effective contrast
to the sullen touchiness which can be detected in his rival's reply:

> My being in Egypt, Caesar,
> What was't to you? [II. ii. 39.]

The thought of Egypt touches on a raw spot in Antony's conscience,
and none is more calculated than Caesar, so ruthlessly devoted to his
public purposes, to aggravate it. The contrast between the two men
and their respective attitudes could not be more tellingly conveyed.

From this initial exchange, Octavius passes to accuse Antony of
inciting his wife and brother to make war upon him. Antony's careless disclaimer of responsibility ends in a suggestion that Caesar is in
fact using his brother's deeds to '*patch* a quarrel' against himself on
grounds which he contemptuously dismisses:

> As matter whole you have not to make it with,
> It must not be with this; [II. ii. 57.]

and to this Caesar, taking up the belittling, contemptuous implication, replies with the counter-accusation that his rival, who now seeks
to justify himself by ascribing 'defects of judgement' to him, 'patched
up' false excuses for his conduct. As the tone of the discussion rises,
Antony shifts his ground more than once, alternating between praise
of the dead wife whom he has himself abandoned –

> As for my wife,
> I would you had her spirit in such another – [II. ii. 65.]

and use of her alleged 'garboils' as excuses to distract attention from

---

[1] *Julius Caesar*, IV. iii. See p. 59 above.

his own neglect; for the 'disquiet' which her 'impatience', allied to 'shrewdness of policy', might have caused Caesar,

> you must
> But say, I could not help it. [II. ii. 74.]

When, finally, Octavius accuses Antony of neglecting his messenger and of insulting him, the latter can only reply with the careless gesture, noble in form but once more too easily made, of the confirmed libertine. The messenger arrived, it seems, unexpectedly, 'ere admitted', when Antony, having newly feasted 'three kings',

> did want
> Of what I was i' the morning; [II. ii. 80.]

but to have explained the circumstances next day was

> as much
> As to have ask'd him pardon. Let this fellow
> Be nothing of our strife; if we contend,
> Out of our question wipe him. [II. ii. 83.]

It is typical of such as Antony to take it for granted that others are as ready as themselves to take a gesture for a reality, to dismiss with careless ease the grounds of the very quarrel which neglect, misplaced confidence, has done so much to exasperate.

At this point, when mutual recrimination seems to have brought the meeting to a dead end, the trend of the argument is changed by one of those sudden shifts of mood which characterize Antony's behaviour throughout. When Caesar presses home his charge of perjury, and Lepidus interposes his 'Soft, Caesar!' he provokes a moment of firm affirmation in which we may feel the presence of Antony's more dignified self: 'The honour is sacred which he talks on now.' The mood, could it only be maintained, is one of steely control; but, followed as it is by a show of self-excuse, it reveals yet another facet of the speaker's constantly shifting personality. His oath to come to Caesar's aid has been, so he can now believe, 'neglected' rather than broken: negligence has always been a prominent feature of his nature, and is now brought forward as an excuse by one who, while not lacking in a certain candour of self-knowledge, is in fact a weak man ready to ascribe his own failing to the machinations of others, working upon him

> when *poison'd* hours had bound me up
> From mine own knowledge. [II. ii 94.]

The 'poison', indeed, has worked more deeply than he is ready to admit. His infatuation for Cleopatra, which he can now recognize as the occasion of his indignity, is at least as much the product as the cause of his self-betrayal. The effort to cover this by a show of dignity –

> As nearly as I may,
> I'll play the penitent to you: but mine honesty
> Shall not make poor my greatness, nor my power
> Work without it – [II. ii. 95.]

cannot disguise the unworthiness of the plea that his wife made wars to have him 'out of Egypt', and that his part in this sordid state of affairs has been that of an 'ignorant motive', who now goes 'so far' to

> ask pardon as befits mine honour
> To stoop in such a case. [II. ii. 101.]

Thus to reveal character in all its complexity through verse at once easy in its flow and full of human variety is in itself a great achievement.

Having thus shifted the blame upon Fulvia, Cleopatra, anyone but himself, Antony's 'honour' is satisfied and he is ready to come to terms. To assist him in so doing, he has the helpless tool Lepidus, whose fear for himself prompts him to grasp at these exculpations as words 'nobly spoken', Maecenas, whose eye is on the 'present need' and its call to unity (which Enobarbus interprets as borrowing 'one another's love for the instant', prior to further 'wrangling' when the threat of Pompey has been removed), and Agrippa, ready as a courtier should always be to whisper the supremely cynical suggestion into his master's ear. To Caesar's expressed wish to find 'what hoop should hold us staunch', the latter responds, after craving leave, with the decisive word:

> Thou hast a sister by the mother's side,
> Admired Octavia: great Mark Antony
> Is now a widower. [II. ii. 124.]

Thus seconded, and with the ground so prepared, the dishonourable project cannot but prosper. It is, indeed, insinuated before it is openly proposed, and Agrippa's implied gibe when he describes Antony as a 'widower', which Caesar cannot resist taking up in his oblique reference to Cleopatra, leads to a further parody of 'honour' in Antony's stiff, self-conscious 'I am not married, Caesar': a false dignity to cover a false situation, and leading to a transaction as cynical as it is clearly destined to be transitory. Agrippa's highly politic stressing of his concept of 'perpetual amity', of the 'unslipping knot' which will unite the triumvirs as 'brothers', has itself the effect of emphasizing impermanence; and the unctuous flattery of Antony which is implied in the suggestion that Octavia deserves for her beauty and virtue

> No worse a husband than the best of men, [II. ii. 135.]

one, moreover, of whom Agrippa, by a crowning adventure into the unreal, can say:

> Whose virtue and whose general graces speak
> That which none else can utter, [II. ii. 136.]

is sufficient to place the entire manœuvre in its true light.

Agrippa winds up his insinuations with gestures of courtly servility towards his master and with a typical involution of the concepts of truth and fairy-tale:

> all great fears which now import their dangers
> Would then be nothing: truths would be tales,
> Where now half tales be truths. [II. ii. 139.]

He then stands aside to observe the effect of his words. These are at first approached, on either side, with characteristic caution. Antony calls upon Caesar to speak; Caesar, for his part, will wait to hear

> how Antony is touched
> With what is spoke already. [II. ii. 146.]

In so doing, he follows his permanent instinct to seek the firm ground beneath his feet; and Antony, not less wary, asks for the authority behind Agrippa's suggestion, his power to 'make this good'. Thus prompted, Octavius is ready to declare himself and, by uttering his final assent, to dispose of his sister; for Agrippa's authority is now declared to be

> the power of Caesar; and
> His power unto Octavia. [II. ii. 149.]

The bargain is struck, and Antony, as befits his nature, turns it into the poetry which is both his redeeming grace and his weakness:

> May I never
> To this good purpose, that so fairly shows,
> Dream of impediment.[1] [II. ii. 150.]

He may even, as he speaks this, believe it; being the man he is, who shall say? At all events, he is ready to call the agreement so

---

[1] Compare, for the phrasing, the opening of Sonnet CXVI:
> Let me not to the marriage of true minds
> Admit impediments.

H

concluded 'an act of grace' and to pray, one knows not whether from simplicity or rooted cynicism, that

> from this hour
> The hearts of brothers govern in our loves
> And sway our great designs! [II. ii. 153.]

The reaction from the preceding distrust is in a very real sense, absurd, and no doubt Antony's words are designed for a public effect; but the fact remains, and is relevant to the later development of his tragedy, that he alone of the politicians of this play is capable of a gesture of this kind. Perhaps the gesture, like the man who makes it, is hopelessly flawed, tied up in vicious circumstances; but the contrast with those to whom it is directed is there to point to a certain implication of redemption.

Caesar's reply, accompanying the appropriate gesture of the outstretched hand, combines a correct assertion of brotherly love –

> A sister I bequeath you, whom no brother
> Did ever love so dearly – [II. ii. 156.]

with a sober and politic plea for the unity of 'our kingdoms and our hearts'; but the thoughts of both turn at once to the coming attack on Pompey, which Antony now finds in some sense unnatural –

> I did not think to draw my sword 'gainst Pompey,
> For he hath laid strange courtesies and great
> Of late upon me – [II. ii. 160.]

but which has been, of course, the object of all these proceedings. The political motives displayed, indeed, remain strangely complex, compounded of contradiction. The only certain fact is, as Lepidus says, that 'time calls upon us', and that the alternatives are to attack or to meet attack:

> Of us must Pompey presently be sought,
> Or else he seeks out us. [II. ii. 165.]

Before finally embarking on the preparations for war, Antony calls for the dispatch of what he describes, not without significance, as 'the *business*' (that of the marriage) 'we have talk'd of'. Caesar, not unlike a merchant anxious to bring off a deal, invites him 'to my sister's view', and Antony, as he follows his new ally, turns to request the company of the half-forgotten Lepidus, who is pathetically ready to be remembered: 'Not sickness should detain me.' The end of the negotiation worthily epitomizes its presiding spirit.

The affairs of the politicians thus concluded, the professionals of war and diplomacy remain to register their hard-headed, disillusioned comments. Their talk turns, by contrast with the political realism of Rome which we have just seen in operation, upon the opulent dissipation of the East and so, through Enobarbus' vivid reference to 'monstrous matter of feast', to the Cleopatra whom Antony has just ostensibly put aside. Maecenas describes her, ominously for Octavia, as a 'most triumphant lady', and the phrase is as relevant to our understanding of her as the picture, already stressed, of her ripe maturity, her dubious past, and the corruption which her person undoubtedly represents. A double end of exposure and glorification is, indeed served by Enobarbus' account of her meeting with Antony at Cydnus. The beauty to which he pays tribute bears with it an element of over-ripeness, artificial opulence. The effect of beauty is there, present in the picture of the royal barge as 'a burnished throne' burning on the water, a setting fit for a goddess; but artifice and a cloying sense of luxury also belong to the complete impression. The poop of the barge was 'beaten gold', the oars 'silver', and the queen herself lay in a pavilion 'cloth-of-gold of tissue'; surrounded by 'pretty dimpling boys, like smiling Cupids', her entire person presented itself as an elaboration, wrought less by nature than by conscious artifice, on what is clearly conceived as a deliberate work of art:

> O'erpicturing that Venus where we see
> The fancy outwork nature. [II. ii. 208.]

On this vessel, indeed, nature has no place, and natural feeling correspondingly little; a triumph of artifice, its sails are 'purple' and so 'perfumed' that the very winds, sharing in the prevailing mood of cloying sensuality, are 'love-sick' with them. The smiling boy-Cupids and the 'gentlewomen, like the Nereides' belong, as do their rhythmic motions, to a world of elaborate decoration in which only decadent feeling can have a place; the winds stirred by the motion of the 'divers-coloured fans' did *seem*

> To glow the delicate cheeks which they did cool,
> And what they undid did. [II. ii. 212.]

The sense of artifice, of feelings and sensations caught, as it were, in their opposites ('glow . . . cool', 'undid did') belong to a poetic world most germane to the central tragedy. The barge is steered by a *'seeming* mermaid', the hands that move the elaborately luxurious 'silken tackle' are 'flower-soft', and the entire picture is involved in a perfume – 'strange invisible' – which cloys even as it fascinates. This is beauty indeed, but of a kind strangely and firmly limited by its artifice, in which spontaneous life can have no assured place. If this is the framework in which the love of Antony and Cleopatra has thus far flowered, they will have to be taken out of it (by death and disaster, which its setting already implies) before we can respond fully to whatever value their mutual emotion may have.

Even at this point, however, we need to take into account other, more truly vital elements. If the artificial sensual provocations of Egypt are Cleopatra's background, they do not exhaust her appeal. It is not until she has become involved in the popular acclaim –

> The city cast
> Her people out upon her – [II. ii. 221.]

that we feel her freed from the world of elaborate decoration to which Enobarbus' set-piece has confined her. The effect of the liberation is superb; and it is confirmed when we hear of her, a little later, as given over with racy vitality to the popular diversions:

> I saw her once
> Hop forty paces through the public street;
> And having lost her breath, she spoke, and panted,
> That she did make defect perfection,
> And, breathless, power breathe forth. [II. ii. 236.]

Once again, the balance of contrary impressions – 'defect perfection'; 'breathless, power breathe forth' – conveys marvellously the play's central impression of passion caught in its own weakness, vitality at once issuing from and returning to the death it bears within itself; and once more we shall be careful to give due weight to every element in the balance. The whole account is beautifully contrived round this sense of precarious but essential equilibrium. It is apparent in Enobarbus' further description of the mutual deference of the invitations to supper, where Cleopatra's generosity –

> she replied
> It should be better he became her guest – [II. ii. 228.]

is answered by Antony's 'courtesy', and this in turn most subtly qualified by the touch of irony implied in Enobarbus' aside:

> our courteous Antony,
> Whom ne'er the word of 'No' woman heard speak, [II. ii. 230.]

with its devastating judgement of character and the effeminacy of 'barber'd ten times o'er' to give it final confirmation. Antony on this occasion loses himself, 'pays his heart' (but it is perhaps in his favour that, unlike his political rivals, he has a heart with which to pay) for a deception, for 'what his eyes eat only'. In contrast with this intricate balance of feelings, loss and delusion at the heart of life, Agrippa's comment on the past relationship between Cleopatra and Julius

Caesar, and on the birth of Caesarion, conveys the disenchanted estimate of appetite which prevails in the world which surrounds the royal pair.

As the scene closes, it is clear that Antony's separation from Cleopatra cannot be permanent. The compensating swing of the pendulum is, in fact, anticipated at what seems to be the climax of its Romeward thrust. When Maecenas recalls that he has just sworn to leave her 'utterly', Enobarbus' retort is a forthright 'Never: he will not.' In support of this conviction, he goes on to stress her attraction in one of the finest of all the play's affirmations of her appeal:

> Age cannot wither her, nor custom stale
> Her infinite variety: other women cloy
> The appetites they feed, but she makes hungry
> Where most she satisfies; for vilest things
> Become themselves in her, that the holy priests
> Bless her when she is riggish. [II. ii. 243.]

Once more we are in the presence of the play's marvellous blending of opposites, its confirmation of mortal weakness (and, worse than weakness, corruption) in the act of raising it to the heights of poetic energy. The attactions of Cleopatra are celebrated in terms of her '*infinite* variety', which seems to defeat the circumstances of 'age' (which are, however, present) and the contradiction by which 'appetite', directed upon other women, fatally 'cloys' the very emotion which it provokes. Hunger and satisfaction, 'appetite' and satiation, are held together in a common emotion, and it is part of Cleopatra's equivocal but genuine triumph that, even in her 'riggish' moments, she can make the 'holy priests' bless her. The presence of contrasted elements of life and death, exaltation and corruption, answers to the essential diversity of the character. Cleopatra, though the creature of the world which surrounds her, can at times emerge from it, impose a vitality which is not the less astonishing for retaining to the last its connection with the environment it transcends. This combination of 'nature' with artifice, vitality with corruption in a single, infinitely complex dramatic creation, is the key to the conflicting estimates which her relations to Antony impose on the course of the tragedy. For the moment, it is enough to say that the contrasted virtues of Octavia – the 'beauty, wisdom, modesty' which Maecenas ascribes to her – will have no power, 'blessed lottery' though they may be to him, to deflect Antony from his determined course.

IV

The agreement between Antony and Octavius is followed by a series of episodes which correspond to a point of balance attained by the contrasted fortunes which the play is concerned to follow. Once more, the dramatic structure is both intricate and revealing. The central incident (II. vii) may be taken as the feast on Pompey's galley which, ostensibly cementing the new-found amity between the triumvirs and their one-time enemy, in fact insinuates the precarious nature of the agreement between them. On either side of this episode the principal threads of the action are grouped in their contrasted realities. Before, it, they seem to point (though with numerous reservations, glances towards other and contrary truths) to a new ordering of things. Antony, with some show of sincerity, declares his reformation to Octavia (II. iii), and the forces of the triumvirs are shown as united in the prospect of decisive action (II. iv); Cleopatra, informed of Antony's Roman marriage, seems to have lost her grip on him and to be plunged into hysterical despair (II. v), whilst Pompey, after coming to make war (II. vi), accedes to clasp the hands of his enemies in a gesture of peace. Up to the brittle convivialities on the galley, in fact, the primary direction of events seems to imply the consolidation of a new world order; after this tipsy apotheosis, on the other hand, the elements of rivalry and division come into their own. Antony, his impulse towards Rome exhausted, turns his wavering thoughts to the East, where Ventidius replaces him on the battlefields of Syria (III. i). Octavia leaves her brother to accompany her new husband (III. ii), and Cleopatra, still alone in Egypt, shows signs of recovering her control over her lover (III. iii). Finally, Antony himself, in revealing to his helpless wife (III. iv) his resentment against Octavius, anticipates a new state of things in which, after Pompey's murder and Lepidus' imprisonment (III. v), Caesar is free to greet his sister's return with the full expression (III. vi) of his determination to eliminate his rival.

The structure of this part of the play is not, of course, as simple as this bald summary might indicate. If the trend of the earlier episodes is towards the consolidation of an apparent unity, it is accompanied at every stage by the presence of discordant elements. This is evident in the scene (II. iii) which, very briefly, shows Antony making some effort to fit into his new life with Octavia. It opens with him foreseeing separation, pointing out that the 'world' and the calls of his 'great office' will at times separate them; but there is about his following self-estimate –

> I have not kept my square; but that to come
> Shall all be done by the rule – [II. iii. 6.]

a certain boyish candour, even an innocence which – while it lasts – strikes an attractive note. It does not last long. The entry of the Soothsayer does more than bring a breath of Egypt to the scene. In warning Antony to keep away from Caesar, it stresses the element of fatality which presides over his entire career. Fatality, indeed, in the form of a rejection, with moral responsibility and self-respect, of the distinctively human privilege of exercising some measure of control over individual destiny, is the essence of the tragic process in this play; and Antony's ruin is its supreme embodiment. The sense of his inferiority to Caesar obsesses him throughout, though it is typical that he should reflect the feeling in terms of gambling, of luck at the dice, and of cock-fighting. It is in talk of these things that Antony announces what is in effect – in spite of his recent words to Octavia – an open-eyed surrender to sensual inclination:

> I will to Egypt:
> And though I make this marriage for my peace,
> I' the east my pleasure lies. [II. iii. 38.]

It will be hard, after this brief revelation of weakness and undisguised self-indulgence, to accept Antony at the romantic estimate which some critics, taking him too readily at his own words (or some of them), have been ready to allow him.

After a short scene (II. iv) between Lepidus, Maecenas, and Agrippa, which recalls the continued pressure of public events, we return (II. v) to Cleopatra who, though momentarily neglected by her lover, will again exercise upon him the charm of her 'infinite variety'. That variety is now presented, realistically and even sardonically, in action. The tone as the scene opens is one of sultry brooding, steeped in unsatisfied sexuality and surrounded by notes of music,

> *moody* food
> Of us that trade in love; [II. v. i.]

the adjective, with its sense of smouldering feeling, the reference to appetite implied in 'food', and the implications of 'trade in love' are all significant. The presence of the eunuch Mardian, saluted by the bitter and frustrated indifference of

> As well a woman with an eunuch play'd
> As with a woman, [II. v. 5.]

further sets the tone for what is to come. Caught in a mood of frustration, deprived of the satisfaction upon which her being is anchored, Cleopatra is ready for an outburst of one kind or another; whether that outburst will be finally tragic or, as the event shows, absurdly revealing, will depend upon the stimulus provided by external events.

First, however, Cleopatra indulges herself in an affectionate parody of her relations to Antony, recalling her descent to the river with the 'music playing far off' to

> betray
> Tawny-finn'd fishes, [II. v. 11.]

and leading up to the playfully ironic bitterness of her conclusion:

> I'll think them every one an Antony,
> And say 'Ah, ha! you're caught'. [II. v. 13.]

Charmian's answering reference to the 'salt-fish' drawn up by Antony 'with fervency' contains a note of satire beneath the recalling of past pleasure tirelessly indulged; but the conclusion –

> That time – O times! –
> I laugh'd him out of patience, and that night
> I laugh'd him into patience; and next morn,
> Ere the ninth hour, I drunk him to his bed – [II. v. 18.]

gives the typical note of poetic transformation, in terms of tireless energy, to what is in fact – and the description also makes this clear – a sordid and life-consuming dissipation.

All this, however, is no more than a prelude, the setting up of an appropriate background, for what is to come. Cleopatra is waiting for reality to intervene, carrying on the mood of her last solitary day-dream; and when it comes, in the form of a messenger with news of Antony (her last scene, it should be recalled, ended with talk of messengers as a substitute for life-giving personal contact), she greets him with an intensity of sexual concentration that makes a most fitting prelude to the following revulsion. She begs him to 'ram' his 'fruitful tidings' into her ears, that have been so long 'barren'; and the following gesture of royal generosity, the offer of gold and, beyond this, of her 'bluest veins to kiss' –

> a hand that kings
> Have lipp'd, and trembled kissing – [II. v. 29.]

is at once absurd and oddly, if incongruously, magnificent. The magnificence is, however, at best precarious, balanced by a note of wanton cruelty which springs from insecurity and frustrated desire:

> But, sirrah, mark, we use
> To say the dead are well: bring it to that,
> The gold I give thee will I melt and pour
> Down thy ill-uttering throat. [II. v. 32.]

Volatile in her every reaction, Cleopatra's cruelty is as intense, imaginative, as the passion which is, in a very real sense, its opposite aspect. A realistic estimate of the imagination which it exalts into tragedy is indeed one of this play's outstanding features. At one moment she is promising to set the messenger in 'a shower of gold', to 'hail rich pearls' upon him; at the next, as the news of Antony's betrayal at last breaks upon her, her anger expresses itself in the depths of sensual incoherence:

> I'll spurn thine eyes
> Like balls before me; I'll unhair thy head:
> Thou shalt be whipp'd with wire, and stew'd in brine,
> Smarting in lingering pickle. [II. v. 63.]

The sadistic note is, as we shall have occasion to see,[1] common to both these lovers, though Cleopatra's expression of it is tense and volatile where Antony's will be heavy with dangerous resentment.

None of this can disguise the fact that, in this scene at least, Cleopatra is the victim of her passions. Her readiness to accept a change in words for a change in reality – 'Say, 'tis not so, a province I will give thee' – breaks against the messenger's bleak reiteration of the intolerable fact: 'He's married, madam'. Faced by this reality, her imagination collapses into the mixture of fertility and poisoned corruption implied in her evocation of chaos:

> Melt Egypt into Nile! and kindly creatures
> Turn all to serpents! [II. v. 78.]

There is a certain recovery into self-knowledge when, as she recalls the messenger, she comments:

> These hands do lack nobility, that they strike
> A meaner than myself: since I myself
> Have given myself the cause; [II. v. 82.]

but even this is the prelude to a further unreasoning effort to extract a denial of the truth, and leads, in a further association of the fertile flooding Nile with the breeding of serpents –

> So half my Egypt were submerged and made
> A cistern for scal'd snakes! – [II. v. 94.]

[1] Compare the episode of Thyreus (III. xi). See p. 149 below.

to what is in fact a following of passion into the depths of irresponsibility. Only her final instructions to Alexas, bidding him report upon
Octavia's 'feature', her age, height, and 'the colour of her hair',
show human curiosity – however unworthily directed – feeling its
way to the revival of hope. If Antony's conduct paints him 'one way
like a Gorgon', it is none the less true that for her – whose life depends
upon it – 'the other way's a Mars'. The combination of extreme
emotional resilience with passionate hysteria, caught here at the
ebb of fortune, will be carried a stage further, shown in the process of
recovery which her restoration to Antony will confirm, upon her
next appearance.

The next scene (II. vi) returns to the main political action, now
tending to a momentary balance. Pompey's statement of his grievances combines rhetoric with free, natural phrasing and rhythm;
Antony, on his side, has put his recent past behind him and become
reincorporated to the greater austerity of the Roman world:

> The beds i' the east are soft; and thanks to you,
> That call'd me timelier than my purpose hither;
> For I have gain'd by it. [II. vi. 50.]

Yet, behind the appearance of harmony, a note of malice persists. It
is felt in Pompey's observation to Antony about 'your fine Egyptian
cooking', and in the twice repeated insinuation 'I have heard',
aimed at recalling Julius Caesar's past relations with Cleopatra and
the adventure, necessarily galling to Antony, that, by means of
Apollodorus, brought 'A certain queen to Caesar in a mattress'. The
cynicism of Enobarbus is happy at the prospect of no less than 'four
feasts' before him; but his judgement remains clear and, when he is
left alone with Menas, the comments of the two seasoned cam-
paigners at once restore the sense of disillusioned realism.

Pompey, in fact, has blindly thrown away his fortune. 'Thy
father', Menas says, 'would ne'er have made this treaty', and the
following exchange amounts to a realistic comment on the warrior's
condition in this world of scorned or exploited values:

> ENOBARBUS ... you have been a great thief by sea.
> MENAS And you by land.
> ENOBARBUS There I deny my land service. But give me your
>   hand, Menas; if our eyes had authority, here they
>   might take two thieves kissing. [II. vi. 93.]

These considerations lead to a dispassionate assertion of human
duplicity which casts its shadow over surrounding events; for 'All
men's faces are true' – including those which have just faced one
another in uttering words of peace – 'whatso'er their hands are', and,

on the other hand, 'there is never a fair woman' – including Cleo-patra – 'has a true face'. The entire scene, moreover, is dominated by a perversion of the simple soldierly values, as Menas ruefully recognizes when he replies to Enobarbus' 'We came hither to fight with you' by saying 'For my part, I am sorry it is turned to a drink-ing'. Over all, politicians and soldiers alike, there lies the shadow of an inscrutable fatality; if, as Menas asserts, 'Pompey doth this day laugh away his fortune', Enobarbus knows that, in the order of things, 'he cannot weep't back again'. Finally, when Menas says of Antony's marriage of convenience, 'I think the policy of that purpose made more in the marriage than the love of the parties', Enobarbus carries this true observation one stage further when he affirms that 'the band that seems to tie their friendship together will be the very strangler of their amity', and justifies his prophecy by pointing to Octavia as 'holy, cold, and still' by disposition, whereas Antony 'is not so':

> He will to his Egyptian dish again: then shall the sighs of Octavia blow the fire up in Caesar; and, as I said before, that which is the strength of their amity shall prove the immediate author of their variance. [II. vi. 133.]

This sardonic estimate rests upon a true understanding of Antony's motives – 'Antony will use his affection where it is: he but married his occasion here' – so that the scene which has seemed to cement a lasting peace ends in fact on a note of foreseen dissolution.

The great scene of drunken festivity to which all this part of the play has been leading (II. vii) is a supreme achievement of its kind. Proceeding by a superb counterpointing of contrasted themes and situations, it balances the witless conviviality of the triumvirs, engaged in celebrating their newly-found unity by a collapse into forgetfulness, against the 'quicksands' of sober treachery represented by Menas and rejected by his master less through honesty than through infirmity of purpose. The opening remarks of the servants – 'some o' their plants are ill-rooted already; the least wind i' the world will blow them down' – refer as much to the farce of reconcili-ation now being enacted as to the business in hand; and the further comment upon the unenviable situation of Lepidus –

> To be called into a huge sphere, and yet not to be seen to move in't, are the holes where eyes should be, which pitifully disaster the cheeks – [II. vii. 16.]

adds its own contribution to the note of hollowness and sinister fatality which the whole episode is aimed to convey. The description of Lepidus himself as 'alms-drunk' indicates most realistically the state of utter indignity in which he stands with relation to his more resolute colleagues.

The conversation between Lepidus and Antony, interwoven as it slips further into incoherence with Enobarbus' caustic comments and the asides between Menas and Pompey, has the double effect of taking the episode further from common reality and of stressing its continued presence. Prefaced by Antony's evocation, for Caesar's benefit, of the 'swelling Nile', his dwelling – in characteristically Egyptian fashion – upon the fertility of the 'slime and ooze' which the seedsman, as he scatters his grain, raises to harvest, it unfolds by contrast with the corrupt opulence of the East a scene of sterility, intrigue, and personal degradation. Lepidus insists that this same fertility breeds serpents ('your serpent of Egypt', he says, 'is bred out of your mud by the operation of your sun' : we recall that Cleopatra has already described herself as 'serpent of old Nile' and that it is by the bite of an Egyptian, Nile-bred snake that she will die), and the culminating point of a confused and fuddled discussion is reached in Antony's phrase,

> These quick-sands, Lepidus,
> Keep off them, for you sink, [II. vii. 66.]

just at the moment when sober calculation returns in Menas' efforts to draw his master aside and in the blunt offer which so effectively follows it : 'Wilt thou be lord of all the world?'. At this point the two worlds of illusion and reality are most admirably poised, set in the balance. Menas, unlike those around him, has 'kept himself from the cup'. His offer is directed to Pompey's capacity for bold, practical decision :

> Thou art, if thou dar'st be, the earthly Jove:
> Whate'er the ocean pales, or sky inclips,
> Is thine, if thou wilt have't. [II. vii. 74.]

It is an offer, however, made to a drunkard whose state reflects a deeper collapse of the personality, who has already lost, even in his sober moments, the will to see his situation clearly and to act in accordance with what he sees. This condition has already been insinuated, to an attentive judgement, in Pompey's earlier appearances; here – morality apart – it finds issue in an ambiguous refusal to accept the moment of decisive choice. Menas has to oblige Pompey to concentrate what remains of his capacity for attention on the matter in hand; his whispers barely penetrate the surrounding conviviality and, when they do, they find a master whose principal anxiety is to be allowed to return to his cups : –

Go hang, sir, hang! Tell me of that? away!
Do as I bid you. – Where's this cup I call'd for? – [II. vii. 60.]

whilst the appeal to him to rise, 'for the sake of merit', is met by the
contemptuous rejoinder 'I think thou art mad'. Meanwhile, with the
issue of world domination thus hanging upon a besotted politician's
indecision, the triumvirs pursue their empty discussions on the
qualities of the fabulous Egyptian 'crocodile', until Lepidus, suc-
cumbing to 'quicksands' of a less insidious nature than those around
him, collapses into complete witlessness.

When Pompey is at last obliged to face the choice set before him,
he refuses to take it up. His refusal carries something less than conviction, represents the weak man's combination of a desire to achieve
ends which his conscience tells him to be unworthy with unreadiness
to accept the means offered for this achievement. The blame for the
refusal is placed upon his servant:

> Ah, this thou should'st have done,
> And not have spoken on't! In me, 'tis villainy;
> In thee 't had been good service. [II. vii. 80.]

Pompey is in fact flinching from what is, however disreputable, a
political choice, upon which his own fortune in a world of ruthless
public realities depends; and, as the previous scene has already
indicated, it is his own fate that he is rejecting. Shakespeare found,
in embryo, in Plutarch the statement that it is 'honour' which has led
him to refuse –

> Thou must know,
> 'Tis not my profit that does lead mine honour;
> Mine honour, it – [II. vii. 82.]

but he conferred upon it an insight all his own into the combination
of vanity and self-distrust which determines this display of weakness.
That Pompey's rejoinder to Menas is no more than a gesture to cover
inner confusion is made clear by his following words of uneasy
reproof:

> Repent that e'er thy tongue
> Hath so betray'd thine act: being done unknown,
> I should have found it afterwards well done,
> But must condemn it now. [II. vii. 84.]

Pompey's attitude typifies the world which this scene is concerned to
show in so pitiless a light: a world whose leaders are, for all their
aspirations to establish control over it, in various degrees the puppets
of an inscrutable development. One and all, these are characters

divided between reality and the appearance they present to the
world. Their seeming reconciliation covers the presence of deep
rivalries, and their drunken conviviality reflects a show of friendship
which cannot, of its nature, be maintained, but must collapse into
renewed conflicts.

Confronted with his master's attitude, Menas at least knows that a
decision has in fact been taken for him and that his own future course
must be shaped accordingly. He announces, to himself, the determination to abandon Pompey's palling fortunes, because

> Who seeks, and will not take when once 'tis offer'd,
> Shall never find it more, [II. vii. 90.]

a decision which will later find a certain parallel in Enobarbus'
betrayal of Antony. Meanwhile, the theme of political realism thus
resolved, the descent into drunken chaos proceeds apace. Lepidus,
'the third part of the world', is carried away to the accompaniment of
Menas' revealing comment to Enobarbus:

> The third part then is drunk: would it were all,
> That it might go on wheels. [II. vii. 99.]

'Increase the reels': 'strike the vessels, ho!'; though not yet, in the
judgement of Pompey, freshly relieved from the necessity for choice,
'an Alexandrian feast', it already 'ripens towards it'. Even the self-
control of Caesar, thus undermined, affirms its consciousness of lapse
in a typical expression of distaste:

> It's monstrous labour, when I wash my brain
> And it grows fouler, [II. vii. 106.]

condemning 'Egyptian' excess, but in a manner which, while it may
explain his success, scarcely adds to his stature. In this situation,
which reflects – however dimly, however separated from its glamour
– the sensuous life of the East, only Antony is in some sense at home.
When he calls upon his companions to

> take hands
> Till that the conquering wine hath steep'd our sense
> In soft and delicate Lethe, [II. vii. 113.]

he maintains a certain transforming poetry even in the descent to
dissipation. Caesar, by contrast, frowns upon levity. Immediately
after Enobarbus, invoking 'plumpy Bacchus', has set the company to
song –

> Cup us, till the world go round! – [II. vii. 124.]

he takes his leave, but not, significantly, without some admission
that his own tongue is in danger of betraying him:

You see we have burnt our cheeks : strong Enobarb
Is weaker than the wine ; and *mine own tongue*
Splits what it speaks : the wild disguise hath almost
Antick'd us all. [II. vii. 129.]

His departure is both an indication of the continued relevance of the
real, the sober world, and a defence of his own consistency, of the
appearance he has made it his business to offer to that world. He
leaves behind him no more than the shadows of men. Pompey,
vaguely conscious of what he has lost –

O Antony,
You have my father's house – [II. vii. 134.]

is yet ready to add, weakly and inconsequently, 'But, what? we are
friends'; and, as they go down together into the boat which is to
take them ashore, he asks for the support of Antony's hand, while
Enobarbus adds the realistic warning : 'Take heed you fall not'. The
scene ends on a last echo of dissipation, the external flourish of drums
accompanying the last farewell to the 'great fellows' who have taken
their indignities ashore.

In the scenes which immediately follow this sinister display the
disruptive elements in the political action lead remorselessly to the
decisive conflict at Actium. Antony's marriage to Octavia turns out
to be a device without substance or possible permanency. Separated
from her, he returns fatally to Cleopatra, and by so doing rejects the
obligation, which his moral nature as a man imposes upon him, to
choose in some measure his own destiny; the return is followed
inexorably by the decline in his public fortunes which he has in part
himself willed and which provides the necessary background to his
personal tragedy.

A brief interlude in Syria (III. i) shows the professional captains
carrying on the real business of war and provides, by implication, a
merciless comment on the tipsy convivialities of their betters. The
leaders of the Roman world, indeed, have little personal responsibility for the successes which have won them their reputation. As
Ventidius puts it, they have 'ever' won 'more in their officer than
person'; but the fact remains, evident to the eye of realism, that the
soldier

Who does i' the wars more than his captain can
Becomes his captain's captain, [III. i. 21.]

and ambition, 'the soldier's virtue' in a world where more disin-
terested loyalties appear to have no place, 'rather makes choice of
loss' than presses rashly on to a 'gain' which, by rousing his master's

envy, can only darken his future prospects. 'Ambition', indeed, rather than 'honour', has become the mainspring of the martial action, and Ventidius, arguing with a candour not far removed from cynicism that he 'could do more to do Antonius good', foresees that to do so would be to 'offend' him and so to undo the effects of his own performance. Praised by Silvius for his possession of that realism

> Without the which a soldier and his sword
> Grants scarce distinction, [III. i. 28.]

he agrees to write to Antony informing him 'humbly' of the victory won in his name – 'that magical word of war' – by 'his banners' and, above all, by his '*well-paid* ranks'. The brief episode serves as a revealing prologue to the clash of personalities and interests which follows.

The main business of the next scene (III. ii), the parting of Octavius and Antony, is preceded by the ironical comments of Agrippa and Enobarbus on the unhappy Lepidus. Lepidus 'loves' the one and 'adores' the other, balances against 'the Jupiter of men' his praise of 'the god of Jupiter'; in so doing, it is in reality his own uneasy position that he strives to maintain. The conclusion to this caricature, however, lies in an estimate sharply realistic to the point of cynicism. 'They are his shards, and he their beetle', as Enobarbus sums up the matter, and once more the effect is to pass an implicit comment upon the political values of the world in which Antony will so conspicuously fail to maintain his standing. The exchange between these two 'worthy soldiers', confessed adventurers in a world where self-interest is the supreme conviction, ends fittingly in Agrippa's salutation and wish of 'good fortune' to the man who is now his comrade and appears so clearly destined to become, in the near future, his enemy.

Their entry so prefaced, the principal protagonists appear in the act of bidding one another farewell. Caesar's commendation of his sister to her husband is, like everything he does, dignified, admirably calculated to make the desired impression; but, though we need not interpret it as consciously insincere – for such as Caesar are so convinced of their rectitude that the need for insincerity does not occur to them – it is noteworthy that the emphasis lies, as ever, upon himself. Octavia he describes as 'a great part of myself', whom Antony is bidden to cherish, to 'use *me* well in't'. She, for her part, is recommended to him as befits the reputation of Caesar himself:

> Sister, prove such a wife
> As my thoughts make thee, and as my farthest band
> Shall pass on thy approof; [III. ii. 25.]

the sister, in short, is envisaged as an essential part of her brother's reputation, a contribution to the dignity and virtue which his vocation requires him to present to the world. Already, however, a note of foreboding imposes itself, which even the sober and chaste beauty of the expression cannot entirely cover. Set between the triumvirs as a 'piece of virtue' to 'cement their love', Octavia may yet become

> the ram to batter
> The fortress of it; for better might we
> Have loved without this mean, if on both parts
> This be not cherish'd. [III. ii. 30.]

Beneath the appearance of unity and concord there is a sense of unease, an awareness of fatal and approaching dissolution; nor, in view of the nature of the transactions which led up to this marriage, could it be otherwise.

Antony, indeed, is hurt in his self-esteem by these expressions of doubt. He requests Caesar not to offend him by such mistrust, and receives in reply the typically laconic, non-committal 'I have said'. Always it is Antony's part to respond to the dry brevity of his rival with a facile flow of feeling, which often attains poetry but may also degenerate into the display of emotion. Here he protests (and we need to remember that he has already revealed to himself, and to us,[1] the intention of returning to Egypt) that Caesar, however 'curious', scrupulous he may be, will not find 'the least cause' for what he seems to fear. In all these uneasy exchanges, the one element that remains pure is the capacity of Octavia to strike from those around her a redeeming note of poetry. Caesar, elaborating his farewell, says to her:

> The elements be kind to thee, and make
> Thy spirits all of comfort, [III. ii. 40.]

and receives in return an ascription of generosity which in her eyes alone can be beyond suspicion: 'My noble brother!'

If Caesar is moved to dignity, Antony is characteristically inspired to a gesture of emotional poetry:

> The April's in her eyes: it is love's spring,
> And these the showers to bring it on. [III. ii. 43.]

The concluding injunction – 'Be cheerful' – is perhaps, under the circumstances already familiar to himself and us, too easily uttered, but, while the effect of it lasts, it provides the simplicity of Octavia's dedication to her new husband with a background which enhances its effect as the only statement of unambiguous feeling in a situation

[1] II. iii. See p. 119 above.

I

otherwise already charged with potentialities of guile and mutual deception. Last of all, Antony's genius for the right phrase, his capacity for catching the decisive moment of emotion, expresses itself in lines full of the play's distinctive intuition of beauty:

> Her tongue will not obey her heart, nor can
> Her heart inform her tongue, the swan's down-feather,
> That stands upon the swell at full of tide
> And neither way inclines. [III. ii. 47.]

Whatever Antony's defects – and we must surely at this moment be acutely aware of them – his capacity to respond to an emotional situation marks him out in a world otherwise dominated by cynicism and intrigue. The response is without doubt too readily made, stands in odd and inconsistent contrast to other, more sinister strains in his nature. It is a gift of weakness, but a gift none the less, and one which here reflects a universal point of equilibrium reached by the action and conveyed in the tender balance of Octavia's loyalties. Released in defeat of the need – and the possibility – to support a fictitious greatness, it will achieve full expression in his final tragedy.

The pathos of the scene, however, is not allowed to stand alone. We are to be aware of the presence of other, discordant realities. These are made plain once more in the sardonic asides of Enobarbus and Agrippa. Antony's display of emotion is damagingly related to that which showed him, at Julius Caesar's death, crying 'almost to roaring' and weeping over the corpse of Brutus; whilst Octavius would be the worse, 'were he a horse', for the 'cloud in's face', and is still more so, by his own standards, being a man. Yet the poetic note persists to the last, with Antony striving with Caesar for Octavia's affection –

> I'll wrestle with you in my strength of love – [III. ii. 62.]

before he gives her 'to the gods', and with even Lepidus moved, as his last word, to a surprising display of feeling:

> Let all the number of the stars give light
> To thy fair way! [III. ii. 65.]

It is typical of the overmastering power of this play, of its emotional completeness, that even such a minor episode as this should flow so readily, without sense of strain or lack of truth to human nature, into most splendid poetry.

The return of Cleopatra, which at once follows (III. iii), though placed appropriately after Antony's farewell to Octavia, is not one of the most interesting episodes in the play. We may feel that Shakespeare has been obliged by the paucity, at this stage, of his Egyptian material (which must, however, be kept before us in its fundamental contrast with Rome and as the reality to which Antony is impelled by his own nature to return), to stretch a little unduly the exchanges, in which a brittle sense of comedy seems to prevail, between the solitary queen and the messenger who brings her news of Antony's marriage. Yet, when compared with the previous meeting between them, the new episode does show development, reveals a Cleopatra recovering with characteristic resilience from the blow inflicted upon her. The flattery of Alexas –

> Herod of Jewry dare not look upon you
> But when you are well-pleased – [III. iii. 3.]

is balanced by the off-hand, posed 'majesty' of her comment –

> That Herod's head
> I'll have – [III. iii. 4.]

which, however, the reference to her absent lover –

> but how, when Antony is gone,
> Through whom I might command it – [III. iii. 5.]

modifies in the direction of true feeling. The pitting of herself against Octavia which follows ('Is she as tall as me?'), and the subsequent flow of eager questioning, are effectively set against the flattery of Charmian and the messenger's willingness to provide the kind of information she desires. By the end of the exchange, when Octavia has become a 'widow' and nearly or quite 'thirty', the scene has almost fallen into farce; but, we must add, the farce is in character, and it is the achievement of this play to assimilate even this type of reality into its final purposes. By the time she leaves the messenger and by a combination of her own volatile resourcefulness and Charmian's flattery, Cleopatra is clearly on the road to recovery, ready to believe that, as far as her hold over Antony is concerned, 'All may be well enough'.

The very next scene (III. iv) shows Antony in the process of parting from Octavia, to the accompaniment of rising resentment against Caesar. Chief among his accusations is that Caesar has held him in contempt:

> Spoke scantly of me: when perforce he could not
> But pay me terms of honour, cold and sickly
> He vented them; most narrow measure lent me;
> When the best hint was given him, he not took't,
> Or did it from his teeth. [III. iv. 6]

The hurt self-esteem of Antony expresses itself here in tense immediacy of phrase. Octavius has spoken after his character, so
opposed to Antony's own, 'scantly', 'cold and sickly', with phrases
disobligingly 'vented' forth; given the opportunity to flatter, he has
either neglected it or, what has been almost more galling, spoken
with notable unwillingness, 'from his teeth'. Two characters are
represented here, the touchy, resentful Antony, aware of his own
indignity and ready to hide it in indignation at his treatment by his
equals, and the cold, purposeful Octavius, essentially void of human
sympathy, dedicated to the necessary impersonality of his political
ends.

Placed to her own misfortune between them Octavia can only
plead for moderation. She urges Antony to 'believe not all', or – if
he must believe – not to 'stomach' the insults offered him. The
division forced upon her finds expression in phrases of rare pathos:

> A more unhappy lady,
> If this division chance, ne'er stood between,
> Praying for both parts. . . .
> Husband win, win brother,
> Prays, and destroys the prayer; no midway
> 'Twixt these extremes at all. [III. iv. 12.]

Octavia's situation is a measure of the remorseless nature of the
issues now in process of being worked out over her unhappy person.
As such it marks a particular turning-point in the play's greater
structure, and to it Antony, even as he commits his act of cynical
desertion, can respond on the plane of feeling:

> if I lose mine honour,
> I lose myself: better I were not yours
> Than yours so branchless. [III. iv. 22]

Our reaction to this will not be simple. Whilst he speaks at any rate,
Antony believes that he is moved by true emotion. Octavia is for
him 'gentle', a victim to be pitied and worthy to be offered the gift
of the speaker's 'honour'; but – we must add – that 'honour' has
long ago been tarnished in the eyes of the world and is now being
exalted as a source of self-respect by one who is planning, even as
he speaks, a most shameful desertion. Having thus made his gesture to sentiment, Antony is ready to use Octavia as a pawn, a 'go-
between' in his political game; and, having decided this, he turns,
as his principal concern, to preparations for the approaching war.
Octavia, in her last reply, stresses the universal scope of the issues at
stake:

War twixt you twain would be
As though the world should cleave, and that slain men
Should solder up the rift. [III. iv. 30.]

Against this vision of a universe dedicated to mutual destruction she can only pray, vainly, to the gods to make her, 'most weak, most weak', a reconciler between the mighty opposites dedicated to the intolerable resolution of war.

The short scene which follows between Enobarbus and Eros (III. v) mirrors the onward march of events towards this resolution. Caesar and Pompey, so lately reconciled, have been once more at one another's throats, and Lepidus has been eliminated from the game in which he never played more than a negligible part: 'the poor third is up, till death enlarge his confine'. To this report by Eros Enobarbus adds his own sardonic vision of the future, expressed in terms at once world-embracing and grotesque:

Then, world, thou hast a pair of chaps, no more;
And throw between them all the food thou hast,
They'll grind the one the other. [III. v. 14.]

Octavius and Antony, in other words, are destined to seek one another's downfall; but there is something ominous for his future, a sense of abandoned control, in the hysterical outburst with which Antony, as reported by Eros, denounces Lepidus as a 'fool' and, as he walks in the garden, spurning the rushes before him,

threats the throat of that his officer
That murder'd Pompey. [III. v. 19.]

Lepidus awaiting death in prison, Pompey dead: it is not an edifying comment, thus evoked in passing, on the recent reconciliation between the leaders of the Roman world. Nor does Antony himself appear well in it. Having allowed his servant to murder Pompey, he regrets the act and threatens to exact vengeance upon his own tool; having habitually treated Lepidus with contempt, he accuses him of folly in an outburst of unreasoning hysteria that can do nothing to strengthen his position or ward off his fate.

The last episode before Actium (III. vi) opens with Caesar's indignant comments upon Antony's behaviour in Alexandria. This serves both to underline, from a severe and strictly practical Roman viewpoint, the atmosphere of luxurious corruption which surrounds Antony's excesses and, by implication, to stress an ungenerous, mercantile element in Octavius' own position. His account of the enthronement of his rivals is intended to evoke a false and corrupting luxury, implied already in the reference to the 'silver'd' tribunal set

up in the market-place and the 'chairs of gold' upon which Antony
and Cleopatra presented themselves to the public acclamation. The
crowning indignity offered to Octavius is shown in the reported
presence, at the foot of the opulent throne, of Julius Caesar's bastard,
'Caesarion, whom they call my father's son', together with

> all the unlawful issue that their lust
> Since then hath made between them. [III. vi. 7.]

From this grotesque posture, Antony is described as indulging in
ample, yet finally vacant gestures of royalty ('His sons he there
proclaimed the kings of kings'), and the volatile Cleopatra, upon
whom these 'kings' were bred, as dressed 'in the habiliments of the
goddess Isis'. In all this, Octavius combines just criticism of a
mockery enacted 'i' the common show-place' with a frigid air of
self-contained contempt for the wayward behaviour of his rivals.

Maecenas and Agrippa, realizing that the public effect in Rome of
these reports will favour their master, urge that they be published
abroad; and Agrippa, commenting that the Roman people are
'queasy' at Antony's conduct, adds a note of his own to the cold distaste which prevails throughout. It is not long before more mercenary
grounds of quarrel emerge. Antony has accused Caesar of having
withheld a share of Sicily, conquered from Pompey, and of 'detaining'
the entire revenue of the fallen Lepidus. 'Sir, this should be answer'd'
urges Agrippa, with an eye upon the public effect rather than
upon the truth of these accusations; and in Caesar's off-hand reply
('I have told him Lepidus was grown too cruel': the charge is taken
from Plutarch, but its application to the Lepidus presented in this
play is remote) and in his determination to bargain Sicily against
Armenia, we have a clear indication of the course which the following
negotiations will take:

> MAECENAS   He'll never yield to that.
> CAESAR Nor must not then be yielded to in this. [III. vi. 37.]

Hard bargaining is clearly to be the order of the day, and – on
Octavius' side at least – the aim will not be to restore a peace
already shattered but to urge on the final resolution of the conflict.

The entry of Octavia, now openly abandoned by Antony, might
have been the occasion to substitute personal feeling, a brother's
intimate concern for his sister's wrongs, for frigid political calculation. In point of fact, her arrival strikes Caesar less for the unhappiness which it implies than for the outrage against his own
indispensable dignity.

> You come not
> Like Caesar's sister, [III. vi. 42.]

nor, indeed, he adds – but this, perhaps, is not his primary concern – like 'the wife of Antony'. Typically, we may feel, it is the public slight that really moves the speaker; that and an undercurrent of resentment at having been deprived of the opportunity to make a suitably ostentatious display of his affection. 'You have', he goes on, almost as though accusing Octavia of a certain neglect,

> prevented
> The ostentation of our love, which, *left unshown*,
> *Is often left unloved*: we should have met you
> By sea and land, supplying every stage
> With an augmented greeting. [III. vi. 51.]

This assumption of personal emotion into public effectiveness is one of the most constant features of Shakespeare's political characters, and seems to have been regarded by him as a necessary accompaniment of the political vocation. Henry V, as prince and king, already shows something of it;[1] but it is never expressed more self-sufficiently, more divorced from the claims of intimate feeling, than in Octavius.

Against this brotherly reproof, Octavia's simplicity stands out with a dignity as unaffected as it is, finally, pathetic. She was not, she pleads, 'constrain'd' thus to appear, but did so of her own free will and with her husband's permission; though, we must add, Caesar's bitter comment on the latter point is hardly answerable:

> Which soon he granted,
> Being an obstruct 'tween his lust and him. [III. vi. 60.]

Octavia's desire to believe, against all reason, that the truth is otherwise is brushed aside by her brother's all-seeing competence:

> I have eyes upon him,
> And his affairs come to me on the wind; [III. vi. 62.]

the vivid strength of the phrase shows that it is here, and not in the intimacies of family feeling, that the speaker's true interest lies. When Octavia goes on to express her belief that Antony is still in Athens, there is a note of complacency mingled with contempt for his rival, in the way in which he produces the news that she has been irrevocably betrayed:

> No, my most wronged sister. Cleopatra
> Hath nodded him to her. He hath given his empire
> Up to a whore; who now are levying
> The kings o' the earth for war. [III. vi. 65.]

[1] For the spirit of Octavius' calculation we might compare Prince Hal's opening soliloquy (*Henry IV – I. I ii.*)

Caesar speaks here, justly and firmly indeed, as befits his position, but with his own purposes in view; and in relation to these the breaking of the last remnants of his sister's faith is finally irrelevant.

Octavia, not surprisingly, is shattered by the truth thus bluntly brought home to her. She reacts with the bewilderment of one caught in a catastrophe beyond her comprehension or control. 'Ay me, most wretched!', she exclaims, and adds, in a phrase where even the most natural resentment has no part:

> That have my heart parted betwixt two friends
> That do afflict each other! [III. vi. 76.]

Caesar, rather than reacting to her personal situation, takes his stand upon more universal grounds:

> Be you not troubled with the time, which drives
> O'er your content these strong necessities;
> But let determined things to destiny
> Hold unbewailed their way. [III. vi. 82.]

This is essentially a dispassionate, public philosophy in which individual grief is barely relevant. Caesar holds it the more easily because he is certain that 'destiny' will, in the long run, bring him to victory and the universal rule of the principles of justice and decorum for which he stands. This victory, at all events, he is determined to ensure by action faultlessly conceived and firmly executed; and, having thus placed – from his point of view, which is never negligible – first things first, he is ready to relax in a more intimate gesture which combines dignity with the calm confidence proper to a truly imperial figure:

> Welcome to Rome;
> Nothing more dear to me. You are abused
> Beyond the mark of thought; and the high gods,
> To do you justice, make them ministers
> Of us and those that love you. [III. vi. 85.]

The dignity of the expression is not in question, and Maecenas' following references to the 'abominations' of the 'adulterous Antony' drive a true contrast home with added force. Caesar has all the dignity of empire, which must be maintained if peace and order are to reign in society. He has also the felicity which can utter, in its proper place, the genuine expression of affection, the correct gesture to the 'gods'. We should not, even remembering how he previously bargained his sister's happiness for his political ends, accuse him of insincerity. The conception is more complex than this. The public figure acts, of necessity, with public ends in view, and

private emotion can only express itself when the necessary dispositions have been taken, the desired effects obtained. If this is a cold
conception, which can only meet Octavia's bewildered response to
his denunciation of Antony – 'Is it so, sir?' – with a calm, impassive
'Most certain', it is one which the public good seems to require; for
virtues other than those publicly conceived, and for the vices which
correspond to them, we shall need to look elsewhere.

v

The presentation of Caesar's campaign against Antony, compressed by Shakespeare into three days, corresponds to a rhythm of
loss, partial recovery, and confirmed defeat. This rhythmic conception of events answers admirably to the impression of see-sawing
alternatives, of rise and fall respectively, which has been throughout
characteristic of Antony's emotional states. Carried for short
periods on temporary waves of success, of seeming recovery from the
world of illusion into which on each occasion he relapses, these
episodes of battle convey perfectly the ruin of the warrior, the decline
of the man into self-indulgence and contempt. They sum up all that
has gone before, being indeed its logical fulfilment; but they also
prepare the way, through the desolation and abandonment to which
they lead, for what is to follow.

The first scene (III. vii) in this new phase opens with Enobarbus'
candid comments to Cleopatra, dissuading her from taking part in
the war. Her presence, he argues, must needs 'puzzle' Antony, distract him from the serious business of soldiery. His arguments
culminate in the blistering accusation, retailed from Rome, that
Antony's wars are being waged by 'Photinus, an eunuch, and your
maids'. Antony himself, when he appears, shows himself bemused by
the rapidity of Caesar's advance; as Cleopatra, with one of her
characteristic touches of candour, puts it:

> Celerity is never more admired
> Than by the negligent. [III. vii. 24.]

They conclude, against all reason, to meet Caesar at sea, on no better
grounds than that 'he dares us to't'. The cogent arguments of Enobarbus against this course end in his pointing out that Antony is in
fact proposing to 'throw away'

> The absolute soldiership you have by land;

but the last word is left to Cleopatra, who emerges clearly as his evil
genius. As the news of Octavius' advance presses upon the action, it

remains for Canidius to make yet again the plain soldierly comment
upon his master's self-destroying folly:

> his whole action grows
> Not in the power on't: so our leader's led,
> And we are women's men. [III. vii. 68.]

All, meanwhile, Canidius not less than Antony, are amazed by the
decisive pace with which Caesar advances to meet them.

> This speed of Caesar's
> Carries beyond belief: [III. vii. 74.]

and, indeed, the brief episodes which follow (III. viii) are only
remarkable in so far as they show, by contrast with Antony's impulsive reactions, Octavius' confident and far-sighted control of the
situation:

> Strike not by land; keep whole, provoke not battle,
> Till we have done at sea. [III. viii. 3.]

Brevity, energy, and firmness of decision are the qualities which,
advancing remorselessly upon Antony, will effect his ruin.

These preliminaries lead directly to the consummation of Antony's
first defeat at sea, for which the desertion of Cleopatra is, as Scarus
recognizes, directly responsible:

> we have kiss'd away
> Kingdoms and provinces. [III. viii. 17.]

Cleopatra, far from being accepted at Antony's infatuated estimate,
is made the object of ribald comment, culminating in the comparison
of her flight to the vagaries of 'a cow in June' or 'a ribaudred[1] nag
of Egypt'; Antony himself, meanwhile, is reduced to the status of 'a
doting mallard', 'the noble ruin of her magic'. The emphasis is
throughout upon the shameful loss of manliness to which Scarus
most clearly refers when he says:

> I never saw an action of such shame;
> Experience, manhood, honour, ne'er before
> Did violate so itself. [III. viii. 31.]

In other plays, and elsewhere in this tragedy, Shakespeare has cast
doubt upon the validity of the verbal concept, as distinct from the
substance, of 'honour'[2]; but here it is the substance that is in
question, a reality, a source of self-respect, without which Antony is

---

[1] The text here is in question.

[2] See, on this point, my *Shakespeare: from 'Richard II' to 'Henry V'*, more especially
in relation to Falstaff.

but the ruin of his former self. His example, moreover, is inevitably corrupting. Canidius, following 'six kings' before him, announces his intention of embracing Caesar's cause, and though Enobarbus decides still to follow 'the wounded chance of Antony', he does so in spite of his knowledge that reason 'sits in the wind' against him.

At this moment of ruin and degradation, Antony once more appears (III. ix). Undisguised shame prevails in his thoughts: a shame which expresses itself, not untypically, in the personification of the very 'land' to which he should have entrusted his fortunes and which is now 'ashamed' to bear him. His first reaction is to drama- tize himself, calling upon his friends to share in his disgrace:

> I am so lated in the world that I
> Have lost my way for ever; [III. ix. 3.]

though it is perhaps worth making the comment that, unlike Caesar, his nature is such that the idea of friendship is conceivable to him. To dramatize themselves as simple men of feeling lost in the com- plexities of the world is a favourite device by which such as Antony seek to conceal from their own selves the magnitude of their personal disaster and the extent of their own reponsibility for it. Equally typical is the gesture of selfconscious generosity with which he turns to these same friends and offers them a ship 'laden with gold' which they may use to make their peace with his victorious rival. This, again, is a semi-conscious device to cover the bitterness of defeat; but – it is fair to add – Antony has, even in this moment of self-exposure, enough left to him of the power to inspire devotion for the offer to be, at least whilst he speaks, repudiated by those who still respond to the magnetism of his person.

It is, indeed, typical of Antony, faced by the ruinous consequences of his own choices, to dramatize his position, to relieve himself, as far as may be, of the bitterness and self-accusation of his intimate feelings by stressing his indignities, piling them upon his own head:

> I have fled myself, and have instructed cowards
> To run and show their shoulders. [III. ix. 7.]

Urging his supporters once more to desert him, he emphasizes yet again his shame – 'I follow'd that I blush to look upon' – and rounds off the picture, with a strange compound of irony and pathos, true feeling and its naïve exhibition, by a bitter reference to his advancing years:

> My very hairs do mutiny, for the white
> Reprove the brown for rashness, and they them
> For fear and doting. [III. ix. 13.]

His destiny is, in fact, in the process of being dramatized into self-conscious 'despair', as is the generosity which, at bottom, he desires to present to the world as a saving grace:

> let that be left
> Which leaves itself.
> .... indeed, I have lost command. [III. ix. 19.]

Always the creature of impulse, Antony is here giving way to his emotions whilst waiting for the arrival of the external stimulus which he craves, which alone can give him the illusion of self-respect. Thus waiting, he is conjuring his shame by giving it expression, where another man, more honest but less resilient in his reactions, would have withdrawn more simply into himself; here there lies at once an indication of his weakness and of a certain capacity for recovering from impossible situations which the later stages of his tragedy will confirm.

The entry, immediately after this outburst, of Cleopatra, 'led' by her attendants like a kind of decoy, is not devoid of comedy[1]. The exchanges between them, on either side, and their respective followers, urging them to meet in broken, embarrassed exclamations, admirably convey the position at this moment of crisis. If anything should follow logically from Antony's recent declaration of his shame it is the repudiation of its external cause. It is therefore a sign of the inconsistency, of the weakness of the man, that the end of the exchange so inauspiciously begun should have brought them once more in some measure together. This does not happen at once. Whether through embarrassment or tact, or possibly on account of a mixture of both, Cleopatra is at first tongue-tied; this is a situation which her accustomed arts cannot directly meet, and it is therefore appropriate that her only words in answer to the exhortation of those around her should be: 'Let me sit down. O Juno!' Nor has Antony at this moment much time to devote to the thought of his love. Broken by the consideration of his shattered greatness, he turns back in bewilderment to the past, to a contrast between his own martial prowess at Philippi and the inexperience of Octavius:

> he alone
> Dwelt on lieutenantry and no practice had
> In the brave squares of war. [III. ix. 38.]

This, once more, is a characteristic effort to seek compensation in the recalling of past glories; as such, it cannot be finally successful. 'Yet now – no matter': the end of the short speech amounts to a confes-

---

[1] This point has been well made by H. Granville Barker in his study of the play (*Prefaces to Shakespeare*, Second Series, 1930).

sion that there can be no valid way of avoiding the bitter realities of
the present.

In this very depth of shame, however, lies Cleopatra's opportunity.
In the present, Antony has nothing but his feeling for her to fall back
upon; he can renounce this feeling for the part it has played in his
ruin, but the ruin itself will not thereby be avoided. Iras realizes
this, implicitly, when she says that Antony is 'unqualitied with
very shame' and urges the fact upon her mistress as a reason for
approaching and speaking to him. Shame, indeed, will bring them
together for mutual support. The persuasions of those who surround
the two central figures of fallen greatness urge them together in
phrasing that gradually adds to the original note of comedy a
deeper content of feeling; to Iras' plea to Cleopatra corresponds the
intervention, on Antony's side, of Eros:

> Most noble sir, arise; the queen approaches;
> Her head's declined, and death will seize her, but
> Your comfort makes the rescue. [III. ix. 46.]

To this combination of emotion and enticement – for we may doubt
whether Cleopatra is to be brought so easily within reach of death –
Antony at first refuses to respond. He remains fixed, not without a
kind of perverse self-satisfaction, in the enormity of his shame – 'I
have offended reputation' – and adds a reproach to Cleopatra that
is at once the reflection of his downfall and an attempt to thrust the
responsibility for it on to her shoulders:

> O, whither hast thou led me, Egypt? See,
> How I convey my shame out of thine eyes
> By looking back what I have left behind
> 'Stroy'd in dishonour. [III. ix. 51.]

The entire exchange at this point needs to be considered with some
care. Antony is at once admitting his own responsibility –

> Egypt, thou knew'st too well
> My heart was to thy rudder tied by the strings,
> And thou should'st tow me after – [III. ix. 56.]

and seeking to excuse himself. He is also turning his situation into a
self-conscious pathos that is theatrical, revealing of weakness, at the
same time as it rises, more especially in the personification of Cleopatra as 'Egypt', to a certain transforming intensity:

> o'er my spirit
> Thy full supremacy thou knew'st, and that
> Thy beck might from the bidding of the gods
> Command me. [III. ix. 58.]

The last phrase is very close to the central experience of this many-sided tragedy. The infatuation that has called the former 'pillar of the world' from 'the bidding of the gods' is finally a renunciation of the hero's full stature; but that it could have this effect, that Cleopatra could establish over him her 'supremacy', is a sign of the force, the certain, if perverse, influence which it exercises, through her, over its victim. It would be a fatal error to seek to sentimentalize Antony at this, the moment of his recognized and necessary shame. To follow him in his attempts at emotional self-evasion is no part of the play's intention; but neither is it to minimize the power of the feeling here involved and the sense of its significance, real if limited, for life.

Throughout the whole of this first crisis Cleopatra remains silent, limiting herself to craving pardon for the ruin she has caused. Antony, still self-obsessed, involved in the contemplation of his shame, sees nothing but further disgrace before him. He will have to humiliate himself before the 'young man' whom he so recently treated with a contempt which his words still echo; it will be his ignoble fate to 'dodge' and 'palter in the shift of lowness', he who formerly with regal irresponsibility,

> With half the bulk o' the world play'd as I pleas'd,
> Making and marring fortunes. [III. ix. 64.]

To this aspect of Antony Cleopatra will later give its most superb expression[1], but only after he is dead, once the contrast with reality is no longer directly relevant. For the present, his subjection to her and the implied reproach, the reiterated effort to thrust responsibility upon the object of his passion –

> You did know
> How much you were my conqueror – [III. ix. 65.]

can lead only to a most damning confession of the facts:

> My sword, made weak by my affection, would
> Obey it on all cause. [III. ix. 67.]

The decline of strength into weakness, life into death, energy into self-regarding pity, is an essential aspect of the tragedy, and one which here, in the first hour of defeat, begins to assert its presence. Nothing in Antony's final reaction can contradict it.

The suggestion of collapse having thus been made, Cleopatra's barely articulate request for pardon prompts from Antony one of those typically sudden shifts of feeling which amount, in this case, to an effort to seek comfort, the forgetting of his shameful situation, by clinging to the only type of experience, reality or illusion, still

[1] In her account of her 'dream' to Dolabella. See V ii. and p. 194 below.

open to him. 'Fall not a tear, I say', he exclaims, when practically everything he has said since his defeat has been so far directed to exacting the tribute of tears from those around him. Absurdity, together with the familiar strange shadow of generosity, emerges from the phrase to which this reference to tears gives rise:

> one of them rates
> All that is won and lost; [III. ix. 69.]

a single kiss will, he seeks to believe, repay all that has been ruined for him. From this false stimulus, Antony swings, equally typically, to a corresponding depth of despair. 'Love, I am full of lead': no longer willing to contemplate his situation, he clings to Cleopatra as to an illusion of comfort and, reanimating however artificially the fires of epicurean sensuality by calling for 'wine' and 'viands', ends the scene on a note of faded bravado:

> Fortune knows
> We scorn her most when most she offers blows. [III. ix. 73.]

This is the mood of Macbeth faced, at the last, with the consequences of his own choice: the mood of those who have left themselves with nothing more positive to fall back upon. No more than in the earlier tragedy should we take this kind of comfort at its own valuation; but – we must add – this is not for Antony, as it was for Macbeth, the last word, and his love – for all its stressed weaknesses – will have other and finer opportunities for expression before the death it has willed for itself overtakes it.

The shift to Caesar's camp (III. x) shows, by contrast, the successful leader preparing to exploit his advantage. Antony has just mentioned the 'schoolmaster' whom he has sent to beg for terms; for those round Caesar, the arrival of such a messenger proves that the former triumvir is 'plucked' of the greatness which has hitherto afforded him 'superfluous kings' for envoys. A generous 'superfluity', indeed, accompanies greatness in this play, and Antony, even in his ruin, bears memories of it about him; such memories live, however pathetically, in the envoy's statement that he was

> of late as petty to his ends
> As is the morn-dew on the myrtle leaf
> To his grand sea. [III. x. 8.]

The power to rise effectively to the heights of poetry is conceded in this tragedy even to its most minor figures; the full force of this nostalgic assertion of past splendour is only apparent in the light of the sad depreciation of the phrase which precedes it: 'Such as I am, I come from Antony'.

Evocations of past glory, however, have little relevance to Antony's present situation. Caesar thrusts them curtly aside with his brief 'Be't so : declare thine office'. The message itself is calculated to point still further the contrast between Antony's great past and his abject present. He 'salutes' Caesar and begs permission to live in Egypt; if this is 'not granted' he is ready to 'lessen his requests' to the extent of living 'a private man in Athens'. Cleopatra, less simply, asks for rather more. She 'confesses' the greatness of the conqueror, 'submits' to him, and begs at his hands

> The circle of the Ptolemies for her heirs,
> Now hazarded to thy grace. [III. x. 18.]

Caesar, glimpsing the signs of a split between the pair, proceeds on the path he has chosen. For Antony he has no further use ('I have no ears to his request') ; but the queen, should she be ready to betray her lover, may yet – though his promises remains carefully vague – be an instrument to his hand. Having accordingly announced coldly that Cleopatra, to ingratiate herself, must drive from his last sanctuary 'her all-disgraced friend' or, if necessary, bring about his death, Caesar proceeds to strike while he feels the iron still hot. Thyreus is dispatched to win Cleopatra from her allegiance to Antony; to accomplish this, he may promise in Caesar's own name and add whatever further enticements his own 'invention' may inspire him to. The instructions are accompanied by a typically cynical depreciation of the moral value of women, uttered by one who is, we feel, nothing if not a man of the world :

> women are not
> In their best fortunes strong, but want will perjure
> The ne'er touch'd vestal; [III. x. 29.]

a truth, we feel, which the speaker, as he enunciates it, finds oddly attractive, a confirmation of the element of meanness which exists, with other and more impressive qualities, in his own nature. Above all, Thyreus is to exercise the politician's primary gift of 'observation', to watch Antony for signs of the weakness which, duly exploited, will bring him to destruction.

The scene which follows (III. xi) pitilessly displays Antony's disintegration in the hour of defeat. The tone for it is set by Enorbarbus' laconic advice to a thoroughly chastened Cleopatra :

> – What shall we do, Enobarbus?
> – Think, and die. [III. xi. 1.]

He goes on to lay the blame for the recent disaster squarely upon Antony himself. Antony has made his perverse will 'lord of his reason', has in effect betrayed his manhood for 'the itch of his affection'; and if the result has been the negation of his 'captain-ship' at the moment when the fate of a whole world rested upon his decisions –

> half to half the world opposed, he being
> The mered question – [III. xi. 9.]

the primary fault has not lain with Cleopatra but is his alone. To this bitter truth Cleopatra can only reply by what is in effect less a command than a plea for merciful silence: 'Prithee, peace'. Scarcely again in the course of the tragedy shall we see her volatile and re-sourceful nature so shattered, so ready to confess the irrevocable reality of their common ruin.

Antony, entering with the 'schoolmaster', passes to Cleopatra the news of Caesar's offer. This he does with a typical combination of ingenuousness and generosity – 'Let her know' – backed immediately by self-conscious pathos in his reference to the 'grizzled head' which she may, should she so desire, surrender to one who is ready to

> fill thy wishes to the brim
> With principalities. [III. xi. 18.]

The motives which begin to be outlined at this point are of some intricacy. If Antony, in reporting Caesar's terms, combines pathos with a certain exploitation of feeling, Cleopatra's reply – 'That head, my lord?' – is at once hesitant, uncertain, and a first intima-tion that there are values at stake which the unilateral competence of the conqueror may fail to compass. For the moment, however, Antony seeks relief in the quixotic gesture of an absurd personal challenge; a gesture which, although worded with some nobility, is none the less set in its true light by Enobarbus' devastating comment. 'High-battled Caesar' is, in fact, being asked to 'unstate his happi-ness', to make a spectacle of himself for the benefit of a 'sworder', a soldier of fortune. So considered, the challenge is decisive proof that Antony's 'judgement' has been finally subdued:

> I see men's judgements are
> A parcel of their fortunes, and things outward
> Do draw the inward quality after them,
> To suffer all alike. [III. xi. 31.]

In the world of practical realities postulated by this most realistic of tragedies there is, indeed, no truth more relevant than this.

The arrival of Caesar's messenger draws from Cleopatra a com-ment which associates her adverse fortune with the suggestion of age and decline:

K

> Against the blown rose may they stop their nose
> That kneel'd unto the buds. [III. xi. 39.]

It emphasizes decay at the same time as it anticipates that transformation of corruption into ripeness which will become increasingly evident in the poetry of the play. To Enobarbus, the messenger's reception is one more confirmation of Antony's ruin, and he begins to adjust his thoughts to the practical necessity of desertion. 'Mine honesty and I begin to square': the loyalty which clings beyond reason to the fortunes of a 'fool' is itself folly, and yet allegiance to 'a fall'n lord' has about it an illogical validity that even this hard-headed soldier cannot ignore[1]. As Antony's fortunes crumble, mirroring his personal disintegration, the devotion which he inspires in followers to whom his manifold weaknesses are abundantly clear will play an increasing part in the tragic development.

Thyreus now enters to convey, with the brazen effrontery proper to the servant of a conqueror, his message to the queen. His attempt to separate her from Enobarbus produces from the latter yet another realistic estimate of the situation. Antony, aware that he has no prospects of recovery, will – if allowed to do so – 'leap' to be Caesar's friend; and, as for his followers, including the speaker:

> for us, you know,
> Whose he is we are, and that is Caesar's. [III. xi. 51.]

Thyreus, having received this admission with a laconic 'So', turns to Cleopatra and delivers his message with a confidence of which we can only say that it covers profound contempt:

> He knows that you embraced not Antony
> As you did love, but as you fear'd him. [III. xi. 56.]

Here, indeed, is the voice of worldly success, of Caesar's own capacity to regard as relevant only those realities which suit his purpose. This expression of cynicism, however, marks the beginning, still hesitant and tentative, of a reaction from Cleopatra herself. Thus far she has been overwhelmed by events, crushed in the presence of a defeat in which her own and her lover's weaknesses have been so pitilessly revealed; but to this simplification of her motives she replies, first with an 'O!' which is at once non-committal and full of implicit

---

[1] It is interesting to compare the similar statement of illogicality by the Fool in *King Lear*:

> But I will tarry: the fool will stay,
> And let the wise man fly:
> The knave turns fool that runs away;
> The fool no knave, perdy.
> (*King Lear*. II. iv. 83.]

irony, and then, when Thyreus goes on to refer unctuously to 'the scars upon your honour' (what a depth of indelicate contempt the phrase reveals!) as 'constrained' blemishes, with a more subtle combination of submission and implied rejection:

> He is a god, and knows
> What is most right: mine honour was not yielded,
> But conquer'd merely. [III. xi. 60.]

Cleopatra is here feeling her way through an intricate situation, covering with a barely perceptible irony her intention to keep open all possible lines of action, not excluding that of surrender. This will be from now on the course by which she steers; but Enobarbus, who knows her as well – and only as well – as one may do whose values are exclusively male, soldierly, accepts her words at their face value as a surrender and comments accordingly:

> To be sure of that
> I will ask Antony. [III. xi. 62.]

The surrender, as he interprets it, confirms him in his resolve to leave to its 'sinking' the 'leaky' boat of Antony's fortunes, though it is typical that, in expressing this resolve, it is the image of the rat and the sinking ship that enters his mind.

The reality, however, is more complex than male commonsense can entirely perceive. Cleopatra's attitude is varied, even contradictory, and her apparent surrender contains within itself the first indications of recovery, combines self-knowledge and some measure of inner reserve with essential opportunism. To Thyreus' final invitation to 'warm' Caesar's heart by putting herself under his protection as 'universal landlord' she replies with a most subtle combination of the deferential and the non-committal. To Caesar her attitude is one of political subjection: –

> Tell him, from his all-obeying breath I hear
> The doom of Egypt; [III. xi. 77.]

but the direct request to betray Antony is left unanswered. Thyreus, however, has obtained enough to think he has conquered, and commends Cleopatra for following what he describes, not without irony, as her 'noblest course'. Appealing, as the man of the world he believes himself to be, to her 'wisdom', he is emboldened to accept the invitation implied in her previous request for his name. Kissing her hand, he receives one of those regal gestures which are in her the counterpart to Antony's self-animating evocations of his former greatness:

> Your Caesar's father oft,
> When he hath mused of taking kingdoms in,
> Bestow'd his lips on that unworthy place,
> As it rained kisses. [III. xi. 82.]

This exaltation of sensual experience is, in fact, Cleopatra's equivalent to Antony's gesture in challenging Octavius. Aimed at restoring
her own confidence in herself, it is made, however, with a more
conscious eye on the effect to be produced upon Thyreus; and it is,
in addition, peculiarly calculated to rouse the anger, the sense of
forfeited self-respect, that has rankled in Antony since the moment of
his defeat.

Antony's return at this inauspicious moment speedily brings out
the element of sadistic resentment which is a principal sign of his
collapsing integrity. Thyreus' complacent reply to his challenge, in
which he affirms himself to be

> One that but performs
> The bidding of the fullest man and worthiest
> To have command obey'd, [III. xi. 86.]

carries an implied reference to Antony's own decline; as Enobarbus
at once sees, it is an invitation to the punishment he receives. The
immediate reaction is one of outraged hysteria, in which the mastery
just affirmed on behalf of Octavius is bitterly contrasted with the
reality indicated in his own phrase, 'Authority melts from me',
and with the glorious past when

> kings would start forth
> And cry 'your will?'. [III. xi. 91.]

'Melting', indeed, and a sense of deliquescence repeatedly emerge in
the poetry used to convey Antony's decline, and here they lead at
once to bitter denunciation of Cleopatra ('Ah, you kite!') and to the
hysterical invocation of 'god and devils'; on the verge of incoherence,
he grasps at the limited, senseless action still in his power and sees in
it the desired confirmation of his crumbling identity: 'I am Antony
yet!' Rage and resentment at his own failure express themselves, indeed, in an inconsequent overflow of emotion. Evocations of cosmic
imagery ('Moon and stars!') combine with broken rage at the
betrayal he fears from his mistress –

> she here, – what's her name
> Since she was Cleopatra? – [III. xi. 98.]

to reveal the collapse of personality into ruin. The command to
whip Thyreus in which this outburst culminates is wrapped in

sadistic fury. 'Whip him!', he cries, and stresses the need to humiliate the instrument of his rival in the repetition which follows:

> Whip him, fellows,
> Till like a boy you see him cringe his face,
> And whine aloud for mercy; [III. xi. 99.]

and the final contemptuous reference to 'this Jack of Caesar's' clearly affords him a typically perverse, and senseless, pleasure.

Having thus grasped at the only means of self-assertion in his power Antony turns upon Cleopatra. It is typical of him that only in hysteria can he bring himself to look upon his situation in its true light. His first words contain an implacable evaluation of the object of his infatuation. Cleopatra was 'half-blasted' before he knew her, and for her he has sacrificed his self-respect in 'the getting of a lawful race' by one whom he has come to see in retrospect as 'a gem of women', only to be

> abused
> By one that looks on feeders. [III. xi. 108.]

The contrast with what might have been is, at the same time, an effort at emotional self-compensation, which proceeds in great part from the desire to hide even from himself his responsibility for the position in which he finds himself. There is, however, a deeper truth, a truer estimate of his condition, in the clear-eyed statement which follows of the hardening of the moral vision which accompanies the persistent surrender to the compulsions of appetite:

> when we in our viciousness grow hard –
> O misery on't! – the wise gods seel our eyes;
> In our own filth drop our clear judgements; make us
> Adore our errors; laugh at's while we strut
> To our confusion. [III. xi. 111.]

This is perhaps the clearest judgement yet indicated in the play upon Antony's moral nature, and in the light of it all merely sentimental approbation is ruled out of court. Antony, seeking to console himself, to place elsewhere the responsibility for his disaster, is driven in his own despite to a very clear comment upon his condition. He is, indeed, one who has grown 'hard' in his 'viciousness', lost sensibility by his wilful submission to 'appetite'; and the result has been to close his eyes, as though by a dispensation of fate, apparently cruel, but just, appropriate to the nature of his choice, to moral realities. The 'judgement' which should have been his distinctive quality as a man, a purposeful reasoning being, has been dropped into 'filth' of his own creation; his 'errors' have been turned into a cause for complacency, and the result has been to reduce him to an absurd figure 'strutting'[1] in a caricature of self-approbation to his final confusion. The stroke which brings this moment of self-revelation out of hysteria and attempted auto-deception is one of the most revealing in the entire play.

Cleopatra, indeed, has no answer to offer to this statement of bare truth. Her single phrase – 'O, is't come to this?' – is, beyond fiction and artifice, the contemplation of a ruin, the poignant realization of an illusion irretrievably shattered. After it, Antony's tirade against her, and through her against fate and circumstance, is rounded off in incoherent but unanswerable abuse. She has been 'a morsel',

> cold upon
> Dead Caesar's trencher, [III. xi. 116.]

a 'fragment' of Pompey's, one who has spent, unknown to him, other 'hotter hours', 'luxuriously prick'd out' and 'unregister'd in vulgar fame'; the speaker's own sensuality, and his feeling of being thwarted, are combined in what is in effect a distorted outburst of unconfessable emotions. Side by side with this hysteria, most illogically, comes a reference to

> My playfellow, your hand, this kingly seal
> And plighter of high hearts, [III. xi. 125.]

where the very hand that he has just proclaimed as common, stale, dishonoured, becomes the object of his own – supposedly – regal and transforming passion. The entire tirade ends on a note of collapse, in which the sense of having been betrayed projects itself in a hysteria that borders on the ridiculous:

> O, that I were
> Upon the hills of Basan, to outroar
> The horned herd! for I have savage cause;
> And to proclaim it civilly, were like
> A haltered neck which does the hangman thank
> For being yare about him. [III. xi. 126.]

The vehemence of this is a reaction against the intolerable moment of self-revelation which Cleopatra's reception of Thyreus has brought home to Antony. The collapse of his integrity is rounded off in a grotesque image of animality and cuckoldry combined. The meaningless passion of the bull, the sense of a 'savage cause' for irrational

---

[1] Compare, for the spirit of this,

> Life's but a walking shadow, a poor player
> That *struts* and frets his hour upon the stage
> And then is heard no more. (*Macbeth*, V. v. 24.]

resentment, the repudiation of 'civil' behaviour, all combine to
produce an impression which borders on the breakdown of all the
normal features of human personality. Faced by it, Cleopatra can
only maintain silence.

The return of Thyreus, 'soundly' whipped, stimulates Antony's
jaded emotions and gives him further outlet for his confusion in
hysterical abuse. The suffering of his victim clearly affords him a
satisfaction reflected in his insistent questioning ('Cried he? and
begg'd he pardon?'); and the pleasure he feels at the power thus
exercised is associated in his mind with the thought that, by
this irrational and disproportionate act, he is somehow finding
a substitute for his inability to revenge himself upon Caesar in
person:

> be thou sorry
> To follow Caesar in his triumph, since
> Thou hast been whipp'd for following him. [III. xi. 135.]

This, and the following sneering reference to 'the white hand of a
lady', proceed from depths greater than the speaker can entirely
understand. What is certain is that, at the back of this inarticulate
rage, lies resentment at his rival's success and a sense, which he is
unwilling or unable to relate to the true indignity of its causes, of his
own failure:

> He makes me angry with him; for he seems
> Proud and disdainful, harping on what I am,
> Not what he knew I was. [III. xi. 141.]

Excusing himself for what he knows, at bottom, to be unworthy
behaviour, Antony goes on to imply a bitter contrast between his
present shame and the galling memory of his former reputation. He
then proceeds to refer to 'the good stars that were my former guides',
which now – reflecting the chaos in which he feels his emotional
being immersed –

> Have empty left their orbs and shot their fires
> Into the abysm of hell. [III. xi. 146.]

Antony is at this moment a man who, in the process of looking into
himself, has discovered only chaos and ruin, and who, appalled by
what he has glimpsed there, has taken refuge in expressions of incoherent rage. There is meaning in the confession that Caesar has
angered him at a moment when his defences are down, when 'most
easy 'tis to do't'. After this glimpse of chaos he rounds off his message
for Caesar with a last expression of senseless defiance:

> If he mislike
> My speech, and what is done, tell him he has
> Hipparchus, my enfranched bondman, whom
> He may at pleasure whip, or hang, or torture,
> As he shall like, to quit me. [III. xi. 147.]

The revelation of character in weakness is here as varied as it is
remorseless in its realism. One scarcely knows whether to emphasize
the callousness, the contemptuous cruelty of the offer of his bondman
as a substitute to meet Caesar's wrath, the latent sadistic impulse in
'*at pleasure* whip, or hang, or torture', or the vain gesture of defiance
with which the outburst opens. 'Hence with thy stripes, begone!';
it is doubtful whether anything in Antony's previous behaviour has
left him more effectively stripped of the last shreds of nobility to which
he desperately, and here so vainly, clings.

The marvellously varied content of this scene is not, however, yet
exhausted. Cleopatra's quiet 'Have you done yet?', the most effective
and revealing foil to the preceding hysteria, is met by one of those
touches of sublimation into poetry which will from now on, under
the shadow of approaching death and dissolution, play an increasing
part in the play:

> Alack, our terrene moon
> Is now eclipsed, and it portends alone
> The fall of Antony. [III. xi. 153.]

The poetry apart, the word 'alone' stresses once more Antony's need
for pity, his sense of betrayal; and after Cleopatra has interposed her
brief, resigned 'I must stay his time', he proceeds to a direct attack:

> To flatter Caesar, would you mingle eyes
> With one that ties his points? [III. xi. 156.]

Cleopatra's reply, however calculated it may be – and there is no
real answer, here or elsewhere, to the charge of betrayal, only an
attempt, which is successful, to turn it aside – shows a more firm
confidence – 'Not know me yet?' – which will be the prelude to a
semblance of recovery. Once more, the change of mood is related to a
further extension of the elemental poetry, combining life and
fertility with death and corruption in one continuous process:

> Ah, dear, if I be so,
> From my cold heart let heaven engender hail,
> And poison it in the source, and the first stone
> Drop in my neck; as it determines, so
> Dissolve my life! The next Caesarion smite!
> Till by degrees the memory of my womb,

> Together with my brave Egyptians all,
> By the discandying of this pelleted storm
> Lie graveless, till the flies and gnats of Nile
> Have buried them for prey. [III. xi. 158.]

A proper reading of the speech brings us very close to the spirit in which this tragedy is conceived. The astonishing poetic power involved is not open to question, nor is the fact that it contributes, within certain limits, to an assertion of constancy in love: but the emphasis is at least equally on decay, and the emotional compensation offered to Antony is significantly couched in terms of death and dissolution. Dissolution, indeed, the 'melting' of a personality into its component elements of corruption, has been the essence of the entire episode, and here Cleopatra is engaged in turning it into her own kind, at once intense and equivocal, of poetry. 'Discandying' imparts a sense of melting sweetness to corruption, and 'dissolve', whilst presenting the end of the corrupt process itself, gives it an ease and inevitability which looks forward to the final aspic scene; and 'the memory of my womb' again suggests the full fertility associated with the speaker's desires, the reflection of a certain richness of life (real or fictitious?) which seems to blend with its foreseen conclusion, the decay so vividly implied in 'the flies and gnats of Nile'. Within these subtle variations, at once hauntingly lyrical and ruthless in their evocation of corruption, the speech contains the whole range of an emotion particularly relevant to this stage, combining disenchantment with a first, flushed anticipation of the conclusion, of the play's development.

Antony, at all events, begins to show under this influence a certain appearance of recovery. 'I am satisfied', he comments at the end of Cleopatra's outburst, and one cannot, in registering the change of mood, refrain from pointing out how it reflects the attitudes of one whose life consists, from now on, in a grasping at baseless, but to him *necessary*, compensations. His 'satisfaction' rests on self-deception, and he knows this even as he accepts it; but, without such deception, he cannot face even that butt-end of life which is now left to him. He announces his readiness to oppose Caesar's 'fate', and on sea and land alike there are intimations of recovery which, illusory as they are, answer to a spurious rallying of confidence in his nature. The values of love and war, so brutally shattered in the recent hysteria, begin to come together again in the mind of the declining warrior:

> If from the field I shall return once more
> To kiss these lips, I will appear in blood;
> I and my sword will earn our chronicle:
> There 's hope in't yet. [III. xi. 173.]

No doubt, this represents the same process of 'cheering up', of finding comfort in his own words, to which we have already seen Antony so addicted; but, while it lasts, and by contrast with the preceding ruin, it stands for a recovery, for a show of positive emotion which can be incorporated, together with so much else that is weak and unworthy, into the final resolution.

The recovery, however, remains artificial, no more than the shadow of a lasting and effective reaction. In the lines which immediately follow, the emphasis is upon strained effort, upon bodily sinews stretched in desperation:

> I will be treble-sinewed, hearted, breath'd,
> And fight maliciously . . .
>   now I'll set my teeth,
> And send to darkness all that stop me; [III. xi. 177.]

and the end is the calling together of his 'sad captains' into the illusory conviviality of 'one other gaudy night', reliving as their shadow the opulent excesses of the past and doomed finally to a ruin which cannot be effectively countered by the injunction to

>   fill our bowls once more:
> Let's mock the midnight bell. [III. xi. 183.]

All this is, in fact, on the political level – and even on the moral – no more than illusion. Without an external and unworthy stimulus Antony is in no position, here or ever, to make even a show of recovery; the stimulus is needed, finally, to help him to hide from himself what he has in fact become. It must, however, always be associated for him with the person of Cleopatra; we may say, indeed, that his passion for her is no more, seen from one viewpoint, than the instrument of this self-deception.

His revival of spirits does, however, rouse Cleopatra – though not without a touch of stratagem, indicated in her convenient reference to her 'birth-day' – to a shadow of their former mutual love:

> I had thought to have held it poor, but since my lord
> Is Antony again, I will be Cleopatra. [III. xi. 185.]

In this same spirit she calls his 'noble' (no longer 'sad') captains to their lord, and he – by a characteristic feat – achieves the momentary transformation of revelry into poetry:

>   to-night I'll force
> The wine peep through their scars. [III. xi. 189.]

However falsely, the imagery of life, of a kind, begins to rise again: 'There's sap in't yet', and the values of love and death are joined in a way which, at least while the resonance of the words lasts, carries conviction:

> The next time I do fight
> I'll make death love me, for I will contend
> Even with his pestilent scythe. [III. xi. 191.]

Even now, however, we should not take this reaction at anything like its face value. Set against the preceding disintegration, it will carry Antony through the second day's battle to an appearance of success, before finally leaving him naked in the face of disaster; but, outside this temporary fluctuation, this rhythm of real defeat and the shadow of recovery, it is a hysterical resolve which here emerges, one which is based on artificial stimulation and which therefore, when the stimulus dies, cannot fail to collapse. The last word lies once more with Enobarbus: 'Now he'll outstare the lightning'. Antony has, in fact, assumed this show of confidence because he has been 'frightened out of fear', roused to a mood in which real distinctions no longer count and in which 'the dove will peck the estridge'. As Enobarbus sees clearly, Antony's 'heart' has been restored only by a 'diminution' of his brain, and 'valour', preying upon reason, is in a state in which it may be said of it that it 'eats the sword it fights with'. The time has come for his most faithful followers to abandon Antony; the tragic recovery, in so far as it effectively takes place, will not be found to depend upon success in war, but rather on the recognition of failure.

A brief return to Caesar (IV. i) underlines, by contrast, the hopelessness of Antony's position. Openly contemptuous of his rival's challenge –

> Let the old ruffian know
> I have many other ways to die – [IV. i. 4.]

Caesar is ready to accept Maecenas' advice urging him on to further action:

> Give him no breath, but now
> Make boot of his distraction. Never anger
> Made good guard for itself; [IV. i. 8.]

the penetrating psychological comment amply reinforces the effect of the episode we have just witnessed. This is the voice of cold sufficiency, ever on the watch for weak spots in the enemy's defences. Against such practical competence Antony's hopes are vain; indeed, many of his former friends have already abandoned him, and Caesar's last word – after the necessary dispositions have been taken – is an off-hand and contemptuous statement of pity: 'poor Antony!'

'Poor Antony', indeed, when he reappears (IV. ii), registers the failure of his gesture, which the common sense of Enobarbus further drives home:

> He thinks, being twenty times of better fortune,
> He is twenty men to one. [IV. ii. 3.]

Antony's reply, in reality the only one open to him, is a desperate resolve to fight 'by sea and land' and in full awareness of the alternatives which face him of 'life' in victory and 'dying honour' in defeat. In fact, they are not true alternatives at all. That the second possibility is in fact the best that can await him is implied by Enobarbus' refusal to respond to his master's mood of despairing exaltation: 'I'll strike, and cry "Take all"'. Antony, grasping desperately at the most tenuous of encouragements, sees comfort in this phrase – 'Well said' – and goes on to confirm his own resolve by a gesture in which generosity and the need to seek for emotional stimulus in a shadow of conviviality are typically mingled:

> Call forth my household servants: let's to-night
> Be *bounteous* at our meal. [IV. ii. 9.]

It would be falsifying the intention of the episode to deny that this is an exposure of careless irresponsibility in a confirmed profligate. There will clearly be no answer here to Caesar's firm command of the practical issues; yet the gesture does serve to preface a momentary recovery in Antony's attitude and to indicate the presence in him of a certain redeeming humanity which, however stained with vice and weakness, stands in effective contrast to his rival's impersonal dedication to his universal purposes.

In the following episode, which covers Antony's farewell to his servants, generosity and weakness are shown in close and characteristic relation, the ostentation of emotion which aims at concealing, even from himself, an awareness of inner failure, is modified by a growing sense of tragedy. Each of the servants is greeted with warmth and a note of personal attachment – 'Thou hast been rightly honest. . . . You have served me well' – though (it must be added) these greetings are joined to a conclusion in which self-flattery plays no mean part: 'Kings have been your fellows'. Cleopatra, still overawed by the disaster which she has brought upon him, is clearly disturbed by these unpredictable vagaries of feeling, which Enobarbus justly places as a by-product of sadness and defeat:

> one of those odd tricks which sorrow shoots
> Out of the mind; [IV. ii. 14.]

the phrase is deeply typical in its combination of realism with the effortless, almost conversational attainment of poetic intensity.

Unbalanced and self-indulgent as he may be in his craving for emotional stimulus, the episode does reveal an Antony able to identify himself with those who follow him. This identification becomes explicit in his next utterance, when he wishes that he 'could be made so many men' and they in turn 'clapp'd up together' in an Antony. The effort to enlist sympathy – for it is that – ends in a gesture of comradeship conceived in a mingling of 'empire' and dissolution:

> Scant not my cups, and make as much of me
> As when my empire was your fellow too
> And suffer'd my command. [IV. ii. 21.]

Antony's memories of empire, like his love, seem to need the external stimulus of drink and luxury to keep them, and thereby himself, in some semblance of life; and it is, at all events, a self-conscious indulgence of the emotion released by defeat that wrings from him this human gesture of comradeship. Once more, Enobarbus has the last word. Antony's aim in all this is 'to make his followers weep', to see his own failure reflected in their tears and so in some measure put out of mind; but the note of generosity, allied though it is to pro-fligacy and implying a perverse dwelling upon the emotional aspects of his impending ruin, is none the less there and will register its effect increasingly in the scenes to follow.

The episode culminates in an effort – of the kind which has been shown by certain of Shakespeare's earlier tragic characters, as far back as Richard II – to extract a self-regarding pathos from the contemplation of ruin:

> Maybe it is the period of your duty:
> Haply you shall not see me more. [IV. ii. 25.]

Antony dwells at this point, with a certain rhetorical complacency, on the 'mangled shadow' of himself which he is in process of becom-ing, and even on the thought that those to whose loyalty he is appealing must shortly abandon him:

> I look on you
> As one that takes his leave. [IV. ii. 28.]

Self-conscious dramatization is the prevailing effect here, but one which in some sense transcends itself in its very surrender to weak-ness, finds issue in the direct and effective appeal with which the speech concludes:

> Mine honest friends,
> I turn you not away; but, like a master
> Married to your good service, stay till death:
> Tend me to-night two hours, I ask no more,
> And the gods yield you for't! [IV. ii. 29.]

Once more, the effect needs to be disentangled with some care. Antony, conscious of his inevitable fate, asks only for 'two hours' in which to cling to the shadow of conviviality, to avoid consideration of what is to come. The effect upon those who hear him is aptly defined by Enobarbus, who confesses himself 'onion-eyed' (with a touch of self-reproving irony in an effort to disguise true emotion), but who also recognizes himself to be an 'ass' for being so moved. It is, finally, an effect of 'shame', reflecting a transformation from martial self-reliance to the state of 'women'. As such, it squares with all the adverse comments that have been made on the effects of Antony's infatuation; but the appeal to friendship and generosity are there too, and demand their place in the complete effect.

Antony's last speech in this scene confirms these considerations. There is the same grotesque lack of sense of practical reality in the admission that he has not seen the inevitable result of his words ('Now the witch take me if I meant it thus!'), though even this admission is in part covered by the following lapse into full emotion: 'Grace grow where these drops fall!'. The scene ends, most characteristically, on Antony's effort to restore confidence by taking back his own words. 'My hearty friends', he exclaims, and the emphasis is placed, in the very utterance, by the forced note of optimism implied in 'hearty', 'You take me in too dolorous a sense'. The retraction, coming from one who has been stressing, almost to the point of emotional exploitation, the 'dolorous' elements in his situation, is naïve indeed; and so is what follows:

> I spake to you for your comfort, did desire you
> To burn the night with torches. [IV. ii. 40.]

It is noteworthy that this comfort is once more allied to dissipation, to the persistent desire to evade reality. Thus lifted momentarily upon an illusory crest of emotion, Antony looks forward to victory in a cause which he himself, in his glimpses of sober fact, knows to be beyond hope:

> know, my hearts,
> I hope well of to-morrow, and will lead you
> Where rather I'll expect victorious life
> Than death and honour. [IV. ii. 41.]

Yet again, Antony prefaces his appeal with the intimate gesture
implied in 'my hearts'; but the underlying emphasis is not where he
desires to place it, upon 'victorious life, upon 'hope', but upon
meeting his inevitable death with 'honour'. In the subtle rhythmic
construction of this part of the play, this mood will carry him through
the brief recovery of the next day's fighting: thus far and, because it
is finally based upon illusion, upon an artificial simulation of new
life, no further. It is significant that the last words of the scene, confirming its deepest implications, should be an invitation to supper
and an appeal to 'drown consideration'.

The brief scene which now follows (IV. iii), poised between the
first day's disaster and the momentary recovery of the second, marks
most effectively the present state of the action. The quick, trenchant
exchanges between the soldiers on their watch correspond to a point
of balance in the minds of men – 'It will determine one way' – and to
an emphasis upon things 'strange', mysterious and unrealized. There
is a sense of partial recovery which corresponds to Antony's own
equally partial revival; he has still at his command a 'brave' army
and, if the navy which has been throughout the doubtful element in
his fortunes can hold, there is 'absolute hope' that the 'landsmen will
stand up'. The element of fate, however, introduced to the sound of
music, presages otherwise, penetrates air and earth with the sad
premonition of Antony's fallen manhood:

> 'Tis the god Hercules, whom Antony loved,
> Now leaves him. [IV. iii. 16.]

There are few scenes more effective than this, in its tense economy of
expression, in evoking the sense of human life against a background
of fatality and in conveying the pathos which accompanies, in
Antony's approaching tragedy, the dissolution of his heroic integrity.

Against this grave interlude, Antony's recovery of confidence is
seen in relation to what is, after all, its final cause, his return to
Cleopatra (IV. iv). The scene carries a stage further the emotional
swing of the pendulum which aims at a momentary reversal of the
prevailing trend to ruin and disintegration. The page Eros, binding
on his master's arms in the inspiring presence of his mistress, serves
to unite the values of love and war; whilst Antony's own mood
finds expression in an ambiguous declaration of confidence:

> If fortune be not ours to-day, it is
> Because we brave her. [IV. iv. 4.]

To 'brave fortune' is, indeed, to some extent a sign of moral recovery;
but whether this is enough, or whether 'fortune', in her inscrutability,
will not rather evade those who 'brave' her, almost in defiance and

because no alternative is open to them, remains to be seen. The following brief exchanges with Cleopatra are charged with effortless poetry. There is, more especially, deep pathos in the juxtaposition of 'the armourer of my heart' – referring to Cleopatra – with the murmured repetition 'false, false', which at once follows; though the latter refers to Eros' buckling on of his mail, it contains a more universal tragic implication. Taken as a whole, this is perhaps the most unequivocally romantic episode in the play; in its romanticism lies at once its justification and the certainty of its impermanence. Putting on the armour which symbolizes his manhood, Antony also dons a brief confidence – 'We shall thrive now' – whilst Cleopatra's question 'Is this not buckled well?' makes her, for the moment, a handmaid of Mars, an inspiration to the warrior about to advance gaily upon his fate.

In Antony, the mood of the moment finds expression in a longer utterance. 'Rarely, rarely' is his reply to Cleopatra's question (the adverb is one to which the play more than once returns[1] in its moments of emotional fulfilment), and he goes on to stress his new confidence:

> He that unbuckles this till we do please
> To daff't for our repose, shall hear a storm. [IV. iv. 12.]

This in turn leads to an explicit identification of the values of love and war:

> Thou fumblest, Eros, and my queen's a squire
> More tight at this than thou: dispatch. O love,
> That thou couldst see my wars to-day, and knew'st
> The royal occupation! thou shouldst see
> A workman in't. [IV. iv. 14.]

In such speeches, which characterize the lull before the approaching resolution, we can feel Antony's confidence returning in poetry which, ultimately founded though it is on deception, serves to carry a new note, related to the final tragedy, into these later scenes of the play.

The entry at this point of a soldier in arms enables Antony to extend still further his new confidence. The warrior, like the lover, has the morning at his back to illuminate his hopes:

> To business that we love we rise betime,
> And go to't with delight. [IV. iv. 20.]

Words that might have been spoken of Cleopatra are thus transferred to the martial business in hand and the soldier's reply,

[1] Compare Agrippa's comment on Enobarbus' description of Cleopatra at Cydnus: 'O rare for Antony!' [II ii. 213.]

announcing that, 'early though't be', a thousand men, ready with their 'riveted trim', await their leader at the port, carries on the same note. When a captain also enters with the salutation 'The morn is fair', he prompts Antony to reply, amid the flourish of his trumpets:

> 'Tis well blown, lads;
> This morning, like the spirit of a youth
> That means to be of note, begins betimes. [IV. iv. 25.]

The entire exchange gains its effect through a contrast with the nocturnal feasting, the artificial animation stressed in the preceding scenes. Both elements have their part to play in the complex unity which makes up his contradictory nature. Now, indeed, in his farewell to Cleopatra, he responds to the summons of the trumpets as to an augury of growing confidence, transforming to a momentary intuition of youth the spirit of this ageing warrior, elsewhere wrapped in dissolution and emotional evasion of the truth. The brief instructions of those who are arming him for war – 'So, so; come, give me that; this way; well said' – radiate intimacy and confidence, and are rounded off in the rueful simplicity of the farewell to his inspiration to which they lead:

> Fare thee well, dame, whate'er becomes of me. [IV. iv. 29.]

It is recognized here that the revival of spirit cannot in itself alter, mould to ends of its own, the iron course of external events; but the scene does ally humanity and tenderness with recent memories of dissolution to produce an effect of its own. Meanwhile, come what may, there is still to be given the 'soldier's kiss', prelude of departure to a more inexorable order of reality:

> I'll leave thee
> Now like a man of steel. [IV. iv. 32.]

Taking his leave, Antony embraces his followers in his new-found confidence:

> You that will fight,
> Follow me close: I'll bring you to't; [IV. iv. 33.]

and Cleopatra, left behind, sums up with perfect clarity the impression which the entire episode has left. Antony has to some extent recovered his manhood: 'He goes forth gallantly'. She is moved by this recovery, which is owed – like the preceding disgrace – in no small measure to her influence upon him; but she is well aware how little it will be able to project itself upon the course of events:

> That he and Caesar might
> Determine this great war in single fight. [IV. iv. 36.]

L

'Then Antony', indeed, might achieve victory; 'but now – Well, on'. There is no alternative but to follow the coming battle to its foreseen conclusion.

The practical limits of Antony's recovery are, indeed, clearly shown in the next scene (IV. v), in which his past follies are recalled in the exchange with a soldier:

> Would thou and those thy scars had once prevail'd
> To make me fight at land! – [IV. v. 2.]

and where it is learned that his appeals to his followers have not prevented Enobarbus from abandoning his cause. Even at this point, Antony's quixotic mixture of generosity and unpracticality is revealed in the gesture which enables him to send the traitor's treasure after him and in the 'gentle advice and greetings' which he offers to one who, though he has now deserted him, was formerly a friend. No doubt these decisions answer in part to Antony's need to live up to his own impression of himself as generous, open-handed, in a world of calculation in which he is singularly ill-fitted to succeed; but there is more than pose here, an openness of character which can still command at least a shadow of respect and which the final bitter comment –

> O, my fortunes have
> Corrupted honest men! – [IV. v. 16.]

enforces with pathos and a frank admission of the truth.

In contrast to the mixture of dissolution and emotional excess which characterizes these scenes, the next stage in the rich pattern of contrasts show Caesar proceeding upon his destined path (IV. vi.). Firmly in charge of events, he disposes – 'our will is' – that Antony be taken alive; and, we must add, if his progress seems, and is, hard and inhuman in its concentration, it is in the name of true values, of peace and order, that he is fighting:

> The time of universal peace is near;
> Prove this a prosperous day, the three-nook'd world
> Shall bear the olive freely. [IV. vi. 5.]

Until this noble aspiration has been gained, the emphasis is upon the sternly practical. The immediate effect falls upon those who have sought to save themselves by deserting their former master. Of them Caesar has no more than this to say:

> Plant those that have revolted in the van,
> That Antony may seem to spend his fury
> Upon himself. [IV. vi. 9.]

The immediate effect is to bring home to Enobarbus the truth that treachery bears within itself the seeds of its own destruction. Alexas, for his pains in 'revolting', has been hanged; Canidius and the rest

have entertainment, but
No honourable trust. [IV. vi. 17.]

This 'honest' traitor, in short, is left only to accuse himself of his own actions, can 'joy no more'. The ruthless realism of vision which accompanies this play's moments of poetic exaltation is never better displayed.

At this moment the news of Antony's generosity ('his bounty over-plus', added to the restitution of Enobarbus' goods) comes with double effect to celebrate the presence in this darkening world of at least one redeeming grace. In the words of the common soldier, and by comparison with the frigid Octavius, Antony 'continues still a Jove', moving Enobarbus to confess himself 'the villain of the earth' and to exalt his former master as 'a mine of bounty'. It is only left for him to seek out for himself in his desolation 'some ditch wherein to die'. The effect is once more to contribute to a certain limited re-habilitation of the fallen hero.

As if to follow the same course, the battle itself now engaged (IV. vii) stands at a balance. Agrippa confesses that Caesar's forces have 'engaged themselves too far' and that Caesar himself 'has work' beyond his expectation. The fortunes of Antony, still for a brief moment 'brave emperor', are such that, on land at least, they seem to be in the way of recovery. His exultant followers express them-selves in imagery of the chase –

Let us score their backs
And snatch 'em up, as we take hares, behind:
'Tis sport to maul a runner – [IV. vii. 12.]

which corresponds to the new spirit that animates them in this part of the action.

Immediately afterwards (IV. viii), Antony, on the crest of the wave, returns to Cleopatra. 'We have beat them to their camp', he affirms, and his first impulse is to keep her informed of what has been achieved. 'Let the queen know of our gests': the choice of the romantic word 'gest' corresponds to the transformed, typically heightened emotion. The mood of confidence carries Antony to anticipate further victories on the following day:

To-morrow,
Before the sun shall see's, we'll spill the blood
That has to-day escaped. [IV. viii. 2.]

In the meantime, the first reaction is, characteristically, a gesture of ample generosity. All must participate in the celebration of success; all have served the hero's cause, all have shown themselves 'Hectors' in the field. Once more, as the warriors dispose themselves to return in triumph to Alexandria, Antony unites the emotions of love and war in a single transitory exaltation:

> Enter the city; clip your wives, your friends,
> Tell them your feats; whilst they with joyful tears
> Wash the congealment from your wounds and kiss
> The honour'd gashes whole. [IV. viii. 8.]

Antony's emotion expresses itself here, as it does so often, with typical excess, but dangerous as this excess is, carrying within itself the seeds of a reaction to despair, it bears us momentarily with it in opulent confidence.

The entry of Cleopatra, whom Antony, in his mood of realistic dejection, has so recently greeted with a resentment that reduced her to silence, now crowns his mood of triumph. She is the 'great fairy' to whom he must present his victorious companion Scarus that he may receive from her nothing less than the blessing of her thanks. The stress laid upon light and the dawn is now crowned by the apostrophe to her as 'thou day o' the world', and her arms are called upon to 'chain' the warrior's 'armed neck', and she herself to 'leap',

> attire and all,
> Through proofs of harness to my heart, and there
> Ride on the pants triumphing! [IV. viii. 14.]

Cleopatra's reply is one of those gestures which, by surpassing common reality, convey simultaneously the intensity and the remoteness, the dangerous, because impossible exaltation of the passion which will accompany both Antony and herself to death. Antony she hails as 'lord of lords', and further – by a marvellous withdrawal from the reality of every day which, however, precisely on account of its unreality, cannot last – as 'infinite virtue'; whilst the apostrophe which follows –

> comest thou smiling from
> The world's great snare uncaught – [IV. viii. 17.]

triumphs, again for the moment, by sheer imaginative force over its very implausibility as addressed to the middle-aged reveller who now confronts her in his decline. Antony, responding, combines frank romanticism ('My nightingale!') with a rueful confession of his advancing years:

> though grey
> Do something mingle with our younger brown. [IV. viii. 19.]

In the mood of triumph, however, which follows the proud claim
that 'we have beat them to their beds,' Cleopatra can still be
addressed as 'girl' and Antony see himself as the equal of youth:

> yet ha' we
> A brain that nourishes our nerves and can
> Get goal for goal of youth. [IV. viii. 20.]

In the light of this illusory transformation of common reality,
Scarus is raised before Cleopatra to a status which approaches that of
a god; he has fought, we are told,

> As if a god in hate of mankind had
> Destroy'd in such a shape, [IV. viii. 25.]

and is accordingly to be commended to the life-giving, 'favouring'
hand.

To this exaltation Cleopatra, as ever, is able to respond with a
characteristic gesture of generosity that, in this case, borders on the
absurd:

> I'll give thee, friend,
> An armour all of gold; it was a king's, [IV. viii. 26.]

where extravagance and royal carelessness momentarily, and impossibly, meet. The scene ends, after Antony's responding reference
to the 'carbuncles' on 'holy Phoebus' car', on a note of martial
music –

> Through Alexandria make a jolly march – [IV. viii. 30.]

which is at once gaily optimistic and oddly inconsequent, and on a
heroic display: 'Bear our hack'd targets like the men that own
them'. This mood, so far removed from Caesar's purposeful sobriety,
finds its issue once more in the dissolute companionship of feasting:

> Had our great palace the capacity
> To camp this host, we all would sup together
> And drink carouses to the next day's fate,
> Which promises royal peril. [IV. viii. 32.]

The lines combine admirably the elements of weakness and exaltation which are, at this moment, perilously balanced in Antony's
mind. The fanciful, absurd generosity which leads him, in his
imagination, to throw open his palace to an entire army and to issue
an all-embracing invitation to 'sup' leads directly to the thought of

the 'carouses' in which he invariably seeks to drown consideration of the future, of 'the next day's fate'. In Antony's mind there is less a reasoned conviction of victory than the fascination of a 'peril' which he salutes as 'royal', and which acts upon him for the moment as an exhilarating drug. The background to this exaltation is provided by the 'brazen din' of the trumpeters and by the combination of this with the noise of the 'rattling tambourines', both so united that 'heaven and earth may strike their sounds together' to applaud, in one last appearance of triumph, Antony's approach to Alexandria.

The following scene (IV. ix), returning to Caesar's camp and setting against the optimism just displayed a deeper note of tragedy, adds equally, from its own standpoint, to the partial rehabilitation of Antony. His successes have made an impression, as Caesar's soldier confesses, and now Enobarbus enters to act out the final stage of his foreseen repentance. As he does so, he stresses the generosity of his former master –

> Nobler than my revolt is infamous – [IV. ix. 19.]

and ends his life evoking the name of Antony himself. Here, at least, we have some indication of the feeling which Antony can rouse in others and which Caesar can never attract to himself. The next short episode (in IV. x) stresses Antony's success 'by land', as well as the mood of rash confidence which accompanies it:

> I would they'ld fight i' the fire or i' the air;
> We'ld fight there too; [IV. x. 3.]

turning the play's elemental imagery to a fresh use, Caesar, by contrast, announces his intention to be 'still by land', an intuition which Antony's rash decision to take to the water, Cleopatra's self-chosen element, again confirms.

The recovery which seems to have come upon Antony in the last few scenes cannot, by its very nature, last. Whilst we await the issue of the battle, Scarus confesses as much in his reference to the uncertainty of the augurers, and adds a frank account of the state of mind that underlies his master's many changes of mood:

> Antony
> Is valiant, and dejected, and by starts
> His fretted fortunes give him hope, and fear,
> Of what he has, and has not. [IV. x. 19.]

The resolution of this uncertainty is not long delayed, and, when it comes, is shatteringly complete. The battle itself is barely indicated; as it is decided, the whole structure of Antony's confidence collapses into a ruin: 'All is lost!'. There is never place in Antony's mind for emotional light and shade, or for a sober estimate of realities; his transitions are throughout sudden, without mitigation. The Cleopatra who so recently inspired his mood of triumph now becomes once more the 'foul Egyptian' who has betrayed him (but has he not betrayed himself first, in surrendering his manhood to her?); whilst the friends whom he has so recently saluted, invited to sup with him, have gone over to the foe, in whose ranks

> They cast their caps up and carouse together
> Like friends long lost. [IV. x. 25.]

Never was a heroic ruin more tellingly conveyed through the words so appropriately put into the hero's own mouth.

It is characteristic that Antony's first reaction to his defeat should be to mask his sense of failure by mouthing against the 'triple-turned whore' whom he himself so recently saluted as the inspiration of his material deeds, and by evoking in bitter envy the 'novice' Caesar who has beaten him so utterly at his own game of war. Only a thought of revenge remains to stir him to action and, having once more bidden his followers leave him, he takes refuge in a rhetorical personification of his own dejection:

> O sun, thy uprise shall I see no more:
> Fortune and Antony part here, even here
> Do we shake hands. [IV. x. 31.]

The rest of the speech is a remorseless exposure of tragic weakness, of a personality dissolving in the contemplation of its inner contradictions:

> All come to this? The hearts
> That spaniell'd me at heels, to whom I gave
> Their wishes, do discandy, melt their sweets
> On blossoming Caesar; and this pine is bark'd
> That overtopped them all. Betrayed I am.
> O this false soul of Egypt! this grave charm,
> Whose eyes beck'd forth my wars and call'd them home,
> Whose bosom was my crownet, my chief end,
> Like a right gipsy hath at fast and loose
> Beguiled me to the very heart of loss. [IV. x. 33.]

The sense of dissolution makes itself felt first through the contemplation of those who have abandoned Antony's failing fortunes; those who formerly followed him with dog-like servility in return for his generosity, now 'discandy', '*melt* their sweets', with cloying insistence, on the growing fortunes of 'blossoming Caesar'. By contrast, the 'pine' that was Antony, who formerly 'overtopp'd them all' (and here we look forward to Cleopatra's image of 'the soldier's pole'[1]) is 'bark'd', stripped of its trappings of nobility and honour. This leads Antony to express his sense that he has been betrayed, that the 'grave charm', the superstitious amulet that Cleopatra has been to him, and whose memory is still with him, has become his 'false soul': 'soul', in recalling her former inspiration, and 'false' on account of the ruin to which his infatuation has led him. Even at this moment, Antony confesses to her magnetism and his own subjugation. It has been his tragedy to place his manhood in the hands of one who at once inspired ('beck'd forth') his wars and irrationally, illogically, 'call'd them home'. Upon her, abandoning all sense of his male responsibilities, he rested, her bosom his 'crownet', her love his impossibly exclusive end; and the result has been a betrayal, the 'beguiling' by one who is denounced as a 'gipsy', of his manhood into what he now sees – in a phrase that wonderfully combines haunting emotion with the sense of intimate failure – to be the 'heart of loss'.

Cleopatra, as she enters, is greeted by Antony as a 'spell', as the supernatural cause of his ruin; and, as on a previous occasion,[2] she can only be silent before the force of his rage and the magnitude of his ruin. Antony, plunged into hysteria, finds a certain perverse satisfaction in humiliating her, subjecting her in his imagination to indignity and torture:

> Let him take thee,
> And hoist thee up to the shouting plebeians;
> Follow his chariot, like the greatest spot
> Of all thy sex; most monster-like, be shown
> For poor'st diminutives, for doits; and let
> Patient Octavia plough thy visage up
> With her prepared nails. [IV. x. 46.]

The shift here from the preceding expressions of ecstasy is as complete as it is devastating in its revelation of essential self-indulgence. The speech ends, after Cleopatra's silent departure, with the complete collapse of all the confidence that Antony seemed so recently to have gained into rant and base rhetoric, references – resting on his former pride in his divine ancestor Hercules – to the 'shirt of Nessus' and to the poison that destroyed the god:

> Let me lodge Lichas on the horns o' the moon,
> And with these hands that grasp'd the heaviest club
> Subdue my worthiest self. [IV. x. 58.]

[1] IV. xiii. See p. 184 below.
[2] III. xi. See p. 140 above.

It is now his frantic desire to overcome his 'worthiest' self, to give himself over to a bestiality which he ascribes to a sense of betrayal when he affirms that Cleopatra has sold him 'to the young Roman boy' (how Caesar's youth and success, compared to his own sense oi having lost both, rankle in his mind!), but which covers a sense that it is in reality by his own baser self that he has been betrayed. In executing in his imagination a brutal revenge upon the late object of his infatuation ('she dies for't) Antony grasps as ever at a vain hope of concealing from himself the more intimate causes of his ruin. By the end of this scene of pitiless self-revelation the precarious recovery shown in the preceding scenes has been entirely undone; only once his dedication to death has become complete, in the course of the two great scenes to follow, will it be possible for his relationship with Cleopatra to achieve some measure of restoration.

VI

After the conclusion of these episodes of war, the action of the play progressively narrows, concentrates itself upon the remaining personal issues. As it does so, the prevailing mood moves away from political and moral realism – which are, however, relevant to the last – towards that of a 'metaphysical' balance of love and death in an enriching combination of contraries. To respond adequately to this change, and to its implications in terms of human behaviour, is among the most difficult undertakings in Shakespearean criticism. The poetry which expresses the exaltation of the lovers tends, by its unique magnificence, to impose acceptance: acceptance, moreover, made the more compelling by the fact that it answers to what is undeniably *there*, an essential part of the dramatic situation. It is necessary, however, whilst recognizing this, to realize that we are being asked to balance participation with detachment, to see in the end of the tragic process not merely a certain affirmation of life, even in the acceptance of death, but its opposite, the logical conclusion of an entanglement sought after and accepted, the end of a course which has been from the beginning both perverse and life-destroying. Without maintaining this balance to the last, it is impossible to offer a coherent and meaningful account of the tragedy.

The development of events leading to Antony's suicide can leave us in no doubt that his death follows inevitably from all that has gone before. Nothing that has been asserted in exposure of this pair is softened or palliated as their end approaches. Before he appears, Cleopatra confirms the mood of rage in which he confronted her, associating it with the loss of mental balance –

> O, he is more mad
> Than Telemon for his shield; the boar of Thessaly
> Was never so emboss'd – [IV. xi. 1.]

and takes refuge in a stratagem which will be the direct occasion of
his death. 'To the monument': we can never forget that the last
meeting between this pair, which will occasion one of its supreme
poetic moments, will be the result of a device initiated by Cleopatra
to further the effect by which she aims at retrieving, if nothing else,
her ascendancy over her declining lover.

Against the background of a situation in which tragedy and
falsity are thus compounded, Antony builds up, hesitantly and self-
consciously through the long scene which follows (IV. xii), the
resolution which his situation in fact imposes upon him. Left alone
with Eros he indulges for the last time the impulse, always strong in
him, to escape into a world of fantasy: a fantasy, however, which no
longer reflects memories of victory or martial prowess – things which
have finally eluded him – but rather, through its evanescant image
in the physical shape of things, the dissolution of personality itself.
'Eros', he calls, 'thou *yet* behold'st me': the 'yet' presages a certain
fading of the speaker's being, which the following elaborate word-
picture confirms:

> Sometimes we see a cloud that's dragonish,
> A vapour sometime like a bear or lion,
> A tower'd citadel, a pendent rock,
> A forked mountain, or blue promontory
> With trees upon't, that nod unto the world
> And mock our eyes with air: thou hast seen these signs;
> They are black vesper's pageants. [IV. xii. 2.]

The different elements which make up this shifting fantasy need to
be weighed one against the other. In part, the effect of its elaboration is to facilitate the coming change of mood, to introduce a
necessary pause between Antony's recent hysteria and his coming
assimilation to his fate. Beyond this, however, it is also related to his
personal reaction to his tragedy. The tendency to see the real world
in terms of 'cloud', 'vapour', 'air' exists in the poetry side by side
with a persistent undertone of 'mockery'. Antony, lost in the sphere of
solid reality which his own choices have led him to abandon, seeks
refuge, as he has done before, in the elaborate decoration of his
fancy; but experience itself is now shown as liquefying, losing its
distinct outlines –

> That which is now a horse, even with a thought
> The rack dislimns, and makes it indistinct – [IV. xii. 9.]

to become without identity, 'as water is in water'. The application
to his own state, though vaguely comforting in intention, is in
fact ruthlessly affirmed. 'Thy captain', he confesses, is no more
than 'such a body'. Though still a 'captain', still related to his
former vocation as a leader of men, there is no prospect of his
holding to 'this visible shape', of maintaining his heroic identity
as anything more than a series of shifting illusions doomed to
destruction.

The entry of Mardian with 'news' of Cleopatra immediately recalls Antony to a sense of the shame which has overtaken him. This
shame is, as it were, symbolized in his mind by the imagined loss of
his sword:

> O, thy vile lady,
> She has robb'd me of my sword!; [IV. xi. 22.]

the accusation recalls Othello's gesture of impotence before Desde-
mona's murdered corpse[1], and is scarcely less a confession of failure.
Shame, however, is still compatible with other less direct attitudes.
The Antony who can now say of Cleopatra –

> the queen –
> Whose heart I thought I had, for she had mine – [IV. xii. 15.]

is recalling the appeal of a true devotion which has been irretrievably
shattered; but he is also fishing in his own mind for the pathetic
response which will in some measure answer to his need to lay the
blame elsewhere, and so restore his self-respect. Assimilated though
he is to the idea of his own decline, more than a touch of self-com-
miseration lingers in his utterance; and the final accusation of
betrayal, the assertion that Cleopatra has 'Pack'd cards with
Caesar, and false-play'd my glory', reflects yet again the need to see
himself as the victim, not of his own choices, but of the failure of
those upon whom he has deposited his trust to respond to the
shadowy image of 'glory' to which he obstinately clings. The speech,
in short, is oddly and characteristically ambivalent. Although it
contains an admission of reality and ends in an acceptance of the
death which circumstances are forcing upon him –

> there is left us
> Ourselves to end ourselves – [IV. xii. 21.]

it also carries a faint reflection of this hero's inveterate tendency
to seek comfort through the dramatization of his own state. This

---

[1] Compare Othello's
> I am not valiant neither,
> But every puny whipster gets my sword. [*Othello* V. ii. 241.]

confronting of objectivity with the continued need for self-evasion
is, indeed, a principal element in the tragic effect.

Mardian's reply involves Antony still further in complexity. It
asserts in Cleopatra the constancy upon belief in which, although he
has just denied it in the attempt to justify himself, his own integrity
(or what is left of it) is now anchored:

> No, Antony;
> My mistress loved thee, and her fortunes mingled
> With thine entirely. [IV. xii. 23.]

The assertion offers Antony the only positive comfort now open to
him; and yet, we cannot forget that the news which accompanies it
is *false*, that its effect is compatible with deception and stratagem.
The blending of poetic illusion with recognized falsity is at this point
the basis upon which rests a subtle interplay of contrasted judgements. As much can be said of the brief exchange which follows.
When Antony replies with a last shadowy expression of his former
rage ('She hath betray'd me, and shall die the death'), Mardian's
answer, while it can be said to anticipate the spirit of the coming
encounter on the monument –

> Death of one person can be paid but once,
> And that she has discharg'd – [IV. xii. 27.]

is still based on falsity. Calculation and emotion, deception and
depth of feeling, are here blended; it is most typical of the balance of
judgement for which this play calls that this statement, based on
known untruth, should yet be delivered with the intensity of true
emotion.

As truth, indeed, Antony receives it. After Mardian's speech has
culminated in his statement that Cleopatra 'render'd' her life, 'thy
name so buried in her', thus balancing 'life' and 'buried' in a way in
which, as so often from now on, language takes upon itself a sense of
rhythmic fitness which touches upon the musical, Antony's reply
falls in a contrasted simplicity. 'Dead, then', he says, and Mardian,
with the single word 'dead', confirms what he can hardly credit.
The pause, implying Antony's assimilation of the fact that his last
hold upon life has been taken from him, marks a prelude to the
following speech, which corroborates and deepens what has gone
before. 'Unarm, Eros': the time has come for the soldier to divest
himself of the trappings of his vocation; for he was in any case
Cleopatra's 'warrior', and her 'death' has come to assert finally the
necessity for his own. The speech which elaborates this act of renunciation proceeds with a gravely 'musical' building up of its cumulative effects, the name 'Eros' being threaded through the developing

harmony as a kind of basic theme upon which the most subtle and even contrary variations of feeling are beautifully played. As a prelude to it, Mardian is dismissed with a shadow of Antony's former dignity –

> That thou depart'st hence safe
> Does pay thy labour richly – [IV. xii. 36.]

in which we do not know whether we are in the presence of the fallen hero or of the broken warrior who was ready to inflict his resentment upon the unworthy person of Thyreus.

This, however, is a mere prelude to the full development of harmonies which follows. After the final brief 'go', addressed to Mardian, Antony returns to his principal preoccupations and 'off, pluck off' is incorporated, with marvellous fitness of rhythm, into the dying fall of the line. In the following speech, true pathos and the seeking of compensation in exploited sorrow are still superbly interwoven. The armour of the warrior no longer serves him, 'the sevenfold shield of Ajax' can no longer repulse the 'battery' from his stricken heart. The 'heart' itself, centre of emotion and feeling, is on the point of proving stronger than its 'continent', the frail case of the body which once enclosed it and, enclosing it, upheld the warrior's dignity. Antony is, even as he speaks, conscious of the dilapidation which has left him 'No more a soldier', deprived him of his claim to self-respect; but anxious as he is to complete the process of devesting – 'Apace, Eros, apace' – he still finds it necessary to affirm in memory the impression, half reality and half self-consoling illusion, that his 'bruised pieces' have been 'nobly borne'. The defeated warrior, in other words, even as he approaches death with a new simplicity, a throwing aside of accidental honours and ambiguous prestige, clings to memories of former prowess to cover the present reality of his ignominy. This combination of exaltation with realism, this taking up of former weakness, even as it is stressed, into what will turn out to be a fleeting assertion of human transcendence is essential to the play's achievement.

Immediately afterwards, his own recent accusations of Cleopatra turn, at the thought that she is dead – but we can never forget that this belief is false, and the falsity must colour our reaction to it – into a request for pardon in which the simple effect of a carried-over line answers, beyond weakness, to a sense of pathos:

> I will o'ertake thee, Cleopatra, and
> Weep for my pardon. [IV. xii. 44.]

The effect, combining pathos with a tentative recourse to self-deceiving emotion, is wonderful in its simultaneous truth to feeling

and character. A similar impression is conveyed in the lines which
follow and which, accepting annihilation as the only possible end,
are at once supremely poetic and the last, necessarily remote expression of sensual indulgence:

> So it must be, for now
> All length is torture: since the torch is out,
> Lie down and stray no further: now all labour
> Mars what it does; yea, very force entangles
> Itself with strength: seal then, and all is done. [IV. xii. 45.]

The effect is obtained through the play's characteristic mastery of
verse at once natural in its rhythms, wedded to the rise and fall of the
speaking voice, and capable of an almost unprecedented ease in the
expression of complex states of feeling. The breaking of the rhythm
in the middle of the blank verse lines is perfectly adjusted to the ebb
of an emotion tending deathward, dwelling with a certain complacent weakness upon the release which it can only envisage through
the thought of extinction. To this compound of tragedy and
emotional indulgence corresponds the lingering effect of the play on
'torture' and 'torch', which is at once full of feeling and, somehow
at this juncture, incongruously frivolous. Above all, the lines relate
Antony's tragedy to that intimate balance of contraries tending to
self-annihilation which is perhaps his most consistent sensation.

> All labour
> Mars what it does; [IV. xii. 47.]

the efforts of the tragic protagonists, aiming at life and self-assertion,
have been caught throughout in the deathward, self-frustrating
tendencies implied in their emotional states. The 'very force' of their
aspirations involves them in contradiction, 'entangles itself'; but the
entanglement, it must be added, conveys itself with the 'strength',
the transforming power which all living emotion implies.

From this entanglement death is the only release, and the relief
which the thought, if not the reality, of it brings to Antony is reflected
in the recovery of emotion from its dying fall, summed up in the
ecstatic apostrophe 'I come, my queen', and in the mingling of
pathetic fallacy with a conscious and yet moving effort to compensate
the hopelessness of the present situation with an assertion of happiness
to come:

> Where souls do couch on flowers, we'll hand in hand,
> And with our sprightly port make the ghosts gaze:
> Dido and her Aeneas shall want troops,
> And all the haunt be ours. [IV. xii. 51.]

Like so much else in Antony, this is finally an evasion, the creation of an attractive illusion to cover failure and self-betrayal. The evocation of the souls that 'couch on flowers' is wrought in a weak, a self-indulgent imagination, and the impressing of the ghosts in their pale after-life with the 'sprightly port' of the lovers offers, we may feel, a poor compensation for a real world surrendered. Like the following reference to Dido and Aeneas, this is finally and deliberately litera-ture; but the pathos which it also implies will be taken up, once the necessary death has been consummated, the price of folly paid, into Cleopatra's final apotheosis of her lover.

The return of Eros comes in time for Antony to take a last look at the 'dishonour', the 'baseness', which have so long haunted his thoughts. Once more his reaction is a compound of truth and fiction, recalled nobility and present weakness. In contrast with his great past when, as he puts it, 'I',

> with my sword
> Quarter'd the world, and o'er green Neptune's back
> With ships made cities, [IV. xii. 57.]

(the play's universal imagery is here being incorporated into the tragic effect: Cleopatra, in a still greater speech, will take up these memories of triumph when the obstacle to them represented by Antony's real failure has been removed by death), he finds himself to lack 'the courage of a woman'. In Cleopatra's supposed resolution – even in the resolution to self-destruction – he finds at once a reproach and a call to the only kind of consistency now open to him; for his mind appears to himself 'less noble' than hers,

> which by her death our Caesar tells
> 'I am conqueror of myself'. [IV. xii. 61.]

This is, yet again, a line of thought which Cleopatra will develop[1]. We may stress, if we will, together with the speaker's effort to goad himself emotionally into suicide, the presence of elements of self-deception; but we shall also see the prelude to the other, the more positive side of the balanced effect. Only in the lines which follow, however, and lest we should be tempted to take these heroics too much at their face value, does the speech reveal its foundation in despair and a sense of intolerable isolation. Unwillingly faced by 'the exigent'

> which now
> Is come indeed, [IV. xii. 63.]

[1] Compare
> 'Tis paltry to be Caesar;
> Not being Fortune, he's but Fortune's knave, [V. ii. 2.]
and the lines which follow.

Antony looks upon what his reason tells him is, once the pretences of
'nobility' have been laid aside,

> The inevitable prosecution of
> Disgrace and horror; [IV. xii. 65.]

the deliberate dragging rhythm reflects the depth of the abyss open
before the speaker, and his own unreadiness, even now, to look
steadily into it. The vision of desolation, however, acts as a stimulus
to tragic resolution. Antony steels himself to command his own
death – 'Do't; the time is come' – and seeks to encourage both Eros
and (in reality) himself by a last turn of rhetoric: 'Thou strikest not
me; 'tis Caesar thou defeat'st'.

His next speech shows that Antony has before him no real alternatives between which to choose. The picture of himself as Caesar's
prisoner, put forward to overcome Eros' reluctance to become the
instrument of his death, is unflinching in its realism; it evokes an
Antony 'bending down' his 'corrigible neck', subdued to 'penetrative
shame', his 'baseness' branded beneath the conqueror's chariot
wheels. The prospect of a shame which must end equally in death
leaves Antony resigned to his fate; as he puts it, 'with a wound must
I be cured'. This is not, however, quite all. Though the scene has
been from its first moment an exposure of weakness faced with the
image of its own folly, the devotion of Eros strikes a different note;
when he refers to his master's invulnerability to 'the Parthian darts',
or speaks of

> that noble countenance
> Wherein the worship of the whole world lies, [IV. xii. 85.]

he is also contributing to the picture of an Antony who, precisely
because he now seems so far removed from the possibility of rousing
such feelings, conveys some emotional meaning in the ability to do
so in his followers.

After the drawn-out tension of the leave-taking, Eros' own suicide
comes to Antony as a reproof, a suggestion of moral cowardice
which his own indirect approach has done something to insinuate:

> Thou teachest me, O valiant Eros, what
> I should and thou couldst not. [IV. xii. 96.]

The thought recalls him to a renewed evocation of the 'nobleness' in
which he seeks the stimulus to resolution and to an equally typical
fusion of the ideas of love and death:

> I will be
> A bridegroom in my death, and run into't,
> As to a lover's bed. [IV. xii. 99.]

In the face of death the contrary judgements which this tragedy so consistently invites are maintained and fused. Not for the first time in Shakespeare the tragic hero, as he approaches the moment of resolution, incorporates expressions that proceed from the weakness that is undoing him into an effect that in some respects transcends it. Antony's suicide, whilst remaining the decisive proof of his self-destroying folly, becomes an integral part of the final lyrical assertion of emotional value and therefore, up to a point, of life. It looks forward to its counterpart in the poetry of Cleopatra's death, in which 'baser life' is transmuted, in so far as poetry can suffice to do it, into a compound of fire, air, and 'immortality'.

The scene maintains to the last the balance of impressions upon which it has throughout rested. Even in his suicide Antony is revealed as a botcher, obliged to confess that he has done his work 'ill' and to plead with his friends to

> make an end
> Of what I have begun. [IV. xii. 105.]

Surely there is reached in this last assertion of incapacity something very near absurdity, and a lesser writer would no doubt have hesitated before incorporating this particular reality into his tragic effect. This, however, is not all. The surrounding emotional tone, as the guards convey it in terms which recall the mystery which surrounded Antony's abandonment by his ancestor, 'the god Hercules',[1] is already passing into an intuition of tragic fitness, a certain dissolution into poetry of the more constricting fetters of harsh reality:

> – The star is fall'n.
> – And time is at his period; [IV. xii. 106.]

the phrases anticipate the mood which is shortly to surround Cleopatra on her throne of death.

Meanwhile, we are not to forget that the whole situation is, in the realm of hard fact, based on falsity, and that Antony is surrounded at the last by those whose main eye is to their future good. If the soldiers fail to respond to his plea – 'Let him that loves me strike me dead' – it is not because the spectacle of his ruin inspires awe but rather because, as Dercetas puts it,

> Thy death and fortunes bid thy followers fly; [IV. xii. 111.]

whilst Dercetas himself is not above taking up Antony's sword with the cynical reflection:

> This sword but shown to Caesar, with this tidings,
> Shall enter me with him. [IV. xii. 112.]

[1] IV. iii. See p. 159 above.

M

It would be hard to envisage a more realistic background to the hero's act of self-destruction. The rats are leaving the sinking ship. That they do so is the result, in the last analysis, of Antony's own folly, but their behaviour at least confirms that, on this plane, there is no future open to him. Cleopatra and the emotions she has roused in him are, for all their deceptive one-sidedness, their foundation on wilful neglect of truth, all that he has to build on in the short period of life remaining to him. This being so, the news that she after all lives comes as the last ironic blow of all. The message, received 'too late', finds echo in Antony's words. 'Too late'; 'too late', indeed; but, by a seeming contradiction very close to his own nature, this last proof of error rouses him to a rally, a return to at least the appearance of confidence:

> do not please sharp fate
> To grace it with your sorrows; bid that welcome
> Which comes to punish us, and we punish it
> Seeming to bear it lightly. [IV. xii. 135.]

The final 'thanks for all', allied to the ghost of a proud memory, 'I have led you oft', comes as an echo, muted into tragic acceptance, of that humanity which has always, even contrary to all the appearances of reason, roused the devotion of Antony's followers.

These events lead directly to the last meeting of Antony with Cleopatra (IV. xiii). where death and love, failure and exaltation, are uniquely blended. Here, and not least because this is one of Shakespeare's supreme poetic achievements, we must still avoid the temptation to simplify; for this – in spite of the dignity which tragedy confers upon it – is the logical end of a process which folly, weakness, and dissolution have made inevitable. Nothing can disguise this reality; but – we must add – the poetry indicates the presence of an emotion not altogether limited by the disaster in which it is involved. Failure and dedication are here counterpointed into a single effect. The building-up of intensities towards the highest moments of the scene, in which the bystanders of the central situation are progressively drawn into its prevailing spirit, rises to a climax in which emotion responds to emotion, suggests an elimination of the baser accidents of personality, those who have produced the disaster whose last stages we are now witnessing, into essential tragedy.

Cleopatra's first words – 'I will never go from hence' – and her attitude to Charmian's plea that she should 'be comforted' assert a dignity appropriate to the tragic mood:

> our size of sorrow,
> Proportion'd to our cause, must be as great
> As that which makes it. [IV. xiii. 4.]

The speech, short as it is, has risen to its height as though to greet the arrival of the dying Antony, round whose failing physical presence, as he approaches in the arms of his bearers, the word 'death' weaves its sombre pattern of finality:

> . . . . is he dead?
> . . . His death's upon him, but not dead. [IV. xiii. 6.]

Our reaction to this opening, though fittingly tragic, will be affected by the presence in Cleopatra's words of a sense of strain, a tone bordering, we may feel, upon hysteria. It will also take into account the fact that her presence at this moment on the monument is due to a device of her own making, and represents not only her last refuge in life but her final deception of the lover whom she has led to his ruin and is about to glorify in his death.

Cleopatra's reception of Antony, which at once follows, again tends towards a transfiguration of the object of emotion, a universalizing of her loss in terms of the greater processes of nature –

> O sun,
> Burn the great sphere thou movest in! darkling stand
> The varying shore o' the world – [IV. xiii. 9.]

before it dies again into the simple concentration which brings her back to the person of the dying hero. 'O Antony!', she exclaims and, repeating the name twice in a lingering fall, calls upon her maids to help her in lifting him up to herself. The emotional intensity thus concentrated on the physical effort required to raise the heavy body is once more dissolved in Antony's simple plea for 'peace'. This is followed by his affirmation of a pride which, once rhetorical and self-consoling, has now become, precisely because he can go no further in life, the reflection of a certain greatness:

> Not Caesar's valour hath o'erthrown Antony,
> But Antony's hath triumph'd on itself. [IV. xiii. 14.]

With its former elements of self-deception modified, though never eliminated by the presence of death, Antony's gesture of assertion can take its place, at least while this scene lasts, in the pattern of deep emotional harmonies to which this final meeting tends.

In further contribution to this poetic effect, Cleopatra's response depends principally upon her reiteration of his name in answer to that which he began:

> So it should be, that none but Antony
> Should conquer Antony; [IV. xiii. 16.]

but this proud assertion is immediately followed by the descent into

grief which the reality of her situation demands: 'but woe 'tis so'.
Antony, in turn, takes up and deepens the sense of tragedy by
stressing, once more through repetition, the extremity of his physical
state: 'I am dying, Egypt, dying'. The word 'dying' will be repeated,
find its place in the harmony of interwoven and contrasted echoes
which determine the emotional content of the scene. At this point,
gradually, almost hesitantly, the speaker's mood rises from the contemplation of his mortality to compass, by contrast, one last faltering
expression of his love. 'Only' – the tentative placing of the word at
the end of the line is superbly appropriate –

> I here importune death awhile, until
> Of many thousand kisses the poor last
> I lay upon thy lips. [IV. xiii. 19.]

Once again, the dramatic effect is best approached through the ebb
and flow of rhythm, the faultless placing of the dominating emotional
words. 'I here importune death awhile, *until*': the line lingers over
'importune', presenting the struggle against mortality by which the
speaker is, briefly and vainly, consumed, and finally, in the assertion
to which the break at 'until' so perfectly leads, the contrast between
the splendours of remembered felicity ('many thousand kisses') and
the burden of present pathos conveyed in 'the poor last' is marvellously registered. The entire speech marries the idea of dedication to
which its conclusion – 'I lay upon thy lips' – tends, to a sense of
faltering which the immanence of death imposes.

Cleopatra's rejoinder answers, by a supremely daring stroke, to
aspects of her nature barely compatible with the tragic effect to
which the poetry is so superbly rising. Faced by this expression of a
dying man's devotion, she shrinks, shows herself afraid. 'I dare not',
she hesitates, adding to the confession a superbly intimate 'dear', and
going on, even as she stresses her fear in broken repetition ('dear my
lord, pardon, I dare not'), to confirm its cause: 'Lest I be taken'.
Having thus revealed a wavering resolution, her following words,
with an inconsequence admirably true to life, turn to defy the fate
personified in their common foe. 'The imperious show' of the 'full-
fortuned Caesar' shall never prevail over her:

> if knife, drugs, serpents, have
> Edge, sting, or operation, I am safe; [IV. xiii. 25.]

the quality of this 'safety', at once rhetorical and faintly hysterical,
the utterance of one who seeks in emphasis of assertion refuge from
the emptiness opening before her, is conveyed in the noticeable
acceleration of the rhythm and in the hurried, slightly breathless
bringing together of the instruments of self-destruction and their

ANTONY AND CLEOPATRA 181

'operation'. It is superbly in character that the thought of Octavia
can still inspire Cleopatra to a heartening expression of disdain. Her
rival is still 'your wife Octavia', whose 'modest eyes' and 'still conclusion' – to the last Cleopatra, in speaking of her rival, couples
contempt and envy – will acquire no 'honour' by 'demurring' upon
her fallen competitor.

Once more the expression of emotion is rounded off in action, as
the dying Antony is lifted to his mistress. Cleopatra, engaged in a
race against death, is eager to draw him to her. 'Come, come,
Antony', she says, with urgent emphasis, and calls on those present
to 'assist', whilst the dying man stresses the struggle against time by
his plea 'O quick, or I am gone!'. At this moment, if ever, dramatic
action is married to its 'metaphysical' content, 'lightness' to 'weight',
the precarious joys of passion to the grief which its impending subjection to mortality imposes. Cleopatra's sorrow expresses itself by the
contrast between the lightness implied in her exclamation – 'Here's
sport indeed' – and her answering concentration upon the weight of
the dying man: 'How heavy weighs my lord!'; this heaviness she
goes on to relate to the sorrow of those who are present at this
melancholy resolution:

> Our strength is all gone into heaviness;
> That makes the weight. [IV. xiii. 33.]

'Heaviness' and sorrow, however, do not stand alone in this marriage
of contrasted harmonies. They are modified by the expression, which
at once follows, of a desire as vain as it is intense – 'Had I great
Juno's power' – and beyond that by the affirmation of a wish
which, though unattainable, carries with it a force of transfiguring
emotion:

> The strong-wing'd Mercury should fetch thee up
> And set thee by Jove's side. [IV. xiii. 35.]

The lines that follow, broken to represent intensity of feeling but
bound together by a superb unifying rhythm, reflect most
immediately the fluctuations in Cleopatra's mind. Desperately
anxious as she is to celebrate her reunion with the dying Antony –
'come a little . . . O come, come, come!' – she is aware, even as she
calls him up to her, of the element of vanity which underlies this
restoration. 'Wishers were ever fools': the conclusion serves to place,
in terms of the real world, the high-flown comparison with the gods
which, in her exaltation, she has just expressed. Each of her words is,
moreover, at this moment bound to the successive stages by which
Antony is visibly lifted to join her. As she at last receives him, 'come'
is replaced by 'welcome, welcome', and death and the life with

which it is interwoven are explicitly brought together. 'Die where thou hast lived', she says, and expresses herself in a delusion as splendid as it is manifestly vain:

> Quicken with kissing: had my lips that power,
> Thus would I wear them out. [IV. xiii. 38.]

In the strength of emotion, at least, a 'quickening' power makes itself felt in this greeting; but the speaker herself confesses that this is an illusion when she goes on to say 'had my lips that power' and ends by clinging to the sense of transforming physical contact upon which, but only for a brief moment, her exaltation rests: 'Thus would I wear them out'.

The guards and women present at this final raising of the emotional tension balance it once more with a return to 'heaviness': 'A heavy sight!'; and Antony, taking up words he has already uttered – 'I am dying, Egypt, dying' – sets the reality of the end now upon him against the varied connotations of Egypt, ranging from the opulent evocation of value to intimations of corruption and promiscuity. Under the effect of this brief rally, he calls for a last draught of the wine which he has so often associated with his moments of fictitious confidence, but now needs, in part indeed for the same reason, but also because it will sustain him in rounding off his tragic career in a last assertion of nobility. With his 'let me speak a little', Cleopatra competes in a strangely daring sublimation of the scolding housewife: 'No, let me speak, and let me rail so high'. Once more, at this point, the presence of external factors is introduced into the complete effect. Antony's last advice to Cleopatra, that she should seek 'honour' and 'safety' with Caesar, is met by her blunt 'They do not go together', in which it is hard to say whether out-raged devotion or a keener sense of her true situation prevails. Antony's last practical recommendation – 'none about Caesar trust but Proculeius' – will turn out to be characteristically mistaken[1]; it produces from Cleopatra a reply –

> My resolution and my hands I'll trust;
> None about Caesar – [IV. xiii. 49.]

which is at once noble and, in the light of what we have known and shall see further of her, self-consciously rhetorical.

Whatever may be the flaws still present in the attitude of the central pair, they are now made momentarily irrelevant in a final surge of tragic feeling. Antony's last speech echoes his earlier efforts at self-justification, but does so in a way which, while it lasts,

---

[1] Proculeius, in fact, is the instrument of Cleopatra's final capture. Se V. ii, and p. 192 below.

achieves a genuine measure of transformation. 'The miserable change now at my end' still haunts his thoughts; but it is felt, at this moment, to be no longer a thing primarily to 'lament or sorrow at', but to be eclipsed in the last evocation of his 'former fortunes',

> Wherein I lived, the greatest prince o' the world,
> The noblest; and do not now basely die,
> Nor cowardly put off my helmet to
> My countryman, a Roman by a Roman
> Valiantly vanquish'd. [IV. xiii. 54.]

Reality and emotion here as ever contradict one another, but in the shadow of death the effect of this contradiction is primarily tragic. Clearly Antony's behaviour has not been consistently that of the 'noblest' of princes. It has been on occasions very different; that is why he has now brought himself to the point of death after a defeat, moreover, which has been ignominious for all that he rhetorically describes himself as 'valiantly vanquish'd'. Yet the speech, uttered on the point of death, which overshadows even the most valid public considerations, bears its own measure of conviction. Though Antony has not turned out 'the greatest prince o' the world', we feel that under other circumstances he might have done so; the aspiration is there, confirmed up to a point (one would not wish to go further) by the admiration it has at times inspired in others. At this moment, the justifying gesture having been made, the spirit declines: –

> Now my spirit is going;
> I can no more – [IV. xiii. 58.]

and Cleopatra is left alone.

Her response to his culminating moment is charged with a marvellous complexity. It is an expression of her own ideal of the 'nobility' enshrined for her in Antony, and now cast down: '*Noblest* of men, woo't die'. As such, and in relation to the reality we have known, it continues to rest upon illusion; but with the difference that now, precisely because Antony is no longer alive to limit it by the presence of his real weakness and failure, Cleopatra's idealization of him rises for the first time to full and unimpeded expression. The immediate result of his death is to confirm her in the acceptance of her own end:

> shall I abide
> In this dull world, which in thy absence is
> No better than a sty? [IV. xiii. 60.]

The poetry that follows is marked by an extraordinary range of

imagery and by an equally extraordinary power of fusing it into a
single and continuous effect:

> O see, my women,
> The crown o' the earth doth melt. My lord!
> O, withered is the garland of the war,
> The soldier's pole is fall'n; young boys and girls
> Are level now with men; the odds is gone,
> And there is nothing left remarkable
> Beneath the visiting moon. [IV. xiii. 62.]

The attempt to separate the images which make up this 'knot
intrinsecate' of poetry reveals the extent of the poet's control. 'The
crown o' the earth' carries on the tone of transcendent royalty with
which Cleopatra has emphasized Antony's greatness and to which
the depth of her own grief responds. The verb 'melt', so repeatedly
used in this play with such a varied range of associations, from
deliquescence to spiritualization, is not factually related to 'crown';
it has been chosen at this point because, whilst continuing to suggest
impermanence, lack of solid actuality, it removes the sense of
harshness from Antony's death and so prepares for the sense of value
which, because she so desperately needs it to confirm her own
resolve, she seeks to confer upon the object of her sorrow. 'The
soldier's pole' is probably the Roman standard of war; but 'pole',
taken with 'crown' and the following 'boys and girls', bears a complex suggestion of May Day, when youthful love and the renewed
life of spring meet annually in triumph. If we set these joyful associations against the corresponding depths of desolation, we shall feel
something of the tremendous emotional range compassed by Cleopatra's utterance. The fact that after Antony's death there is nothing
left 'remarkable' beneath the 'visiting moon' not only indicates the
measure of her loss but implies once more that this union, while it
lasted, reduced all earthly things by comparison to a dull uniformity.
This is, if we will, a splendid expression of illusion and, as such,
limited in value; but it represents also the exaltation of a relevant
truth, which the best moments in Antony's past have in some
measure justified and which, on the plane at least of personal
relationships, has its own validity. To this validity, the concluding
scenes of this tragedy, whilst firmly denying it more than its limited
share of value, pay their proper degree of homage.

The peak of emotion thus reached is followed, as it has been at
each stage, by the intervention of the onlookers, aimed at lowering
the tragic tension into a muted quiescence. 'O, quietness, lady!',
urges Charmian, and is followed by Iras with her exclamation that
she, 'our sovereign', is 'dead, too'. 'Lady!' is taken up by 'Madam!',

and this by Charmian's triple 'O madam, madam, madam!' and, at
the climax, by Iras'

> Royal Egypt!
> Empress!; [IV. xiii. 70.]

and this in turn ends in the superb falling effect of Charmian's contrasted 'Peace, peace, Iras!'. On the note of tranquillity so achieved,
Cleopatra is ready for her last speech. Left to descend from the heights
which she has momentarily touched with Antony and which reality
cannot sustain, she stresses the common humanity that binds her to
those who have served her:

> No more, but e'en a woman, and commanded
> By such poor passion as the maid that milks
> And does the meanest chares. [IV. xiii. 73.]

From this, and moved by her own share of this common 'passion',
she rises to a gesture of reproach to fate:

> It were for me
> To throw my sceptre at the injurious gods,
> To tell them that this world did equal theirs
> Till they had stolen our jewel; [IV. xiii. 75.]

where the value of 'jewel', applied to the object of love, and the pride
of 'sceptre' belong to a complete effect which includes at the same
time an idle attempt at defiance towards the 'injurious gods'. For
the gesture is indeed vain, and its end – doubly effective after the
preceding evocation of 'nobility' – is a desolate vision of life:

> All's but naught;
> Patience is sottish, and impatience does
> Become a dog that's mad; [IV. xiii. 78.]

the only course left open, after this realization of desolation, is to
follow Antony in a statement of seeming self-assertion, by rushing

> into the secret house of death
> Ere death dare come to us. [IV. xiii. 81.]

All this is rhetoric and conveys, side by side with a real sense of loss,
an assertion of boldness and decision which covers in reality
emptiness and shame. It is followed by a rally which proceeds,
however, not from reason, but from a further reaction answering to
the ebb and flow of emotion which has throughout characterized
this scene. Cleopatra calls upon her women to be of 'good cheer',
addresses them as 'noble girls'; the idea of suicide has given her a
momentary sense of confidence, of the only kind now open to her.

This confidence is balanced by the desolate reference to Antony:
'Our lamp is spent, it's out!'. It is only left to bury the dead hero, and
then to seek dignity in the acceptance of self-immolation:

> then what's brave, what's noble,
> Let's do it after the high Roman fashion,
> And make death proud to take us. [IV. xiii. 86.]

We should not underestimate the force of this 'nobility', in so far as
the poetry guarantees it; but neither should we fail to see that it is
based on a rhetorical evasion of facts which Antony's last assertion
began, and leads to desolation and self-destruction. Both judgements
are of the essence of the play. The speech ends, most typically, by
balancing reality, itself transformed in recollection, though not
transcended in death ('This case of that huge spirit now is cold')
against the isolation of those who remain – 'we have no friend' – and
the course of action left open to them, which is 'resolution and the
briefest end'.

VII

From the end of the monument scene, the final stages of the
tragedy turn upon the approaching death of Cleopatra. Whilst
Antony was alive, the political action necessarily concentrated upon
the personal and public disaster which his infatuation implies. Now
that he is dead, the way is open for the expression of another attitude,
valid if only within limits, to this same infatuation; the elements of
sublimation present from the first in the exchanges between the
lovers are allowed relatively free play. No longer checked by the
presence of the real Antony in all his imperfections, Cleopatra's
day-dream can be related, in its unique mixture of splendour and
self-deception, to the deathward movement which is at once its
necessary condition and, by implication, a sign of its limited relevance in terms of the real world. The element of calculation and
intrigue, stressed to the last, now becomes the background to an
assertion of 'nobility' which is at once self-conscious and natural, the
last recognition of failure and the instrument of a genuine emotional
release. In so doing, these final episodes, besides bringing the action
to its foreseen conclusion, provide the play with a 'metaphysical'
crown of poetry.

Before this begins to take shape, we return briefly to Caesar (V. i)
who, in complete control of events, comments competently and with
complete truth on the situation in which Antony has involved
himself:

bid him yield;
Being so frustrate, tell him he mocks
The pauses that he makes. [V. i. 1.]

Antony's political career has been, indeed, a process of surrender, an involving of his better self in the toils of his own vanity; but Caesar, as he speaks, is unaware of his rival's death, which has brought with it the only possible release from that indignity. The tidings of this death are now brought to him by Dercetas.

It is noteworthy that Dercetas, in the act of delivering this news, is able to speak of his former master with a dignity that his own actions have so long and so conspicuously lacked:

Mark Antony I served, who best was worthy
Best to be served: whilst he stood up and spoke,
He was my master, and I wore my life
To spend upon his haters. [V. i. 6.]

If, Antony being dead, he now offers his services to Caesar it is with the detachment of one who is ready, if his offer is not accepted, to 'yield up' his life with something like indifference. As he receives the news, which comes to him as a shock, Caesar, besides living up to the 'public' vocation which demands of him an appropriate gesture, stresses once again the world issues which have hitherto hung upon Antony's life. 'The breaking of so great a thing' should have caused 'the round world' to shake lions into the streets and driven terrified citizens to their doors; for

The death of Antony
Is not a single doom; in the name lay
A moiety of the world. [V. i. 17.]

This, too, is a theme which has been stressed from the beginning and is now to find its appropriate relationship to the final tragedy.

Dercetas' account of the manner of Antony's dying dignifies it with a mixture of 'honour' and lingering pathos:

that self hand
Which writ his honour in the acts it did,
Hath, with the courage which the heart did lend it,
Splitted the heart; [V. i. 21.]

the emphasis is on 'honour', courage, as well as on the final cutting of a knot of complications. The comments which follow, put into the mouths of Caesar and those around him, and once more cumulatively phrased, balance faults and greatness, both of which the dead man possessed in exceeding measure, against a picture of fallen nobility;

for this, as Octavius says, with a tendency to tears which, though rare in him, we need not ascribe to insincerity,

> is tidings
> To wash the eyes of kings. [V. i. 27.]

For Maecenas, the 'taints and honours' of the dead man 'waged equal'; and for Agrippa,

> A rarer spirit never
> Did steer humanity; but you, gods, will give us
> Some faults to make us men. [V. i. 31.]

The repeated stressing of Antony's faults should not lead us to deny his greatness, to which death now enables a freer expression to be given; even in the opening speech of the play, Philo had asserted the magnanimity which fits a 'triple pillar of the world' as well as its degeneration into 'dotage'. Caesar himself is now 'touched', not only by something like a generous, if still 'public', impulse, but by a sense of the fallibility which, in 'nature', he shares with his dead rival.

This sense of fallibility now enters increasingly into the complete effect. Agrippa's further observation –

> strange it is
> That nature must compel us to lament
> Our most persisted deeds – [V. i. 28.]

stresses an element of necessity which modifies all conceptions of political competence and control. We should not simplify the spirit of this, either by accepting these valedictory speeches at their own estimate or by denying them all value. The truth, perhaps, is that a common fate is felt to hang over the entire action, to affect the victors scarcely less than the vanquished. As Maecenas puts it, still speaking of Caesar's stirring into emotion,

> When such a spacious mirror's set before him,
> He needs must see himself. [V. i. 34.]

The effect of 'spacious' contributes yet again to the sense of universal issues, world decisions, which has from the first provided this tragedy with an amplitude of its own; the verse, moreover, is throughout superb in ease and power, in its capacity to take the vastest effects effortlessly in its stride. Caesar's epitaph for Antony, to which all these exchanges have been leading, renders still more explicit the references to a common fate. 'O Antony!', he begins, 'I have follow'd thee to this'. Reflecting upon the tragic relationship which at once brought them together as triumvirs and involved them in separation, he finds in it both the signs of a mortal disease –

We do lance
Diseases in our bodies – [V. i. 36.]

and the expression of a rivalry which imposed upon each of them the
necessity either of overcoming his opponent or of falling before him:

I must perforce
Have shown to thee such a declining day
Or look on thine; we could not stall together
In the whole world. [V. i. 37.]

If, behind this attitude, there is a sense of fatality, so that the
speaker feels himself for once to be something less than the complete
master of his destiny, this sense, as expressed in the lines which
follow, binds Caesar in a certain relationship to his 'competitor'.
Once again, the gesture is both public, decorous, and, we may
agree, something more.

Let me lament
With tears as sovereign as the blood of hearts; [V. i. 40.]

this fine expression of grief carries with it its own conviction, justifies
the salute of the dead Antony as 'brother', 'competitor' (but in what
is now, and only now, with Caesar's rival safely dead, seen as a noble
and world-embracing contest) and 'mate of empire'. The apostrophe
rises to its climax in the exaltation of his defeated enemy as

The arm of mine own body, and the heart
Where mine his thoughts did kindle, [V. i. 45.]

before it falls away into the contemplation of the 'stars unreconcili-
able' which have brought as their end death and ruin, dividing 'our
equalness to this'.

Caesar, however, remains, in spite of and beyond these accessions
of feeling, a figure dedicated to his public purposes; and so we are
not surprised when the pressure of business interrupts these more
intimate reflections: 'I will tell you at some meeter season'. The
arrival of the messenger with news of Cleopatra is met with a further
graphic phrase: 'The business of this man looks out of him', in
which we may feel Caesar turning from death to life, from issues that
are wound up to those that still call for his attention. Cleopatra, as
now reported, approaches the conqueror with a wary deference that
seems to contrast with her recent declarations of firm purpose.
'Confined in all she has, her monument' she awaits the declaration
of the conqueror's will, so that

she preparedly may frame herself
To the way she's forced to. [V. i. 55.]

Caesar's reply is expressed in terms of politic generosity, as we by
now expect of him. She shall be treated 'kindly', for Octavius, with
at least one eye on the public effect of his acts,

> cannot live
> To be ungentle. [V. i. 59.]

This, at least, in view of what is shortly to come, is false, and Caesar,
whose future plans are already clear in his mind, knows it to be so.
His attitude represents a return to the world of expediency from
which deeper feelings, of a kind not normally his, have only momentarily diverted him. His instructions to Proculeius ('Go and say . . .',
'Give her what comforts . . .') are clearly spoken in detachment,
with a mind to the stratagems which now dominate his purposes.
Admitting, indeed, the 'greatness' which may lead Cleopatra to
take her own life –

> Lest in her greatness by some mortal stroke
> She do defeat us – [V. i. 64.]

it is none the less the repercussion upon his triumph that remains
uppermost in his cold, clear mind:

> for her life in Rome
> Would be eternal in our triumph. [V. i. 65.]

Public effect and the justification of his own acts are, indeed, the
final impressions with which Octavius leaves us; for the prosperity of
his cause requires that it be proved

> How hardly I was drawn into this war, [V. i. 74.]

and how 'calm and gentle' have been the proceedings which have
brought him victory.

All this is little more than a necessary preparation for what remains
of the tragedy, the purpose of which is the bringing of Cleopatra to
the centre of the stage. This is accomplished in the process which, in
the last great scene (V. ii), leads to the final resolution. It opens,
significantly, with her assertion that the very completeness of her
'desolation' may be the prelude to what she calls – though, in point
of fact, death is her only conceivable goal – a 'better life'; for, after
all, in her relationship with the living Antony there has been from
the first no real possibility of a durable and vital experience. Now in
her isolation, she can begin to persuade herself that Caesar himself,
no less 'Fortune's knave' than any other human being (and we have
seen Caesar himself touching on this theme), is in some sense a
petty' instrument of fortune, a mere 'minister of her will'. There is,

of course, an element of self-deception here, a blindness to reality which conditions the assertion of resolve; and so much is implied in the very fact that the true direction of the scene is set consistently deathward. Everything that is to follow is based, in a very relevant sense, upon illusion, upon the determined exclusion of reality which has from the first been implied in the tragic relationship which has now found in death its natural and appropriate conclusion; but the illusion is after all itself a manifestation of life and as such capable of genuine tragic significance. Whilst admitting at each stage the presence of other, more desolate realities, we need not impose upon an experience the poetic expression of which guarantees its value a unilateral moral interpretation which belongs to, but does not exhaust, the meaning of the play.

The presence of death is indicated, in the first speech, in a manner as complex as it is intensely poetical:

> it is great
> To do that thing that ends all other deeds;
> Which shackles accidents and bolts up change;
> Which sleeps, and never palates more the dug,
> The beggar's nurse and Caesar's. [V. ii. 4.]

Once more we are in the presence of the astounding breadth of reference which typifies the imagery of this play; and once more each element in it contributes to the total effect. That the intention of suicide is, at this moment, and in the mind of this speaker, nobly conceived is beyond doubt. True though it is that Cleopatra is here once more taking up a rhetorical attitude, steeling herself for a decision which has in fact been imposed upon her, and which so much in her intensely vital nature must reject, her expression of this attitude carries its own assurance of tragic magnanimity. The act she envisages is 'great' precisely in that it ends her slavery to the world of contingencies, because – in the splendid emphasis of her own phrase – 'it *shackles* accidents and *bolts up* change'. The emotional conviction thus conveyed, though no more than a part of the total effect, needs to be given its due weight in the whole. The prisoner of her fate now aims to take her own fate captive. She does so, moreover, by an act which she conceives to be as gentle as 'sleep', a sleep differentiated only by its eternity from that enjoyed, in all times and conditions, by the baby at rest on its mother's breast. Only – it is necessary to remember, lest the beauty of the image induces a mood of surrender, of unqualified acceptance – the baby will turn out to be the asp and the sleep, though associated with rest and fulfilment, will be that of death.

Proculeius, entering at the end of this introduction, sets on foot

Caesar's stratagem. Cleopatra, recalling the dying Antony's recommendation, foresees its fallibility:

> I do not greatly care to be deceived,
> That have no use for trusting. [V. ii. 14.]

In this mood, she is still ready, as a last concession to the world of
public realities, to 'beg' on behalf of her child –

> if he please
> To give me conquer'd Egypt for my son – [V. ii. 18.]

though she makes it clear at the same time that she is asking for
'mine own' and as a queen whose right it is to beg 'no less than a
kingdom'. The balance of negotiation and inner reserve is
maintained throughout. Proculeius covers the bare bones of Caesar's
intrigue with a gesture of generosity; Cleopatra need not fear, ior
she has fallen into the 'princely hand' of one

> Who is so full of grace that it flows over
> On all that need, [V. ii. 24.]

who is, moreover,

> A conqueror that will pray in aid for kindness,
> Where he for grace is kneel'd to. [V. ii. 27.]

The effect of imagery of this type, associated throughout Shakespeare's greater plays with the magnanimity of true and beneficent
royalty, must be set against the knowledge that a stratagem, an
opposition of countering intrigues, is being pursued on either side.
Cleopatra's reply is non-committal, even faintly ironical. She is the
'vassal' who can only offer Caesar 'the greatness he has got', who is
'hourly' learning 'a doctrine of obedience' unfamiliar to a queen and
who is now ready to 'look him i' the face'.

The blow which at once falls is made doubly cruel by Gallus'
comment – 'You see how easily she may be surprised' – following on
Proculeius' assurance that his master pities her misfortunes. There
could be no better reminder that in the external world subtleties of
the kind indulged in by Cleopatra have no place. When she protests
that even the release of suicide, of a death 'that rids our dogs of
anguish', has been taken from her, Proculeius admits frankly that
Caesar's gestures of bounty have a public end in view:

> let the world see
> His nobleness well acted, which your death
> Will never let come forth. [V. ii. 44.]

Cleopatra, looking to the future, can only associate regality with

death. 'Where art thou, death?' she exclaims, and adds the invocation which anticipates her end:

> Come hither, come! come, come, and take a queen
> Worth many babes and beggars! [V. ii. 46.]

There follows a piece of railing which might, under other circumstances, appear 'idle talk', but which is also splendidly in character:

> Sir, I will eat no meat, I'll not drink, sir –
> I'll not sleep neither. [V. ii. 49.]

The effect is to combine resolution with something very like the
scolding of a shrew; and the motives revealed are many, outraged
vanity and resentment against 'dull Octavia' being not the least
among them. At the end of the tirade there is, besides more than a
touch of hysteria, a return to the fundamental theme of death,
envisaged, with a trace of morbid complacency, as 'a gentle grave',
and the renewed association of the 'slime' of Nile, loathsome and
corrupt, with the end that so clearly overshadows her:

> Rather a ditch in Egypt
> Be gentle grave unto me! rather on Nilus' mud
> Lay me stark naked, and let the waterflies
> Blow me into abhorring! [V. ii. 57.]

At this point, it is the element of decay that prevails. Death is contemplated not in exaltation but as a refuge, desperately and hys-
terically conceived by one whose entire nature impels her to fear
and repudiate it, from the intolerable realities of life. Proculeius, as
he leaves, can only obtain from Cleopatra that her thoughts are
fixed upon annihilation: 'Say, I would die'.

With the thought of death, however, Cleopatra withdraws, in
order to gain confidence, into a world of dreams, into a last exaltation, through memory, of the Antony whom she has lost in real
life. To the presumptuous and inexperienced Dolabella, who has
replaced Proculeius as her gaoler, she turns with an indifference
calculated to entice, to mould him to her purposes. She 'cannot tell'
whether she has heard of him, being wrapped in 'dreams' which she
knows to be absurd in the eyes of the world:

> I dream'd there was an emperor Antony;
> O, such another sleep, that I might see
> But such another man! [V. ii. 76.]

It is to be noted in what follows that the emphasis is on a dream-like
quality which at once stresses unreality and makes possible, within
limits, the transformation of the common stuff of experience.

N

Cleopatra is, if we will, indulging a day-dream to conceal from herself
the magnitude of her disaster; but – we must add – the quality of the
dream is such that only in tragedy can it find its appropriate consummation.

The account of the 'dream' is, by common consent, one of the
play's culminating moments. Once more the breadth of reference is
only paralleled by the power which can fuse impressions so diverse, so
deliberately remote from common experience, into a single
unstrained effect:

> CLEOPATRA His face was as the heavens; and therein stuck
> A sun and moon, which kept their course, and
> lighted
> The little O, the earth.
> DOLABELLA Most sovereign creature –
> CLEOPATRA His legs bestride the ocean; his rear'd arm
> Crested the world: his voice was propertied
> As all the tuned spheres, and that to friends;
> But when he meant to quail and shake the orb,
> He was as rattling thunder. For his bounty,
> There was no winter in't; an autumn[1] 'twas
> That grew the more by reaping; his delights
> Were dolphin-like; they show'd his back above
> The element they lived in; in his livery
> Walked crowns and crownets; realms and islands
> were
> As plates dropp'd from his pocket. [V. ii. 79.]

Antony the microcosm of the universe whose face was 'as the
heavens', who 'bestrid the ocean' like a Colossus and 'crested the
world' with a heraldic manifestation of splendour: Antony the
supreme example of the munificence which is the crowning glory
of a prince: Antony whose creative eminence showed itself in a
'bounty' to which imagination expressly lends a lengendary remoteness distinguishing it from the natural order by its participation in a
never-failing spring and by the effortless mastery of his 'delights';
all this is felt to be at once emotionally true, the transfiguration of a
conceivable experience, and realistically false, an apotheosis and an
illusion. The image of the dolphin, marvellous in its audacity,
deliberately carries the effect away from reality into the realm of the
imagination to which it belongs; and the figure who is finally evoked
as dropping kingdoms ('realms and islands') carelessly, in easy
generosity, 'from his pocket' answers to a world of fairy-tale, subli-
mated indeed by the tragic imagination, but deliberately placed at a

---

[1] The text at this point is uncertain. The Folio reads 'Antony'; I have followed
the most common, and plausible, emendation.

distance from common reality. This supersession of fact by legend is the essence of the effect. That such an apostrophe can be accepted as natural, unstrained, is a sign that we are dealing with emotions of no ordinary depth; but that Dolabella explicitly denies, when Cleopatra challenges him, that it corresponds to reality –

> CLEOPATRA Think you there was, or might be, such a man
> As this I dream'd of?
> DOLABELLA Gentle madam no – [V. ii. 93.]

warns us against making exclusive claims upon its place in the whole conception. Resting originally upon a kind of hysteria, Cleopatra's emotions are gradually being assimilated to the rising emotional temper of the scene; but the origin in unreality remains, and is relevant to the last. Cleopatra is living in a world – the only one left open to her – which is the projection of her own desires. She defends that world from the imputation of illusion ('You lie, up to the hearing of the gods') because upon its possible validity rests her capacity to believe in herself, to assure herself that her relationship with Antony has been more than a mass of self-deceptions leading to ruin; but it is a world valid only to the imagination, where it alone, without reference to the external circumstances which have already destroyed it, can transform itself by the intensity of its own operation into a kind of reality:

> if there be, or ever were, one such,
> It's past the size of dreaming; [V. ii. 96.]

and again, with more meaning still,

> nature wants stuff
> To vie strange forms with fancy; yet to imagine
> An Antony, were nature's piece 'gainst fancy,
> Condemning shadows quite. [V. ii. 97.]

The vision, while it lasts, is splendidly valid, even vital in its projection of the transformed stuff of experience; but only death, the negation of all vitality, can prevent an awakening from it. For that reason, if for no other, Cleopatra is resolved to die.

The immediate effect of this outburst is to obtain from Dolabella an admission of Caesar's true intentions. When Cleopatra asks 'He'll lead me then in triumph?', the reply, uneasily covered by the phrase 'Though he be honourable', is simple and direct: 'Madam, he will; I know't'. When Caesar himself appears his attitude, deeply scornful in its implications, confirms in effect what has just been said. 'Which is the queen of Egypt?'; this is the real world intruding with a vengeance upon that of the imagination. Octavius, indeed,

whilst making a show of generosity, is at some pains to stress the
indignities to which he has been subjected:

> The record of what injuries you did us,
> Though written in our flesh, we shall remember
> As things but done by chance. [V. ii. 117.]

The gesture of generosity is made, but we know that nothing has in
fact been conceded; whilst Cleopatra's attitude, the only one open
to her at this, her moment of truth, is one of external submission:

>   my master and my lord
>   I must obey. [V. ii. 115.]

The following exchange between the master of the world and his
prisoner covers in reality a fencing for time. Cleopatra is ready to
confess to the 'frailties' which have often 'shamed our sex'; Caesar in
return makes a show of authoritative generosity – 'We will extenuate
rather than enforce' – whilst being careful to insert a touch of bribery
and the suggestion of a threat:

>   if you seek
>   To lay on me a cruelty by taking
>   Antony's course, you shall bereave yourself
>   Of my good purposes and put your children
>   To that destruction which I'll guard them from
>   If thereon you'll rely. [V. ii. 127.]

Both parties to the exchange know that the words they use are
designed to conceal their true intentions and that the resolution of
their mutual situation lies elsewhere.

There follows the odd, and at first sight disconcerting, episode
initiated by Cleopatra's presentation to Caesar of an inventory of her
possessions. The 'omissions' from this list are disclosed by Seleucus
who reveals that she has retained 'Enough to purchase what you
have made known'. Whether what she has reserved denotes a trick
to deceive Caesar by playing for time, as a comparison with
Plutarch's narratives would suggest,[1] or whether it indicates a deeper
instability of purpose, is left, perhaps deliberately, unclear. Caesar,
at all events, takes it as one more proof of weakness and excuses her,
in an off-hand manner, with the contempt proper to a conqueror
who is also a man of the world:

>   Nay, blush not, Cleopatra: I approve
>   Your wisdom in the deed. [V. ii. 148.]

---

[1] Plutarch's account of the incident clearly favours this interpretation; but this is
not necessarily decisive.

Cleopatra reacts more intimately to the exposure, falls into a characteristic surrender to hysteria, not unlike the mood of excess with which she formerly greeted the messengers who brought news of Antony's marriage.[1] Equally typical is her recovery of poise. Turning from the shock of this exposure, she takes refuge in a pose of dignity, seeing herself once more as a queen receiving her conqueror as a visitor – 'thou vouchsafing here to visit me' – and accusing her servant of vile envy. To this return to dignity she adds a picture of herself as a frail woman who has been led to reserve what she calls 'lady trifles' to greet 'modern friends withal' and – more daringly still – to induce the mediation of Livia and none other than Octavia and who has now been shamefully traduced by 'one that I have bred'.

All this fails entirely to move Octavius from the prosecution of his ends. Taking his leave, he once more shows that condescension which is so much in character:

> Caesar's no merchant, to make prize with you
> Of things that merchants sold. [V. ii. 182.]

The gesture costs little to one who, after all, has everything in his hands, and it implies a contemptuous rebuke. His last words to Cleopatra, clashing as they do with what we (and she) know that he has already decided, are consciously false:

> Make not your thoughts your prisons: no, dear queen;
> For we intend so to dispose you as
> Yourself shall give us counsel. [V. ii. 184.]

The final exchange of courtesies – 'my master and my lord!': 'Not so. Adieu!' – is as laconic as it is finally unreal. On either side, a known truth is being carefully kept back, and the parting between Caesar and his prisoner (it is also their first meeting) ends on a note of recognized and accepted fiction.

Cleopatra's first words to her maids after Octavius has taken his leave show that she is aware of her true situation:

> He words me, girls, he words me, that I should not
> Be noble to myself. [V. ii. 190.]

Consistency to herself, even in the death which her relations with Antony have brought upon her, is the only course now open to her. Iras confirms this with another of those responses which, by dissolving fact into poetry, are so often used to build up the crowning effects of this play:

[1] II. v. See p. 121 above.

> Finish, good lady; the bright day is done,
> And we are for the dark. [V. ii. 192.]

The poetic note once more removes the action from the sphere of common reality. Dolabella, returning briefly, confirms that Caesar intends to exhibit her in his triumph. Every way of escape but that represented by self-destruction is now blocked. Cleopatra anticipates her shame, foresees the exposure of 'our Alexandrian revels' and the reducing to indignity of those relations to Antony –

> Antony
> Shall be brought drunken forth, and I shall see
> Some squeaking Cleopatra boy my greatness
> I' the posture of a whore – [V. ii. 217.]

which, however discreditable they have been, are the only thing left to her in memory and have become, after his death, exalted in an imagination from which very self-respect forbids her to contemplate an awakening. From now on, Cleopatra's decisions are directed to the assertion of that 'nobility' which is her only remaining refuge from the awareness of total ruin. The exchange with Iras ends, accordingly, on a renewed note of resolution, on the intent, rhetorical and self-consciously exalted in kind, but not on that account the less capable of being taken up into the final affirmation, to 'fool' Caesar's preparations and to conquer 'his most absurd intents'.

As a first step in putting this determination into effect Cleopatra proceeds to attire herself as a queen, the queen who formerly greeted Antony on her barge of triumph:

> I am again for Cydnus
> To meet Mark Antony. [V. ii. 227.]

Perhaps, being what she is, she needs this pageantry to confirm herself in her resolve; but the effect is, at all events, by now at least as tragic as it is pathetic and self-animating. The maids, from now on grouped round their mistress as acolytes of the mystery of death, are ennobled by their participation in her resolve: Charmian she addresses as 'noble' and the intensity of her emotion finds issue in the sublime homeliness of phrase which has, from time to time, lent its legendary and folk-tale quality to the transmuting effect:

> when thou hast done this chare I'll give thee leave
> To play till doomsday. [V. ii. 230.]

Left alone to await the Clown who is to bring the instrument of liberation, she stresses once more the 'noble deed' which is to bring her 'liberty' and announces the end of all possible vacillation:

My resolution's placed, and I have nothing
Of woman in me; now from head to foot
I am marble-constant; now the fleeting moon
No planet is of mine. [V. ii. 237.]

Even now, however, this is set against a contrary evaluation. The
Clown, entering with 'the pretty worm of Nilus', that 'kills and pains
not', not only makes a most effective break in the growing tension,
but speaks with the voice of a necessary realism against Cleopatra's
entranced contemplation of self-justifying poetic illusion – 'indeed,
there is no goodness in the worm . . . it is not worth the feeding' –
and, by a vital paradox, adds through his very mistakes to the equation of death and immortality that is building itself up, with a rare
mixture of tragedy and self-deception, round her approaching end:
'his biting is immortal; those that do die of it do seldom or never
recover'. There could be no better way of stating the ambiguous
nature of the resolution which Cleopatra now covets, and which she
finally desires because, besides the proof of failure, it is the only
escape from the situation to which an illusion, however intensely
lived, however seemingly transforming in its effects, has logically
and inexorably brought her.

With Cleopatra crowned, and in possession of the 'worm', with her
maids grouped round her to participate in her end, her last speeches
open with an assertion of 'immortal longings'. The immortality to
which she now aspires stands at the opposite pole to the 'dungy
earth' from which her love sprang and in virtue of which Antony's
fall and her death were both inevitable. Yet the 'immortality' thus
evoked, though limited and precarious, has a content of 'nobility'
which memory supplies; it is the highest assertion of her love for the
dead and now exalted Antony, whom she can call – precisely because
he is no longer there, and for the first time in the play – 'Husband!'.
In the light of this association of love and immortality, death
assumes – for the duration of this incident – a fresh poetic function. It
becomes a dissolution, imposes a purging of all the grosser elements
upon which love itself has been based and which are now in the
process of returning to the earth from which they sprang:

I am fire and air; my other elements
I give to baser life. [V. ii. 291.]

On the edge of death, the sense of dissolution acquires a further
significance; only the purest strains of feeling remain in Cleopatra,
and these, by a paradox particularly significant at this moment,
which are most fully, most intensely alive. From a great distance, as
it seems, we are reminded of the other elements of 'baser life', the

earth and fertile slime from which love sprang, with which its degradation was associated in Egypt, and in virtue of which defeat and
death were inevitable; but defeat and death themselves have now
become subdued, at least in the speaker's exaltation, to the 'immortal
longings' which they have brought into being, and the adverse
fortunes of the world are dismissed as

> The luck of Caesar, which the gods give men
> To excuse their after wrath. [V. ii. 288.]

In spite of this note of transcendence, however, the firm foundation
on the senses of the imagery by which the speech achieves its aim is
essential to the full effect. Cleopatra's words convey no abstract
triumph imposed upon what has gone before. The elements of 'fire'
and 'air' which now predominate in her mind represent a continual
refining process from the comparative earthiness of the opening, and
the effect of her longing is reinforced by the keenly sensed reference
to the 'juice of Egypt's grape', suggesting all that is most alive and
delicate in the activity of the senses.

As the play draws to its close, it assumes more and more the quality
of an intense and cumulative building up of echoing responses.
'Farewell, kind Charmian': 'Iras, long farewell'; the action proceeds
to its conclusion in the exaltation which the contemplation of death
now inspires, and the 'farewell' is balanced by the effect of Iras' fall:
'Have I the aspic in my lips? Dost fall?'. The impression of continuity
balanced by infinite remoteness is appropriate to the whole development of a tragedy in which self-indulgence and valid emotion are
brought together in the death which is their common end. Shakespeare has so refined, so intensified his love poetry by a progressive
distillation of sensible experience that it is now able to assimilate the
apparently incompatible fact of death, which is simultaneously
release and the reflection of exemplary moral failure. The exaltation
of sensuality, through and beyond its element of self-confessed
indulgence, is finally complete in the perfection of

> The stroke of death is as a lover's pinch,
> Which hurts and is desired. [V. ii. 297.]

Only Cleopatra could speak thus naturally, remembering her past as
a woman in the very act of assuming 'immortality'; but, in so speaking at a moment when her thoughts are concentrated upon the final
resolution, she transcends her former self. 'Hurts' and 'desired' which
seem so contradictory, which recall the equivocal pleasures for which
she has lived, now reinforce one another in a splendid balance of
sensations which its approaching consummation in death at once
confirms and places; the pain implied in 'hurts' is so delicately, so

intensely felt, that it becomes fused with the keenness of the lover's
desire. An emotion originally corrupt, luxurious in kind, has
become, besides that, something more, a taking up of the sensible
into a world that shadows permanence; a gesture which originated in
rhetoric and deception, and which retains its connection with these
base realities, has been assumed into tragic validity. For the moment,
at least, we can follow Cleopatra when she asserts that, by her death,
Iras has told the world 'it is not worth leave-taking'. The weight of
emotion, which threatens at this point to become intolerable, is
again broken, at once interrupted and sustained, by Charmian's
interjection:

> Dissolve, thick cloud, and rain, that I may say
> The gods themselves do weep, [V. ii. 301.]

where the idea of dissolution assumes a fresh, a more fully natural
sense. To it Cleopatra replies by raising herself further above sub-
lunary 'baseness' and by recalling once more 'the *curled* Antony', in
a final sublimation of what was once indulgent sentiment and has
now become, in her mind and in relation to the resolution she has
accepted, 'noble' dedication:

> He'll make demand of her, and spend that kiss
> Which is my heaven to have. [V. ii. 304.]

The serpent, seen in this fresh light, becomes a 'mortal wretch',
whose 'sharp' teeth will serve to prove great Caesar 'ass unpolicied'.
The death which is the final proof of failure, to which everything in
this equivocal relationship has tended, becomes now an untying of
'this knot intrinsecate' of body and soul, of infinite desires subject,
in life, to earthly limitation and adverse circumstance. This is,
perhaps, the supreme assertion of the 'metaphysical' effect to which
so much of this episode tends.

It is only left for the cumulative force of the balanced antiphonal
utterances to carry the tragic action forward to its consummation.
Charmian's 'O eastern star!' is met by Cleopatra's call to 'Peace',
and by her recourse to the image, so splendid and so illusory, of the
babe at the breast:

> Dost thou not see my baby at my breast
> That sucks the nurse asleep? [V. ii. 311.]

This, of course, is at once peace and self-delusion – for the baby she
has taken to herself is death, and all her past career has led her to
this negation of true life – but the emotion is now so concentrated
on death that it cannot be held, and Charmain's simple 'Break,
break!' is followed by the resolution of 'As sweet as balm, as soft as

air, as gentle', by the last recalling of Antony, and by the sense of
triumph implied in Cleopatra's last broken exclamation: 'What
should I stay –'. Charmian, having completed the phrase by a
reference to 'this vile world', can only straighten the crown which
has been left 'awry' and then, recalling the very words which her
mistress has so recently addressed to her,[1] confirm her own devoted
resolve, with exultant and child-like simplicity, in terms of 'play'.

The entry of Caesar's envoy, bringing back the external, the real
world, breaks against Charmian's triumphant 'too slow a messenger'
and the final confidence of her defiant farewell:

> It is well done, and fitting for a princess
> Descended of so many royal kings. [V. ii. 328.]

Caesar himself, when he arrives, can only utter one of those fitting
epitaphs in which he specializes:

> Bravest at the last,
> She levell'd at our purposes, and being royal
> Took her own way, [V. ii. 336.]

and follow it by the profounder reflection:

> she looks like sleep,
> As she would catch another Antony.
> In her strong toil of grace. [V. ii. 347.]

In this last phrase, something very like the spirit which animates the
entire presentation of Cleopatra finds its summary. For Antony,
Cleopatra's fascination has been a 'toil', a snare leading to the downfall of both of them; which he had accepted for both of them once he
had fallen victim to her enchantment; but it was also a toil of 'grace',
in which beauty and, at the supreme moment of dedication in death,
a certain fitness have made themselves apparent.

The whole development of the play has moved consistently towards this point. The balancing of the generosity which Antony's
folly has at times implied against Caesar's mixture of competence,
public vocation, and successful meanness; the gradual ascent of the
love imagery, in its very progress towards failure and self-destruction,
from earth and 'slime' to 'fire and air'; the corresponding ascent of
Cleopatra herself, provoked by circumstance, from sensual frivolity
to the tragic affirmation of the only 'nobility' left to her; all these
are parts of one great process which has needed death to complete it.
For death, which had seemed to be in Shakespeare's early tragedies
incontrovertible evidence of the subjection of love and human values

---

[1] . . . when thou hast done this chare I'll give thee leave
To play till doomsday. [V. ii. 230.]

to time,[1] has now become an instrument of release, the necessary condition of an experience which, though dependent upon circumstance, is, by virtue of its intensity and by the intimations of *value* which accompany even its more dubious manifestations, in some sense incommensurate with them – that is, even in its stressed weaknesses, capable of a glimpse of 'immortality'. This effect, moreover, is compatible with a vision of death as the inevitable end of a line of conduct in which folly and self-indulgence have consistently played their part. The emotions of Antony and Cleopatra have been built upon 'dungy earth', upon 'Nilus' slime', and so upon the impermanence which the nature of these elements implies; but, just as earth and slime can be quickened into life, briefly and elusively indeed, but none the less truly, by the action upon them of fire and air, so the very elements of waste and vanity which nurtured this tragedy have become, by the time it reaches its necessary conclusion, constituent ingredients in the creation of an intuition of immortality.

[1] See my *Approach to Shakespeare* (London, 1957), and more particularly the chapters on the Sonnets and Problem Plays.

4
Coriolanus

Conclusion

4

Coriolanus

UNLIKE *Julius Caesar* and *Antony and Cleopatra*, there seems to be no evidence that the story of *Coriolanus* attracted any Elizabethan dramatist before Shakespeare turned to it. The fact may testify to the special nature of the interests which attracted him to this episode of Roman History, and which produced a play about which opinion has notably differed. Controversy turns[1] on the play's tragic quality, upon the relation of an admittedly consummate study of public issues to the strangely contradictory figure of the hero. That *Coriolanus* is conceived with admirable dramatic logic is generally recognized; doubt as to the value of the play by the highest standard only seems to arise when we ask ourselves whether it touches the deeper sources of emotion, whether the hero's disaster, so ironic and detached in its presentation, so clearly the result of inadequacies in his own moral make-up, can affect us as truly and universally tragic in its significance.

Irony, indeed, is the key to the play's peculiar effect. Something of its quality imposes itself upon the style which reflects, at the culminating moments, feeling intense indeed, but somehow involved in a struggle against constraint, forcing itself to the surface in passionate and often distorted outbursts of narrow and concentrated emotion. The style, in turn, corresponds to the presentation of human motives. In few plays do the results of action differ so consistently from what the agents, in their imperfect grasp of reality, propose. Coriolanus, convinced that the principles for which he so assertively stands are the only possible foundations for a sound Roman polity, affirms these principles so unilaterally that he transforms himself into the instrument which brings his own city, and himself with it, to the verge of ruin; his enemies, appealing ostensibly to a more comprehensive vision of the public good, are in fact moved by desires primarily selfish in kind and find themselves finally involved in the disaster which they have brought upon themselves. The result is a tragedy unusual, perhaps unique in kind, in which a largely sardonic estimate of human possibilities, personal and political alike, leads to a desolate and disconcerting conclusion.

[1] See the discussion between D. J. Enright (*Coriolanus: Tragedy or Debate?*) and I. B. Browning (*Coriolanus: Boy of Tears*), published in *Essays in Criticism*, 1954 and 1955.

I

It would be hard to imagine a greater gulf than that which separates the Rome of *Coriolanus* from that of *Antony and Cleopatra*. The poetry of the latter play expands with effortless ease to take in the fortunes of a world in conflict; that of the former achieves its effects through intense concentration upon the familiar and the material.[1] The prevailing imagery of *Coriolanus* is rigid and unadorned in its simplicity, more appropriate to a village or a country town than to a capital of historical significance. The aristocratic ladies of Rome sit at home upon their 'stools'[2] and the people carry 'bats and clubs'[3] to their riots; the action abounds in references to simple pastimes, such as 'bowls',[4] or turns upon disputes over the immediate necessities of life, 'coal', 'corn', and 'bread'.[5] To a great extent the difference is imposed by history; whereas the events which provided the background to Antony's fall concerned an empire which spanned the known world, those which condition the tragedy of Coriolanus are concentrated within the limits of a city and its immediate surroundings, reflect the tension between its classes, the threat to its indispensable unity.

This tension, this threat, marks the struggle for power in a world at once restricted and pitiless. The sense of this struggle is conveyed almost immediately by the patrician Menenius when, in order to rebuke the citizenry for their rebellion against constituted authority, he embarks upon a fable which reveals more than he can himself realize of the true situation in Rome. The central image of the fable, derived from Plutarch but considerably developed, is that of the functioning of the human body in its related parts:

> There was a time when all the body's members
> Rebell'd against the belly; thus accused it:
> That only like a gulf it did remain
> I' the midst of the body, idle and unactive,
> Still cupboarding the viand, never bearing
> Like labour with the rest; where the other instruments
> Did see and hear, devise, instruct, walk, feel,
> And, mutually participate, did minister
> Unto the appetite and affection common
> Of the whole body. [I. i. 101.]

The wording of the parable tends to the transformation of a political

---

[1] This aspect of the poetry of *Coriolanus* has been well brought out by G. Wilson Knight in *The Imperial Theme* (Oxford, 1930).

[2] Stage direction to I. iii.   [3] I. i. 59.

[4] V. ii. 20.   [5] I. i, and *passim*.

common-place, a theoretical vindication of natural 'degree', into a criticism, not of this attitude or that, but of Roman society itself. The impression of a general obstruction of all vital activity communicates itself through the unhealthy stagnation of 'idle and unactive', the coarseness of 'cupboarding'. These effects are set against the very noticeable livening of the verse when Menenius turns to the 'other instruments', the senses and active parts of the body which represent, however, not the class he is defending but its enemies. These contrasted elements, thus concentrated, in a manner profoundly typical of the play, upon images of food and digestion, answer to the real state of the Roman polity. Stagnation and mutual distrust, mirroring the ruthlessness of contrary appetites for power, are the principal images by which we are introduced to the public issues of *Coriolanus*.

It does not follow that our sympathies are to lie, as Menenius intends, solely with the patricians. He criticizes justly the failure of the populace to recognize the part played by their betters in the social organism; but there is a sense in which the figure he uses to illustrate his point turns the argument against his own thesis. The patricians are presented in the likeness of the 'belly'; and though this was indispensable to the proper functioning of the body it was also, in the view of its detractors, 'idle and unactive', self-satisfied and complacent in the security of its position. In this connection we should not overlook that brilliant stroke,

with a kind of smile,
Which ne'er came from the lungs, but even thus, [I. i. 113.]

where the fine balance between the ironic and the self-contented implies so much more than the patrician speaker realizes. By making the belly speak 'tauntingly' against the 'mutinous' members, Menenius asserts the invincible self-satisfaction which has already made itself felt in the assumption of infallibility –

Confess yourselves wondrous malicious
Or be accused of folly – [I. i. 93.]

with which he embarks upon his reproof. Thinking of the motives of those who dare to challenge the authority of his own class in terms of sterile 'malice', he fails to penetrate to the causes of a dislocation deeper than any partial vision can adequately compass.

So much is confirmed by the force of the Citizen's rejoinder. His vigorous defence of the superior organs – the 'kingly-crowned head', 'the vigilant eye', 'the tongue our trumpeter' – has indeed little to do with the reality he is defending; but it cuts across the complacency of the patrician rebuke with a force that the patronizing interruption – ''Fore me, this fellow speaks!' – cannot diminish. The total effect of

o

the fable is to convey, through and beyond Menenius' justification of privilege, the condition of the social organism from which the hero's tragedy will spring. We are shown, indeed, a populace incapable of discerning its true good, confirming by its short-sighted behaviour its need for the leadership which only a class recognized to be superior can give it: as Menenius puts it, carrying the prevailing image of 'appetite' to its final consequences:

> digest things rightly
> Touching the weal o' the common, you shall find
> No public benefit which you receive
> But it proceeds or comes from them to you
> And no way from yourselves. [I. i. 156.]

Yet this, though true, is still only one side of the picture. The parable also reveals a patrician caste unreasonably contemptuous of the rest of society (not for nothing Menenius dismisses as 'the great toe of this assembly' an opponent whose arguments have not always lacked cogency), who have forfeited much of their claim to superiority by their attitude towards those upon whose existence and effort their own well-being, in the last analysis, depends. Both the factions thus confronted in sterile obstinacy are set in an iron framework which permits no real contact or community of purpose, nothing but ruthless repression countered by outbursts of animal discontent. So situated towards one another, they cannot fail to come to blows. 'Rome and her rats are at the point of battle': Menenius describes the situation in one, and relevant way, but other possible interpretations suggest that there can be no final victory in this struggle, that the contending factions are involved in a common disaster which their mutual obstinacy has brought upon the city.

In accordance with the spirit of this parable Shakespeare's presentation of the behaviour of the warring parties is from the first remarkably balanced, even dispassionate in spirit. As the play opens, the spokesmen of the people, faced with the prospect of 'dying' or, at best, of 'famishing', express their grievances with reasoned moderation. Authority, in the guise of privilege, 'surfeits' whilst its victims look in vain for the 'relief' to which they have a human right. This intolerable division they find cruelly and unnaturally written into the social fabric which oppresses them:

> .. the leanness that afflicts us, the object of our misery, is as an inventory to particularize their abundance; our sufferance is a gain to them. [I. i. 20.]

The stress in the First Citizen's protest is laid consistently upon

necessity, on the natural desire to survive: 'the gods know I speak
this in hunger for bread, not in thirst for revenge'.

The discussion between the citizens leads to a call for action, which
their desperate situation imposes. 'The other side o' the city is risen:
why stand we prating here? to the Capitol!' The unity of Rome is on
the verge of final disruption when Menenius enters to put forward his
alternative view of the disorders. The First Citizen, moderate as
ever, is ready to admit the newcomer's virtues, describing him as
'honest enough' and adding, as though in distaste for the action
forced upon him, 'would all the rest were so'. The following appeal
to force – 'They say poor suitors have strong breaths; they shall
know we have strong arms too' – does not exclude reason and when
Menenius asserts that the course they are proposing to follow must
lead to their own 'undoing', there is logic in the wry retort that 'we
are undone already'.

Menenius' rebuke, in the first verse speech of the play, is a suitable
prelude to his fable. It assumes that the position by which his own
class stands to benefit belongs to the natural and unalterable order
of things. If, unlike some of his fellow-patricians, Menenius can
show himself benignly human in dealing with those whom he assumes
to be his inferiors, he is none the less the spokesman of a class which
accepts the perpetuity of that close rigid view of social relations
from which it profits. His habitual kindliness should not blind us to
the touch of iron which this first utterance conveys. He takes it for
granted that it is the duty of himself and his like to exercise 'charit-
able care' over the people; but his concept of 'charity', kindly and
condescending so long as it is unquestioned, is compatible with the
denial of responsibility when 'charity' is not enough:

> For your wants,
> Your suffering in this dearth, you may as well
> Strike at the heaven with your staves as lift them
> Against the Roman state; whose course will on
> The way it takes, cracking ten thousand curbs
> Of more strong link asunder than can ever
> Appear in your impediment. For the dearth,
> The gods, not the patricians make it, and
> Your knees to them, not arms, must help. [I. i. 70.]

The effect is more searching in its revelation of complacency than
may at once appear. Rhythm and expression combine to embody
the irresistible motion of an impersonal and overbearing force with
which the speaker finally feels himself identified. The effect of the
division in the earlier part of the speech between 'cracking' and
'asunder', both words which carry a strong sense of violent physical

separation, is to convey an impression of ruthless progress, leading us to partake directly in the advance of the state towards a goal conceived of as barely human, dedicated to an indifferent fatality. The emotional impetus so generated is then brought to a sudden curb after 'impediment': the long period comes to an emphatic pause in the middle of its implacable development and Menenius, turned from the bland counsellor into the mouthpiece of an unrelenting social destiny, throws upon the 'gods' the responsibility for a catastrophe which no thought of human solidarity is allowed to mitigate.

The speech, indeed, in the process of leading directly to the parable which follows, strikes a note which will be almost obsessively present in the following development. Its spirit emerges perhaps most clearly from the phrase 'strike at the heaven with your staves' with which Menenius dismisses the protests of the citizens and the efficacy of their '*stiff* bats and clubs.' These phrases, and others of a like nature scattered through the play, answer to the peculiar sensation of hardness, of utter incompatibility, with which its conflicting attitudes are presented. The rough implements of the people and the iron weapons of their masters threaten one another in a closed and indifferent universe; the 'heavens' remain stonily impenetrable, so that the 'stiff' weapons can almost be heard to clang when raised, not so much against injustice as against the imposition of an impersonal fatality. This sense of hard hostility will find its supreme reflection in the hero's attitude. It answers to an order in which insensibility responds to unworthiness, in which patricians and people are out of contact, hostile and exclusive in positions which seem to have been imposed upon them by the nature of things. If Menenius is right to stress this fatality: –

> You are transported by calamity
> Thither where more attends you – [I. i. 79.]

the fact remains that the prospect of 'calamity' rouses no real echo of sympathy in his mind. When he blandly asserts that his fellow patricians care for the people like 'fathers', he lays himself open to a retort which the facts of the situation in no small measure confirm:

> They ne'er cared for us yet: suffer us to famish, and their storehouses crammed with grain; . . . repeal daily any wholesome edict established against the rich, and provide more piercing statutes daily, to chain up and restrain the poor. [I. i. 83.]

Envy and blind resentment no doubt play their part in the citizen's accusation of patrician egoism; but the concluding answer to so much complacent paternalism is, as far as it goes, blunt and effective:

'If the war eat us not up, they will, and that's all the love they bear us'.

Into the cauldron of dissension thus ominously overflowing, Caius Marcius plunges with a characteristic outburst of uncontrolled and misdirected energy:

> What's the matter, you dissentious rogues,
> That, rubbing the poor itch of your opinion,
> Make yourselves scabs? [I. i. 170.]

From the first, the resentment of the people has been concentrated on this man whom they feel to be their chief enemy. The First Citizen's initial reference to him – 'Let us kill him, and we'll have corn at our own price' – is a vicious and short-sighted simplification which contrasts with the moderation he shows elsewhere; but this inauspicious entry, surely one of the most disconcerting initial utterances ever put into the mouth of a tragic hero, casts a light of its own upon the uneasy balance between his prowess and his failings, between the 'good report' which even his enemies recognize in Marcius and the pride with which he 'pays himself' in isolated egoism for his services. The speech which follows is an unconscious self-revelation, alternating the slow and weighty amplitude proper to his martial dignity with exaggerated plain-speaking, descents into an explosive directness which tells its own tale of imperfect control. A force of over-emphatic denunciation asserts itself through the elaborately sustained marriage of opposites upon which the development of the speech rests; 'peace' is set against 'war', 'lions' against 'hares', 'foxes' against 'geese', 'fire' against 'ice', and 'hailstones' against the sun, as the speaker's indignation imposes itself in scathing bitterness upon the rhetorical framework which answers finally, in its slow, deliberate amplitude, to the dictates of an alien world. The most striking effect is one of intense contradiction –

> Your virtue is
> To make him worthy whose offence subdues him
> And curse that justice did it.
>   ... your affections are
> A sick man's appetite, who desires most that
> Which would increase his evil – [I. i. 180.][1]

a chafing of contrary sensations, as spontaneous in impulse as they

---

[1] Compare, for the conception,
> Our natures do pursue,
> Like rats that ravin down their proper bane,
> A thirsty evil; and when we drink we die.
>   [*Measure for Measure*, I. ii. 137.]

are laboured, unnaturally hard in expression, which rises to the crowning denunciation:

> He that depends
> Upon your favours swims with fins of lead
> And hews down oaks with rushes. [I. i. 185.]

The plain but ponderous images follow one another, fall like sword-strokes, deadly, forceful, metallic, upon the abuses which they repudiate; but the periods in which they are embedded break habitually in the middle of their rhythmic structure, fail to cohere in a cumulative impression of life. The general sense is of a violent torrent of energy concentrated upon a narrow range of ideas and prejudices, deriving finally – as we shall have occasion to see – from an irreparable lack of spontaneity in the intimate relationships which have made the speaker what he is.

The full significance of this attitude will only emerge as the tragedy progresses. In the meantime Coriolanus, convinced by breeding and temperament that to defer to his natural inferiors is to 'flatter beneath abhorring', asserts in its most extreme form the patrician claim to unlimited authority:

> You cry against the noble senate, who,
> Under the gods, keep you in awe, which else
> Would feed on one another. [I. i. 192.]

The claim is one which the facts in part justify, but which is in danger of being turned into a brutal imposition. Menenius backs it with a more reasoned attitude when he dismisses the 'presumption' of those who, standing outside the magic circle of privilege, aspire to know 'what's done i' the Capitol'. Thus supported, Marcius winds up his tirade with a ruthless assertion of force which, directed by the warrior hero against his own people, amounts to a caricature of true valour:

> Would the nobility lay aside their ruth,
> And let me use my sword, I'ld make a quarry
> With thousands of these quarter'd slaves, as high
> As I could pick my lance. [I. i. 203.]

Here, at least, the strength of emotion, hitherto half-strangled by its own indignation, issues in an image close to the speaker's heart; but, though it will become amply clear that the people against whom this anger is directed are weak, worthless and brutal in many of their reactions, this truth cannot lend validity to what remains a barbarous perversion of traditional heroic values.

Marcius' outburst, not unnaturally, leaves the people stunned.

Their reaction will come later, prompted by the tribunes who lead them for ends of their own and matching unreason with their own surrender to passion. Meanwhile, with his opponents momentarily crushed, Menenius lays aside his mask of experienced kindliness and gives open expression to his contempt. The populace, he remarks, 'abundantly' lack 'discretion' and are moreover 'passing cowardly'. Marcius, in turn, parodies the manner in which the demonstrators on the other side of the city *'vented* their complainings' – the verb, which the play will repeat in other contexts,[1] answers to its characteristic sense of emotion forcing itself violently, explosively to the surface – and then, as he recalls the recent creation of the tribunes, passes from contempt to more intense repudiation. There has been, he complains,

> a petition granted them, a strange one –
> To break the heart of generosity
> And make bold power look pale, [I. i. 216.]

in response to which the people 'threw their caps'

> As they would hang them on the horns o' the moon,
> Shouting their emulation. [I. i. 219.]

Apart from the oddly inconsequential outburst of poetry in the reference to the moon, the most notable feature of Marcius' resentment is the association of authority with 'power', which Menenius echoes when he foresees that these concessions will in due course 'win upon power' to overthrow the established order. In this world of closed and conflicting interests force, 'power', is left necessarily with the last word. Meanwhile, unattractive though the tribunes will prove to be, it is significant that the first references to them should be so strongly coloured by contempt. Marcius' indignation at their appointment –

> The rabble should have first unroof'd the city,
> Ere so prevail'd with me – [I. i. 224.]

stands out by its sinister readiness to contemplate the possibility of chaos; it is noteworthy that Menenius, not less hostile to these novelties but more cautious in his reaction to them, is content with the non-committal comment: 'This is strange'.

At this point, news of a new external factor enters the action. The Volscians have risen against Rome. Marcius, true to his nature, welcomes this news as a diversion from internal problems which at heart mean nothing to him. It will enable the authorities to 'vent' the 'musty superfluity' of the state into a foreign adventure. Having

---

[1] See, for example, III. i. 257 and p. 246 below.

thus asserted the advantages of war, as he sees them, he allows
emotion to speak more directly as he foresees a new meeting with his
rival Aufidius:

> I sin in envying his nobility;
> And were I anything but what I am,
> I would wish me only he. [I. i. 236.]

As will always be the case, the expression becomes easier, more
lyrical in tone, as the hero passes from distasteful public conflicts to
his own absorbing concern with private glory. This is the real
Marcius, the vastly developed successor of Hotspur,[1] a soldier for
whom the world is no more than an arena for the pursuit of what
he conceives to be 'honour'. His very next speech shows to what
degree this pursuit has come to outweigh all wider responsibilities in
his mind:

> Were half to half the world by the ears, and he
> Upon my party, I'ld revolt, to make
> Only my wars with him. [I. i. 239.]

Once more, we feel emotion breaking through to spontaneity,
easing itself into the channels of natural expression. It is emotion,
however, which can lead the warrior hero to contemplate civil strife
without qualm or repugnance. To this self-centred and finally
adolescent aristocrat, the world is no more than an instrument to
minister to his pride, his personal enemy

>   a lion
> That I am proud to hunt. [I. i. 241.]

It is significant that this thaw, this loosening into uninhibited
emotion, fails to maintain itself. In the following conversation with
Titus Lartius, the iron stiffness of the warrior once more takes
possession as Marcius asserts his readiness to 'strike at Tullus' face',
and issues the trenchant challenge 'What, art thou *stiff*? stand'st
out?' which provokes the older man's reply: 'I'll lean upon one
crutch, and fight with t'other'.[2] The response to this display of
martial emulation cannot be altogether simple. These are brave
men when compared with the wavering populace whom their
leader has verbally bludgeoned into silence; but they are also
something less than complete or responsible human beings.

---

[1] See my *Shakespeare: from 'Richard II' to 'Henry V'*, and more especially pp. 104–
5.

[2] For the spirit of this, compare Caius Ligarius in *Julius Caesar*, II. i. See p. 40
above.

Menenius' approving comment on the veteran's determination –
'O, true-bred!' – reflects the values on which these virtues are based
and by which they are, humanly speaking, limited. It introduces the
cult of breeding which Volumnia will shortly raise to its most fanatical expression[1] and by which these warriors are so exclusively
united in mutual admiration. As they prepare to leave, they vie
with one another in a deference –

> – Lead you on.
> – Right worthy you priority.
> – Noble Marcius – [I. i. 251.]

which contrasts with their contempt for all who stand outside their
circle; to this contempt Menenius' parting words on the people –

> The Volsces have much corn; take these rats thither
> To gnaw their garners – [I. i. 255.]

gives ruthless and extreme expression.

After the departure of the patrician leaders, the tribunes are left to
insinuate the existence of greater complexities. Their comments,
though prompted by envy, are not immaterial to what has gone
before. Sicinius' emphasis on the hero's pride is coupled with a
premonition of his fall. 'Being moved, he will not spare to gird the
gods' or to 'bemock the moon'; these are at once true statements of
weaknesses which will lead to disaster and expressions of the desire
felt by mean natures to achieve the ruin of one whom they feel
instinctively to be more capable of generosity than themselves.
The bitterness revealed in Brutus' wish, 'The present wars devour
him', points to a lack of public spirit which answers to that of his
enemies; the sense of envy is only in part covered by the excuse that
Marcius has grown 'too proud to be valiant'.

As the exchange between the tribunes proceeds, the dangers which
threaten the unconscious hero are more clearly indicated. They
spring in great part from defects in his own nature. 'Tickled' – the
word, with its contemptuous implications, is deliberately chosen for
its ironic overtones – with 'good success', Marcius can be relied upon
to rise to grotesque heights of arrogance, to disdain

> the shadow
> Which he treads on at noon. [I. i. 266.]

Not altogether unjustly, this pride presents itself to his detractors as
intolerable 'insolence'; though it is Brutus' own cunning, the sys-
tematic belittling of human motives which his envy imposes, that

---

[1] See I. iii. and p. 218 below.

leads him to suggest that the fame which his enemy seeks will be more readily attained in 'a place below the first', in which

> Half of Cominius' honours are to Marcius,
> Though Marcius earned them not. [I. i. 279.][1]

This is not a true account of the way in which the warrior's mind works or of the means by which his reputation has been gained; but it answers ominously to the cynicism of the public world in which he will find himself, with inadequate defences in self-understanding, progressively ensnared.

II

Before Marcius is set in motion on the first, ascendant stage of his career, we are offered a revealing glimpse of his family circle, and more particularly of the mother whose demands upon him will determine the course of his tragedy. The First Citizen has already linked these demands to the hero's martial prowess when he has said, in explanation of his service to Rome, 'though soft-conscienced men can be content to say it was for his country, he did it to please his mother and to be partly proud!' This pride proceeds from a strange mixture of solicitude and ruthlessness, possession and renunciation in Volumnia's own nature. Remembering 'the only son of her womb' as 'a tender-hearted child', the repository of all her affection, whom 'for a day of king's entreaties' she would not 'sell an hour from her beholding', she can yet recall how she found herself 'considering how honour would become such a person' and how she dedicated his youth to a stern and fanatical conception of duty. Fearing that her son might 'picture-like hang by the wall', she willed that he should 'seek danger where he was likely to find fame'; and, as she dwells on this decision, her thoughts rise to a severe exaltation of the sacrifice which she imposed upon her affection and which she is now determined to assert as freely and responsibly taken. 'To a cruel war *I sent him*: from whence he returned, his brows bound with oak'. Seen in this way, the hero's glory becomes the reflection of his mother's purpose, a compensation for the sacrifice which sent him forth, in despite of a mother's natural attachment, to affirm in dedication to 'honour' the unique and exalted destiny she has chosen for him.

Not all the ladies who attend upon Volumnia can rise to this intensity of dedication. Virgilia, moved by a wife's natural fears for

---

[1] Compare the attitude of Ventidius to Antony in *Antony and Cleopatra* III. i. See p. 127 above.

her husband's safety, raises the very question – 'But had he died in the business, madam : how then?'[1] – which the mother has ruthlessly excluded. Because she cannot afford to admit these feelings, the emphasis of Volumnia's reply conveys a sense of distorted and passionate determination :

> Hear me profess sincerely : had I a dozen sons, each in my love alike, and none less dear than thine and my good Marcius, I had rather had eleven die nobly for their country than one voluptuously surfeit out of action. [I. iii. 23.]

Having assumed possession of her son's being, Volumnia has made it her life's work to impose upon his simplicity the imperatives which rule her own life. The sense of insecurity which, in her own despite, Virgilia's diffident plea arouses in her unnaturally concentrated being finds reflection in the tense and narrow emphasis of her reply.

With the entry of Valeria, this concentration rises, as though spurning nature, to a ruthlessly masculine participation in her son's achievements. Her ideal, to which we shall see him amply corresponding, ceases to be human, becomes the exaltation of an engine impersonally dedicated to destruction. Marcius will 'pluck Aufidius down by the hair', be shunned by his enemies as children 'fly from a bear' ; as she imagines him defying the Volscians, it is as if she were herself engaged in the bloody work, sharing in its ruthless fascination. The picture of her victorious son –

> his bloody brow
> With his mail'd hand then wiping, forth he goes
> Like to a harvest-man that's tasked to mow
> Or all, or lose his hire – [I. iii. 38.]

balancing against a touch of more spontaneous poetry the grim aspect of the warrior bathed in blood, is not allowed to deflect her from the dedication which her nature so insistently demands. When Virgilia, in timid protest, pleads 'no blood', her answer is ferociously concentrated on the idea which entirely possesses her. 'Away, you fool' : the repudiation ends in a glorification of bloodshed more fantastic and inhuman than all that has gone before :

> the breasts of Hecuba,
> When she did suckle Hector, look'd not lovelier
> Than Hector's sword when it spit forth blood
> At Grecian sword, contemning. [I. iii. 44.]

[1] Compare Falstaff on 'honour' : 'Well, 'tis no matter; honour pricks me on. Yea, but how if honour pricks me off when I come on ? how then ?' [*Henry IV – Part I*. V. i. 130.]

Even at this moment of supreme dedication to her martial ideal, the thought of maternity lingers on as an obsessive presence in Volumnia's mind. Sacrificed to the masculine notion of 'honour' which possesses her, its survival emphasizes the moral incompleteness which will bring her son to ruin. Meanwhile, this expression of pride is rounded off by a last vision of Marcius, transformed from her child to the engine of wrath –

> He'll beat Aufidius' head below his knee,
> And tread upon his neck – [I. iii. 50.]

which, at a cost still to be determined, she has willed him to be.

These narrow and perverse intensities are not allowed to pass without implicit comment. Valeria, returning to the commonplace, stresses the homely foundations of the patrician feminine outlook: 'how do you both? you are manifest housekeepers. What are you sewing here?'. These domesticities, so strangely set against the savagery that has gone before, lead, by a crowning incongruity, to Volumnia's picture of her grandson in the nursery:

> O' my word, the father's son; I'll swear, 'tis a very pretty boy.
> O' my troth, I looked upon him o' Wednesday half an hour
> together; has such a confirm'd countenance. I saw him run after
> a gilded butterfly; and when he caught it, he let it go again; and
> after it again; and over and over he comes, and up again;
> catched it again: or whether his fall enraged him, or how 'twas,
> he did so set his teeth, and tear it; O, I warrant, how he mam-
> mocked it! [I. iii. 62.]

There could be no better comment on the deadly lack of feeling which has surrounded Marcius from birth and of which his child, in turn, inevitably partakes; the boy is, after all, 'the father's son'. To complete the effect we need only the crushing, if unconscious irony implied in Valeria's observation, 'Indeed, la, 'tis a noble child', and the contrast between these intimate ferocities and the wifely refinement which leads Virgilia, in the name of propriety and good breeding, to refrain from visiting 'the good lady that lies in': a refusal which provokes Valeria to comment acidly on the values which have inspired this retired devotion: 'You would be another Penelope: yet they say, all the yarn she spun in Ulysses' absence did but fill Ithaca full of moths'. The entire episode, with its glimpse of the father's narrow and inhuman concentration mirrored in the precocious savagery of his child, makes a revealing introduction to the episodes of war which follow.

These are observed from a variety of angles in the course of the Volscian campaign. Marcius and his fellow-captains approach the

hazards of battle in a typically sporting spirit: the refusal of Titus
Lartius to sell back to Marcius the horse he has won in a wager[1]
recalls Hotspur's careless generosity and the streak of childish
obstinacy which went with it.[2] To these aristocratic warriors the
perils of war present themselves as motives for mutual admiration,
and the exchanges between them are marked by a mixture of
strenuous brutality and rhetorical glorification. When Cominius has
'come off', panting and with difficulty, at a pause in the engage-
ment,[3] Marcius meets him 'flayed', grotesquely covered in the blood
he has shed and lost. Their meeting is the occasion for a lyrical
exchange which, after dwelling with a certain intense satisfaction on
the shedding of blood –

> – Come I too late?
> – Ay, if you come not in the blood of others,
> But mantled in your own – [I. vi. 27.]

rises, in the hero's greeting of his friend, to an eloquent equation
of the values of love and war:

> O, let me clip ye
> In arms as sound as when I woo'd; in heart
> As merry as when our nuptial day was done,
> And tapers burn'd to bedward! [I. vi. 29.][4]

The capacity to rise to these moments of romantic exaltation, precarious and imperfectly wedded to reality though they are, is a
distinctive patrician quality which we need neither ignore nor take
entirely at its face value. Limited in its range by the operation of
class solidarity, it may be allowed to answer to a certain fineness, a
true generosity; but a corresponding exclusiveness, a narrow devotion to rigid prejudice, is sufficiently stressed to colour the effect and
to balance the final impression.

Marcius' response to these expressions of comradeship is characteristically evasive. Concentrated upon the soldierly business which
dominates his thought, he shrugs off his own deeds with blunt
modesty – 'Will the time serve to tell? I do not think' – and returns
eagerly to the field. The news of Cominius' repulse inspires him to
redoubled effort; he calls for volunteers in terms which, grimly
decorating his bloody work –

> If any such be here –
> As it were sin to doubt – that love this painting
> Wherein you see me smear'd – [I. vi. 67.]

[1] I. iv.   [2] *Henry IV – Part I*, III, i.   [3] I. vi.

[4] Compare, for the spirit of this, Aufidius in IV. v, quoted on p. 262 below.

lead up to a final appeal to his soldiers to show the patriotic spirit
which, at a less critical moment, he would regard as the prerogative
of his peers. 'If any fear', he cries,

> Lesser his person than an ill report;
> If any think brave death outweighs bad life,
> And that his country's dearer than himself: [I. vi. 70.]

let such, and such alone, share with him the burden and the glory
of the day. The appeal strikes home, and Marcius, carried on the
wings of his dedication, feels himself transformed into the 'sword' of
Rome, backed by followers whom his example inspires to bear
against the enemy shields as 'hard', as grimly unyielding, as his own.

For all his military splendour, however, Marcius remains in some
respects a strangely rudimentary human being. The enemy's
obstinate 'disdain' makes him 'sweat with wrath'; after his initial
repulse before the city gates,[1] Lartius refers to his 'exercise' and he
comments: 'My work hath not yet warm'd me; fare ye well'. The
emphasis on these physical reactions, on the gradual warming up of
an implacable machine of destruction, is not without relation to his
heroic stature. The 'noble fellow' who 'sensibly outdares his senseless
sword', whom his devoted followers contemplate with indulgent
affection as they call upon 'the fair goddess fortune' to 'fall deep in
love with him', is also the ruthless engine celebrated in Lartius'
evocation of his 'grim looks' and 'the thunder-like percussion' of his
sword. Both aspects of the hero's martial nature look back finally to
the values which Volumnia has so arrogantly and so dangerously
imposed upon him; the precarious relationship between them will
find reflection in the irony which throughout accompanies his presentation and which accounts for the human disaster of his tragic end.

Marcius' behaviour in the heat of battle is, indeed, frequently
disconcerting. When the troops whom he has invited to share the
honour of his patriotic adventure fall back before the enemy, he
turns upon them like an embittered scold; the diatribe against
'geese', 'apes', and 'slaves' piles up to an inarticulate conclusion
from which any suggestion of martial lyricism is excluded:

> Pluto and hell!
> All hurt behind; backs red, and faces pale
> With flight and agued fear! [I. iv. 36.]

Thus carried away by motions of indignant spleen, Marcius is ready,
for the first but not the last time, to make war on his countrymen.
The energy so generated enables him to turn the tide, and he re-
enters the enemy citadel like an avenging fury; but an unflattering

[1] I. v.

undertone to these scoldings emerges from the cynical comments of
his own men on 'fool-hardiness' and produces the indifference with
which they shrug off concern for his fate: 'To the pot, I warrant
him'. If this is not an elevated attitude, we may reflect that the
'nobility' to which this play refers is invariably a patrician preserve,
that those who thus express their unheroic detachment have been
allowed no share in the self-admiring effusions of their betters.
When, a little later, the soldiers turn to plunder,[1] only to mistake
their base booty for silver, Marcius is neither surprised nor, in reality,
disappointed. He is content to pass judgement with patrician
superiority –

> See here these movers that do prize their honours
> At a crack'd drachma! – [I. v. 4.]

and to return to the serious business concentrated for him on his
personal rivalry with Aufidius.

It is this rivalry that warms up the engine of destruction and
invests it with its peculiarly intense and limited assertion of life.
Overshadowed by this personal duel, the battle becomes the noisy
background for a display of vociferous defiance. 'I hate thee': 'We
hate alike'; 'promise breaker' and 'serpent' are bandied in abusive
emulation across the din of combat.[2] Marcius boasts the solitary
nature of his exploits, as he will again in the hour of his fall;[3] he also
refers once more to his grim appearance 'masked' in the blood of
enemies mingled with his own. Aufidius is content to answer boast
with boast:

> Wert thou the Hector
> That was the whip of your bragg'd progeny,
> Thou shouldst not 'scape me here. [I. viii. 12.]

The tone of these exchanges, precariously poised between heroism
and empty self-assertion, must be taken into account in any balanced
estimate of the values which these aristocratic warriors so arrogantly
proclaim.

The battle over, the hero's companions in arms acclaim these
same values in anticipation of his triumph. In Rome, Marcius will
be welcomed by senators and patricians, and by the great ladies
who

> shall be frighted,
> And, gladly quaked, hear more; [I. ix. 5.]

[1] I. v.   [2] I. viii.   [3] V. v, quoted on p. 288 below.

even the 'fusty plebeians', whose passive presence will be one more
adornment of his triumph, will be forced to revere the hero 'against
their hearts'. Tongue-tied and self-conscious now that the time for
absorbing himself in action has passed, Marcius expresses his confusion in fumbling disclaimers –

> I have done
> As you have done; that's all I can: induced
> As you have been; that's for my country – [I. ix. 15.]

before he falls back, with greater conviction, upon the thought of
the mother whose inspiration can never be far from his mind:

> my mother,
> Who has a charter to extol her blood,
> When she does praise me, grieves me. [I. ix. 13.]

Undeterred by this blunt, awkward sincerity, the chorus of admiration assumes more pressing tones. 'Rome', urges Cominius, must
recognize 'the value of her own'; even to proclaim the hero's virtue
'to the spire and top of praises' is to be modest in respect of the truth.
Thus faced by the prospect of public eulogy, Marcius persists in
uneasy self-effacement, refers to his new wounds which

> smart
> To hear themselves remember'd, [I. ix. 28.]

only to provoke from Cominius one of those vivid outbursts of
emotion upon which, against the harshly solemn grain of its prevailing
rhetoric, this tragedy concentrates its expression of personal feeling:

> Should they not,
> Well might they fester 'gainst ingratitude,
> And tent themselves with death. [I. ix. 29.]

To the hero's clumsy modesty, such intensity of praise represents less
a satisfaction than a danger with which he is particularly unfitted to
cope. 'Sincerity', far from leading him to a proper measure of self-
knowledge, represents a trap into which he will habitually fall. Where
another man, more balanced and self-aware, would accept the praise
of his friends and associates as a normal gesture of solidarity, Marcius
is driven to affirm excessively the isolation which will finally constitute his tragedy. On his return to Rome, this inability to adapt
himself to the requirements of his public position will lead him
implacably to destruction.

Offered as his reward a generous share in the spoils of victory,
Marcius persists in rejecting what he describes, with characteristic
over-emphasis, as bribes. He declares his wish to be treated like his

companions; but when the soldiery are incautious enough to join in
the general acclamation his violent reaction tells its own tale:

> May these same instruments which you profane,
> Never sound more! when drums and trumpets shall
> I' the field prove flatterers, let courts and cities be
> Made all of false-faced soothing!
> When steel grows soft as the parasite's silk,
> Let him be made a coverture for the wars! [I. ix. 41.]

Perhaps the most striking effect of this outburst, so strangely disproportionate to the situation which provokes it, is the sense which it
conveys of friction, of a conflict, intuited but imperfectly understood,
between a certain superior fineness, which the speaker's heroic
stature implies, and the iron rigidity to which it finds itself limited by
the force of personal circumstance. In its most vivid phrase, the
soldier's virtue is related to the unyielding 'steel' in which he is en-
cased, whilst the gracious softness of 'silk', the vesture of civilized
living in 'courts and cities', is repudiated as the clothing, corrupt
and enervating, of the parasite, the symbol of a world whose undermining action upon his treasured simplicity he instinctively fears.
The contrast, as the poetry conveys it, is less simple than the speaker
would have it be. Besides repudiation of the insinuating attributes of
the courtier, the image conveys an impression of life chafing against
an unnatural inflexibility, torn between the discipline to which the
martial hero has vowed himself and an imperfectly developed
appreciation of the distinctive graces of social life. His sense of this
division leads Marcius to take refuge in an excessive plainness –

> For that I have not wash'd
> My nose that bled – [I. ix. 47.]

and to his final rejection, so manifestly disproportionate in tone, of
the 'hyperbolical' praises in which he feels himself enmeshed and the
'lies' in which these are 'sauced'.

Cominius not unnaturally finds something excessive in modesty
carried to this length. He indicates, perhaps more acutely than he
knows, that Marcius is a man 'incensed against himself', who may
have to be treated like a lunatic before he can be brought to reason:

> we'll put you,
> Like one that means his proper harm, in manacles,
> Then reason safely with you. [I. ix. 56.][1]

The hero's future behaviour will give meaning to these sinister fore-
bodings; but for the moment, with the return to Rome still before

[1] For the phrasing here, compare again the passage from *Measure for Measure*
quoted in the footnote on p. 213.

P

him, these incongrous sentiments are drowned in the general acclaim
which leads to the conferring upon him of the victorious title of
'Coriolanus'. To this he responds, not with thanks or an appropriate
assertion of patriotic dedication, but with adolescent 'blushing' and a
brief, ungracious 'I will go wash'. The scene closes upon his typical
gesture of generosity towards a Volscian captive whose name he has,
even more typically, forgotten; and with a request for wine to revive
his tired spirits, and with the blood still drying upon his face, he turns
towards the dangers that await him in his native city.

The episodes which follow show these dangers gathering ominously
to meet him. Not all of them are to be found at home; and so,
immediately after the victory at Corioli, the action turns to a brief
but revealing glimpse of his rival. Aufidius has accepted his defeat
in the open field; but the determination to master his enemy, now
divorced from all honourable dealing, is stronger than ever in his
embittered thoughts. As he confesses,

> mine emulation
> Hath not that honour in't it had; [I. x. 12.]

where formerly he had hoped to prevail in 'equal poise', he is now
ready to 'potch' brutally at his enemy by any means, fair or foul, that
may occur to his exasperated intelligence. If 'wrath' has failed,
'craft' may yet bring victory over a rival whom he describes as
'bolder than the devil', though not, he grimly adds, 'so subtle'.
'Sublety', indeed, of a kind barely compatible with his heroic
reputation, will from now on be Aufidius' strong suit. His sense of
frustration bears fruit in strangely twisted expressions of envy. His
own valour, he affirms, in an image which will be repeatedly in his
mouth, has been 'poisoned' by suffering the 'stain' of unfavourable
comparison. The phrase, and the whole scene with it, points to a
moral degeneration, by virtue of which the normal sanctions of
chivalrous behaviour, seen to rest on nothing more solid than
'rotten privilege and custom', are set aside with venomous intensity.
Even in the most trustful circumstances,

> At home, upon my brother's guard, even there,
> Against the hospitable canon, [I. x. 25.]

Aufidius is ready to indulge his ferocious envy against his rival by
washing his 'fierce hand in's heart'. To the play's peculiar sardonic
intensity this short episode, with its glimpse of traditional restraints
crumbling under the impact of personal resentment, has its own
contribution to offer.

In Rome, meanwhile, where the hero's fate, concealed under
jubilant manifestations of triumph, gathers to destroy him, the

uneasy debate between his enemies and his complacent friends is carried on in dry and disenchanted comment. Menenius, setting the tone for what is to follow, portrays himself as an epicurean cynic, 'a humorous patrician', loving 'a cup of hot wine with not a drop of allaying Tiber in't', 'hasty and tinder-like upon too trivial motion'. 'What I think I utter', he says, and adds, with a gesture of generosity that comes perhaps a little too easily to cover the contempt he feels for those whom he regards as his natural inferiors, that his 'malice' is spent with his breath. Contempt, nevertheless, dominates the exchange with the tribunes which follows and is reflected in his recurrence to the most common bodily processes to describe the activities of those whose sphere is, in his view, necessarily limited to 'controversies of threepence', disputes between 'an orange-wife and a fosset-seller':

> When you are hearing a matter between party and party, if you chance to be pinched with the colic, you make faces like mummers; set up the bloody flag against all patience; and, in roaring for a chamber-pot, dismiss the controversy bleeding, the more entangled by your hearing. [II. i. 82.]

The exchange of mutual abuse which follows shows neither party in a favourable light. If Menenius' careless manner answers to the outlook of one whom his enemies describe as being, by his own account, 'a perfecter giber for the table than a necessary bencher in the Capitol', there is equally a measure of truth in his retort: 'You talk of pride: O that you could turn your eyes towards the napes of your necks, and make but an interior survey of your good selves'. The unwillingness on both sides to contemplate the uncomfortable truths which such a 'survey' might reveal leads directly to the sterile conflict which will bring themselves and their city to the verge of ruin.

These mutually exclusive attitudes clash, inevitably, in contrary attitudes to Coriolanus. Menenius, to whom the opinion of the 'beastly plebeians' and their 'herdsmen' is a matter of indifference, admits that 'the people love not Marcius'; and Sicinius implies that he shares this contempt when he allows himself to say of those whose representation he bears that 'nature teaches *beasts* to know their friends'. Whether the hero is, as Brutus asserts, 'a lamb . . . that baas like a bear', or, as Menenius prefers to think, 'a bear . . . that lives like a lamb', these brittle sarcasms will hardly clarify; but the markedly unheroic nature of the alternatives colours the dispute to which they lead. Whereas, for Brutus, Marcius is 'stored' with 'all faults', 'topping all others in boasting', Menenius finds him 'in a cheap estimation . . . worth all your predecessors since Deucalion, though peradventure some of the best of 'em were hereditary

hangmen'. The one certainty in this acrimonious and empty exchange is that both parties are concerned less with the truth of their
assertions than with fathering upon the victor their own passions and
prejudices.

As the ladies enter with news of Marcius' return, Menenius
hastens back, not without a sense of relief, into the world from
which this unseemly argument has led him. 'My fair as noble ladies',
he greets them, and follows the courtly salutation with a reference to
the moon, symbol in its purity and cold remoteness of the virtue
which has been so absent from what has gone before; but even at this
point a touch of unintended satire colours the oddly goose-like
picture evoked by his eager question to the patrician matrons,
'whither do you follow your eyes so fast?'. The news of Marcius'
approach he greets by foreseeing a party – 'I will make my house reel
to-night' – though there is also a certain dry self-estimate in what
immediately follows: 'I will make a lip at the physician: the most
sovereign prescription in Galen is but empiriceutic, and, to this
preservative, of no better report than a horse-drench'. Before long,
his joy at his friend's return is concentrated on the familiar topic of
his wounds: 'Is he not wounded? he was wont to come home
wounded'. Volumnia, naturally, has no doubts on the point. Brushing aside Virgilia's protest – 'O no, no, no!' – her mood is one of
exultant certainty: 'I thank the gods for it'. The satirical implications of the exchange are admirably completed when Menenius
makes a discreet return to common sense. He will join Volumnia in
thanking the gods for these patriotic gashes, but only 'if it be not too
much'.

The aristocratic attitude to war and honour is further brought to
life when Menenius asks whether Marcius has 'disciplined Aufidius
soundly'. When Volumnia reports that 'they fought together, but
Aufidius got off', the very inflections of his comment echo bluff self-
esteem:

> And 'twas time for him too, I'll warrant him that; an he had
> stayed by him, I would not have been so fidiused for all the
> chests in Corioli, and the gold that's in them. [II. i. 144.]

These are the attitudes which have made the hero what he is, the
world of impossible simplicities which is so dangerously ready to
take him to its heart. This is, at all events, no moment for considering
dangers. When Virgilia continues to express a wife's normal concern
in connection with these reports – 'The gods grant them true! –
Volumnia brushes hesitation aside with delicious forthrightness.
'True, pow, wow!'; the spirit of a class bluntly assertive of its own
certainties finds here an expression that borders on the ridiculous.

Having thus affirmed her conviction, Volumnia returns to the wounds which are for her the proof of her son's heroism: 'Where is he wounded?'. The question, eagerly repeated, leads to an extraordinary competition in which the hero's wounds are listed in fantastic emulation:

> VOLUMNIA He received in the repulse of Tarquin seven hurts i'
> the body.
> MENENIUS One i' the neck, and two in the thigh; there's nine
> that I know.
> VOLUMNIA He had, before this last expedition, twenty five
> wounds upon him.
> MENENIUS Now it's twenty seven; every gash was an enemy's
> grave. [II. i. 167.]

This grotesque inventory cannot clearly be taken at its own estimate. Volumnia herself sets it in its true light when she refers to the trumpets which herald her son's approach. 'Before him he carries noise, and behind him he leaves tears'; the 'noise' carries with it a certain sense of hollowness, of unsubstantial acclamation, but the tears of the victims are real enough in their tribute to human loss:

> Death, that dark spirit, in's nervy arm doth lie;
> Which, being advanced, declines, and then men die; [II. i. 179.]

it is nothing less than a sombre engine of destruction which is about to make its ruthless entrance upon the scene.

Thus heralded, Caius Marcius appears, crowned with the oaken garland of victory. Brushing aside the herald's proclamation and the 'noise' which greets it, he goes straight to the heart of his concern and kneels before his mother with an intense, if publicly restrained, gesture of devotion:

> You have, I know, petition'd all the gods
> For my prosperity. [II. i. 189.]

Volumnia, in reply, refers her 'good soldier' to the wife whose modesty he next greets with a rare outburst of lyrical tenderness:

> My gracious silence, hail!
> Wouldn't thou have laugh'd had I come coffin'd home,
> That weep'st to see me triumph. Ah, my dear,
> Such eyes the widows in Corioli wear,
> And mothers that lack sons. [II. i. 194.]

Infrequent though they are, these lapses into intense lyricism are an essential part of the hero's nature. Our response to his tragedy needs to compass the divergence between this returning husband and the warrior who has so recently moved like an engine of doom over the

corpses he has pitilessly battered to death. The sensation of life
expressed in terms of passionate dedication, so triumphantly
affirmed against other and contrary realities at certain moments in
Antony and Cleopatra, manifests itself in this play under constraint, is
limited by Virgilia's answering diffidence and overshadowed by the
absorbing claims of martial 'honour'. War, glorified by those who
live for it to the exclusion of other values, is seen here as a product of
life indeed, but as one which tends by its nature to the death which is
its opposite. In the case of Antony defeat in war becomes, precariously and for the limited duration of certain scenes of tragic
exaltation, the condition for a triumphant assertion of love; in
Coriolanus, which could almost be interpreted as a counterpoise to
these moments of splendid but dangerous expansion, martial victory
is accompanied by a callous hardening of feeling, which can only
assert itself under constraint, giving a sense of irony, of human
qualities condemned ruthlessly to repression, to the rhetorical
expressions of the hero's triumph. That these same qualities can
nevertheless, at moments such as this, rise to a poetry of rare human
solicitude is an essential part of the tragic effect.

There can be no doubt at this point of Marcius' capacity to inspire
devotion in those who are closest to him. To Menenius' greeting, 'Now
the gods crown thee!', he responds with comradely concern; and
Volumnia is moved beyond her habitual rigidity to express her joy
in almost inarticulate phrases:

> I know not where to turn: O, welcome home:
> And welcome, general; and ye're welcome all. [II. i. 200.]

It is left to Menenius to give full expression to a mood in which relief
and affection combine:

> I could weep,
> And I could laugh; I am light and heavy. [II. i. 202.]

Only the tribunes, 'old crab-trees', are excluded from the general
acclaim, will not 'be grafted to your relish'. Their abstention, however, is dismissed as 'the fault of fools' and the patrician chorus, led
by Cominius and the hero himself, salutes its mentor, not without
self-satisfaction, as 'ever right', 'ever, ever'.

As the group turns to public business, Volumnia recalls that there
remains 'one thing', the consular office, which she has long desired
for her son. Here she touches upon a potential danger, and Marcius,
in his reply, shows unwillingness to set out upon the path she has
traced for him:

> I had rather be their servant in my way
> Than sway with them in theirs. [II. i. 221.]

The rejoinder indicates that this hero, so tied to his mother's affection, senses in her purposes for him the possibility of disaster. This ominous suggestion does not stand alone. Other signs of a change in the direction of events are not lacking, in the muttered comments of Brutus on the consequences of the coming elevation of this enemy of the people –

> Then our office may,
> During his power, go sleep – [II. i. 241.]

and in the comfort which he and his companion find in the 'ancient malice' of the commoners and in the conviction that Marcius can, in the long run, be relied upon to achieve his own ruin.

On this foundation they begin to elaborate their plot. Drawing strength from the hero's refusal to exhibit himself in 'the napless vesture of humility' or to beg the 'stinking breaths' of those whom they profess to serve, they determine to stress his hatred for the populace and the slavery to which his elevation will condemn them; for, as they not unjustly point out, Marcius holds the people

> In human action and capacity,
> Of no more soul nor fitness for the world
> Than camels in the war, who have their provand
> Only for bearing burthens, and sore blows
> For sinking under them. [II. i. 268.][1]

Sicinius foresees that his own character will lead their enemy to ruin; his 'soaring insolence' can readily be roused –

> that's as easy
> As to set dogs on sheep – [II. i. 275.]

to light a fire which, by kindling the 'dry stubble' of popular resentment, must create a blaze 'to darken him for ever'. The dry intensity of the expression anticipates the catastrophe to come; but for the moment Marcius' star is in the ascendant and the returning messenger stresses the unanimous popular acclaim:

> the dumb men throng to see him and
> The blind to hear him speak: matrons flung gloves,
> Ladies and maids their scarves and handkerchers,
> Upon him as he pass'd: the nobles bended,
> As to Jove's statue, and the commoners made
> A shower and thunder with their caps and shouts. [II. i. 281.]

[1] Compare Antony's reference to Lepidus in *Julius Caesar*:
> though we lay these honours on this man,
> To ease ourselves of divers slanderous loads,
> He shall but bear them as the ass bears gold,
> To groan and sweat under the business.
> [*Julius Caesar* IV. i. 19.]

Upon this sea of 'noise' and universal exclamation, shadowed only by the muttered reservations of his enemies, Coriolanus passes on to his perilous apotheosis at the Capitol.

His appearance there is once more preceded (II. ii) by the meaningful comment of the servants. They see the hero as 'a brave fellow' indeed, but 'vengeance proud', quite lacking in regard for themselves and their like; though one of them is ready to add in justice that the 'love' which the crowd demands as its right is habitually offered in calculating flattery – 'there have been many great men that have flatter'd the people who ne'er loved them' – and accepted in complacent ignorance: 'and there be many that they have loved, they know not wherefore'. Whilst the Second Officer is ready to justify the 'true knowledge' which inspires Marcius' 'noble carelessness', his companion points out that he appears rather to 'seek the hate' of the populace and argues pertinently that 'to seem to affect the malice and displeasure of the people is as bad as . . . to flatter them for their love'. The elaboration of the prose answers to the careful balance of judgement which sets the stage for the hero's approaching elevation.

With the ground thus prepared, Menenius calls upon Cominius to pronounce the victor's eulogy. The tribunes, whilst declaring themselves ready to 'honour and advance' the public hero, desire him to show

> A kinder value of the people than
> He hath hereto prized them at. [II. ii. 64.]

The request strikes Menenius as untimely, and his evasive reply to Brutus –

> He loves your people;
> But tie him not to be their bedfellow – [II. ii. 69.]

hovers on the edge of prevarication. Coriolanus, uneasily silent, shows the embarrassment that so often precedes his explosions of wrath. To Brutus, he affects an olympic indifference – 'You sooth'd not, therefore hurt not' – but his words imply contempt for the people ('I love them as they weigh') and, less obviously, a rankling of outraged pride. The effect of his final disclaimer –

> I had rather have one scratch my head i' the sun
> When the alarum were struck than idly sit
> To hear my nothings monster'd – [II. ii. 80.]

is revealing in its graceless intensity. Menenius, seeking to defend an uncouthness which he cannot but feel to be out of place, adds

nonetheless a contemptuous gesture of his own towards the 'multiply-
ing spawn' which, as he implies, no true hero can bring himself to
flatter.

Cominius' great eulogy, to which all these exchanges have been
leading, underlines by its weight and gravity a turning-point in the
action. Combining complexity with ease, elaboration with the
fluency of normal speech, it unites in one superb impression the
energy and life celebrated in the victorious warrior and the brutal
inhumanity which we have already found joined to it, marrying
both realities in a way that touches the heart of the tragic conception.
At this dangerous moment in the hero's career, where his triumph
and his ruin stand face to face, it stresses with rare concentration
and force the energy, the splendour of superabundant power, made
manifest in his victorious campaign. This impression of life is conveyed not only in the triumphant image which mirrors his youthful
rise to glory – 'he waxed like a sea' – but in the intensity which
records in terms of living sensation his inexhaustible response to the
challenge of danger :

> the din of war 'gan pierce
> His ready sense; then straight his doubled spirit
> Re-quickened what in flesh was fatigate. [II. ii. 120.]

This magnificent rousing of the spirit to the sounds of conflict
carries us back to the nostalgia once felt by Othello for 'the spirit-
stirring drum, the ear-piercing fife';[1] both passages convey, in their
respective evocations of what is, for each of these heroes, life and
fulfilment, a sense of the imagination reaching out to the confines of
sensual intensity. The exaltation of the warrior as he advances
towards his goal, the crowning of triumph with the 'garland' of
victory, express themselves through a fine keenness of sensation, this
play's parallel to that which, at certain moments, transfigures the
utterances of passion in *Antony and Cleopatra*.

Just, however, as *Antony and Cleopatra* does not finally invite to
uncritical romantic surrender, so the celebration of the soldierly
virtues in *Coriolanus* is balanced by a contrary impression. Side by
side with its superb sense of vital energy, Cominius' speech asserts
the presence of a dead heaviness, an almost grotesque insensibility.
The expansive splendour of 'he waxed like a sea' is immediately
qualified by the ponderous, dead impact of

> in the *brunt* of seventeen battles since,
> He *lurch'd* all swords of the garland; [II. ii. 105.]

[1] *Othello* III. iii. 353.

even as the hero attained with manhood the complete martial assertion of his being, the power so revealed converted itself into a heavy
indifference to life, an exclusion of the very qualities which victory
should have crowned. From the comparison, at once splendid and
sinister, of the warrior to a 'vessel under sail', bearing before him the
lives which he already regards as 'weeds', we pass to the evocation
of his sword as 'death's stamp', invested with the destructive weight
of a battering-ram. As the eulogy draws to its close, its object is converted into a mechanical instrument of carnage, indifferent to the
ruin he has caused:

> from face to foot
> He was a thing of blood, whose every motion
> Was timed with dying cries. [II. ii. 113.]

The impression of inhumanity is further reinforced by the irresistible
impact with which the hero 'with a sudden reinforcement' *struck*
(the placing of the verb at the end of the line imposes a pause which
adds to its sense of implacable weight) Corioli 'like a planet'; the
effect is to make Coriolanus no longer a mere soldier but an instrument of 'shunless destiny', an inhuman and impersonal force
launched against 'the *mortal* gates of the city'. In the word 'mortal' is
contained finally not only a sense of the frailty, the helplessness of
those who sought to bar his progress, but the protest of down-
trodden life against the power which began as an affirmation of
vital energy and has now ended in ruthless dedication to the ends of
destruction. Then, to balance the effect yet again, the machine
quickens remarkably in response to new perils –

> by and by, the din of war gan pierce
> His ready sense; then straight his doubled spirit
> Re-quickened what in flesh was fatigate,
> And to the battle came he – [II. ii. 120.]

a quickening followed, however, by the renewed callousness of

> he did
> Run reeking o'er the lives of men, as it
> 'Twere a perpetual spoil; [II. ii. 123.]

and we are left, as Cominius bows to the acclamation which greets
his close, with a final picture of Coriolanus pausing to 'pant' like a
hot-blooded bull after his orgy of carnage.

These complexities, though implicit in the speech, have no
immediate public effect. On the tide of emotion which it rouses,
Coriolanus is lifted to the culmination of his public glory. His true
enemy lies finally, not in those around him, hostile though some of

them are, but in himself. The prospect of addressing himself to the people produces in him a deep-seated, almost physical repugnance associated with the fear of finding himself 'naked,' intimately exposed in his hidden weakness:

> I cannot
> Put on the gown, *stand naked*, and entreat them
> For my wounds' sake. [II. ii. 141.]

In this reaction, the tribunes see an opportunity which they hasten to press home. The people '*must* have their voices'; they will never 'bate one jot' of the 'ceremony' which they know to be their due. The growing rift is healed for the moment by Menenius and the hero is left to 'blush' boyishly, and to express an unwillingness to 'brag' which, however creditable in itself, answers to motives deeper than he can readily understand. The entire situation is already variously and impossibly fragile. The demagogic demands of the tribunes are balanced by an unreasoning obstinacy in the warrior who is being compelled, against every instinct of his stubborn nature, to exhibit his most intimate feelings to further ends which others, using friendship and affection as instruments of persuasion, have imposed upon him.

Having obtained the approval of the senate, Coriolanus passes (II. iii) to his greater ordeal. His meeting with the citizens brings out the contradictions and uncertainties which both parties are seeking to disguise beneath an exaggerated obstinacy. The people, for their part, are still willing to grant the honours for which they are being approached, though their readiness covers a sense of puzzlement which their mentors have not been slow to foster: 'we ought not to deny him', argues their spokesman, for, though 'we have power in ourselves to do it . . . it is a power that we have no power to do'. The phrase sums up shrewdly one aspect of the fiction which underlies the forms of Roman political life. Uneasily aware of it, the citizens accept by implication Coriolanus' estimate of them as 'the many-headed multitude'; and their representative, in his final word before the herd's entry, combines a kind of democratic fatalism – 'But that's no matter, the greater part carries it' – with a recognition, at once rueful and realistic, of his own confusion: 'I say, if he would incline to the people, there was never a worthier man'.

As Coriolanus appears in 'the gown of humility', the citizens proceed to follow the instructions which they have received. They are to require the hero to request approval 'by particulars'; 'everyone' who hears him is to have 'a single honour' in giving him 'our own voices with our own tongues'. It would be hard to find a formula better calculated to rouse Coriolanus to angry repudiation: and from the first moment there is menace in his tongue-tied approach to his ordeal. His attitude is wrapped in the ferocious irony which shadows heroism throughout the play. His reply to Menenius' persuasion, 'The noblest men have done't', is a bleakly helpless 'What must I say?', which leads to a grotesque rehearsal of the coming interview. Of all the indignities he foresees, this exhibition is the hardest to stomach, and not even respect for his friend and mentor can keep him from an outburst of irrepressible bitterness:

> I got them in my country's service, when
> Some certain of your brethren roar'd and ran
> From the noise of our own drums – [II. iii. 57.]

and from a final snarl –

> Bid them wash their faces,
> And keep their teeth clean – [II. iii. 65.]

in which the voice of patrician superiority is heard in strange divorce from the dignity which it so arrogantly claims.

All this paves the way for the interview upon which so much depends. Coriolanus opens it on a note of defiant assertion: 'You know the cause, sir, of my standing here': ''twas never my desire to trouble the poor with bragging'. The tone is a grotesque mockery of the aristocratic intention, and the citizens in their reply insist upon the price they mean to exact for their approval. 'If we give you anything, we hope to gain by you'; the mood is one of bargaining, but there is, after all, a measure of reason in their request to be asked 'kindly' for what they are still disposed to give. Coriolanus replies with an offer, clumsily ungracious, to exhibit his wounds in private; but he continues to show his contempt by referring to 'voices' rather than to persons, and so leaves his hearers uncertain before a situation for which they feel themselves unprepared. 'An 'twere to give again – but 'tis no matter'. The conflict of ill-adjusted motives, in which neither side remains faithful to its declared intentions, is mirrored in the strained and sardonic quality of these exchanges.

The second pair of citizens show more of their own mind when they reply to Coriolanus' supercilious request for their 'voices' with an outspoken rebuke of pride. Coriolanus, a 'scourge' to his country's enemies, has been scarcely less a rod to his own countrymen: 'you have not indeed loved the common people'. The reproof is perfectly calculated to elicit the hero's arrogant response: 'You should account me the more virtuous, that I have not been common in my love'. Determined to buttress his doubtful position by violent assertion, he dismisses his own previous words as 'flattery' and ends with what amounts to an unwitting confession of insincerity:

since the wisdom of their choice is rather to have my hat than my
heart, I will practise the insinuating nod, and be off to them
most counterfeitly. [II. iii. 103.]

When the citizens capitulate uneasily before this arrogance, they
receive only a blunt refusal to be shown the wounds they have come
to see: 'I will not seal your knowledge with showing them'.

Left to himself, Coriolanus gives vent to the sense of humiliation
into which this false situation has led him:

> Better it is to die, better to starve,
> Than crave the hire which first we do deserve. [II. iii. 120.]

From now on, unheroically arrayed in what he describes as the
'woolvish toge' of hypocrisy, he will hardly open his mouth without
involving himself further in contradiction; but for the moment, after
seeking relief in a further bitter repudiation of 'Hob and Dick', he
agrees to carry on the fiction which has been so impossibly pressed
upon his simplicity:

> I am half through:
> The one part suffer'd, the other I will do. [II. iii. 130.]

The people, scarcely less bewildered, meekly endorse his elevation to
the supreme office, and even the tribunes confess that he has played
his part, only to receive in reply a series of brief questions leading to
the thought which is uppermost in his mind: 'May I change these
garments?'. The query has, for him, a deep personal meaning; only
when he has divested himself of the garb of indignity will he be able
to 'know himself' for what he is.

Left with the people, Brutus and Sicinius show that they at least
know where they stand. After reproving their followers for having
yielded their precious 'voices' for so little visible return, they proceed
to build up resentment against their enemy. Brutus, accusing him of
hatred for the mass of his countrymen, emphasizes his point with a
characteristic assertion of force as the final social arbiter:

> do you think
> That his contempt shall not be *bruising* to you
> When he hath power to *crush*?; [II. iii. 209.]

the shadow of the engine of destruction so recently celebrated by
Cominius now lies darkly over Rome. Thus confirmed in their
doubts, the people declare themselves ready to raise 'twice five
hundred voices' to take back their late concession. Brutus exasperates
their mood by further insinuations, and Sicinius relates the enemy's
pride still more explicitly to the 'inveterate hate' he has always

shown to the populace. The latter are urged, by a particularly cunning stroke of policy, to lay the fault of the election upon their own representatives, and the final emphasis rests upon Sicinius' admission that he and his companion have 'goaded' onwards what has been indeed, but only 'partly', the people's own determination. The stage is set for a culminating clash of conflicting wills and passions.

III

During the course of the public episodes which follow and which constitute the pivot upon which the entire dramatic construction turns, the differences which separate Coriolanus from his country-men are brought to their disastrous conclusion. The moment in which he attains the eminence for which he is so clearly unprepared is also the moment of his fall; and, in compassing the ends which envy and ignorance have between them dictated, the tribunes achieve in effect their own ruin. They are shown, in fact, to be less the agents they suppose themselves, than the victims of their short-sighted pursuit of mean and ill-considered purposes; whilst, in a scene (III. ii) which penetrates deeply into the nature of his intimate dilemma, Coriolanus is seen turning to his mother for support only to find himself, at the very point where he has placed the centre of his being, incomprehensibly abandoned. A sense of betrayal, of inadequate intentions perverted and falsified in action, colours with a distinctive and remorseless irony the tragic development of the play.

As the action is renewed in the forum (III. i), a brief conversation between Coriolanus and Titus Lartius reminds us that the issues being so dramatically worked out in Rome have as their background the continued existence of an external threat. The Volscians are once more on the move; Aufidius, maintaining his implacable hatred for his rival, is ready to 'pawn his fortunes' even to the point of 'hopeless restitution' to accomplish his revenge. Coriolanus' own interests are, as ever, absorbingly engaged in this rivalry. He asks for nothing better than a 'cause' to meet Aufidius at Antium so as to 'oppose his hatred fully'; it is true to the spirit of his tragedy that such a cause – though not of the kind he has in mind – is already at hand.

With the entry of the tribunes, whom Coriolanus hails con-temptuously as 'tongues o' the common mouth', we return to the central public conflict. It is their intention to exasperate his dangerous frame of mind by insisting that he has not 'pass'd the common'; and Sicinius, in a burst of arrogant confidence which goes beyond his previous calculated cunning, goes so far as to threaten a civil outburst in which all 'will fall in broil'. From this inauspicious opening, passion rises rapidly and inevitably to the final clash of wills. Coriolanus sees in the changed attitude of the tribunes 'a purpos'd thing', a conspiracy aimed at the overthrow of patrician authority and, with it, of established order in the city. This conspiracy must end, in his view, by setting up a 'curb' to the 'will' of the nobility and lead them to

> live with such as cannot rule
> Nor ever will be rul'd. [III. i. 39.]

To this mixture of truth and prejudice, Brutus replies by accusing the hero of having 'mock'd' the people and of having revoked the gift of corn already granted to them; the latter assertion, indeed, Coriolanus cannot deny, though he dismisses the tribune as a base 'informer' and is met, in turn, with a blunt assertion of defiance:

> – You are like to do such business.
>   – Not unlike,
> Each way, to better yours. [III. i. 47.]

From this point, and in spite of Menenius' plea for 'calm', the rise of tension towards an irrevocable break dominates the development of the scene.

To Coriolanus, the defiance of the tribunes presents itself as a negation of the office which he is about to assume. 'Why should I then be consul?' he asks, with what he regards as impeccable logic. If the claims of the popular leaders are to be admitted, it only remains for him to surrender his authority, sinking to the indignity of 'a fellow-tribune'. The argument, though appealing to a valid conception of 'degree', of lawful subordination, is advanced in a spirit of self-assertion, used to justify the exclusive domination of a class; and, as such, it is driven home with a ruthlessness that fatally provokes a contrary reaction. Carried beyond all thought of moderation, Coriolanus brutally asserts the intransigence in which he seeks, without knowing it, the confirmation of his own integrity. Convinced that the concessions made by his equals to 'the multiple, rank-scented many' amount to a betrayal of the necessary distinctions upon which all ordered society rests, he emphasizes his point with a self-assertive arrogance that tells its own tale:

> In soothing them, we nourish 'gainst our senate
> The cockle of rebellion, insolence, sedition,
> Which we ourselves have plough'd for, sow'd, and scatter'd.
>   [III. i. 68.]

Thus moved by emotions which reflect, in the manner of their expression, the play's concentration on basic, elemental realities, he allows his feelings to break forth in a mixture of proper pride and crude, embittered self-assertion:

> As for my country I have shed my blood,
> Not fearing outward force, so shall my lungs
> Coin words till they decay against those measles,
> Which we disdain should tetter us, yet sought
> The very way to catch them. [III. i. 75.]

As always, it is repudiation, the unreflecting reaction to contradiction, which in Coriolanus opens the flood-gates of emotion. Clumsy in his directness, inelegant in his vain efforts to command the passions which so excessively move him, he only gradually loosens, surrenders to the bare force of indignation. 'My lungs coin words . . . decay . . . measles . . . tetter us': the sequence of ideas, rising to its climax, shows emotion, naked, gross, and material, fretting against restraint, contributing its own strain of stressed corporality to the elemental concentration which Menenius' fable introduced as a distinctive feature of Roman life. A vehemence akin to physical disease, answering to the infection which threatens the body politic with the disastrous reality of civil strife, is visibly taking possession of the hero's mind.

Such intensity of denunciation invites a retort. Unworthy though he be, there is unmistakable point in Brutus' comment:

> You speak o' the people
> As if you were a god to punish, not
> A man of their infirmity; [III. i. 80.]

that this 'god', far from showing a divine serenity, has so violently repudiated 'soothing' in terms of material grossness and functional disorder is essential to the complete effect. Meanwhile, such arrogance can only be exasperated by attempts to impose upon its irresponsible operations the curb of reason. When Menenius seeks to pass off as products of ill-considered 'choler' these unhappy outbursts, the hero proceeds to dig his own grave by thrusting the apology aside:

> Were I as patient as the midnight sleep,
> By Jove, 'twould be my mind! [III. i. 84.]

By this insistence, he strengthens the determination of his declared enemies to see that, as Sicinius puts it, this mind 'shall remain a poison where it is' and not, by proceeding to the enslavement of the

people and the overthrow of their representatives, advance further
to the ruin of the commonweal.

As he hears the word 'shall', coming, to his mind, so inappropriately from this 'triton of the minnows', Coriolanus turns bitterly
upon the patricians who accompany him. Once again his utterance
becomes more sustained, stretches itself beyond its initial tonguetied brevity, as ill-considered passion assumes control of his being.
The senators have been 'good, but most unwise' in conceding
authority to the empty voices ('the horn and noise o' the monster')
which now so monstrously threaten them through his own person.
The diatribe, gathering weight, launches powerfully into tense, vivid
concentrations of metaphor –

> he'll turn your current in a ditch,
> And make your channel his – [III. i. 95.]

in defence of the speaker's conviction, bluntly and unilaterally
affirmed, that the choice before his fellow-patricians lies between the
firm exercise of power and the surrender of all constituted authority.
The argument, capable of cogent expression, turns in Coriolanus'
mouth into an emotional outburst as he elevates the compulsions of
his imperious and unnaturally concentrated nature into a universal
rule of polity. By allowing the tribunes to share the authority which is
theirs by necessity and established right, the senators have consented,
in his view, to become 'plebeians':

> they are no less,
> When, both your voices blended, the great'st taste
> Most palates theirs. [III. i. 101.]

The choice by the people of a magistrate who dares to utter the word
'shall' against his natural betters amounts to a fatal confusion of true
order and will end by introducing the anarchy which must follow
from the existence of 'two authorities' in rivalry and conflict.

Not unnaturally, Brutus affirms that the people will never give
their 'voices' to a consul who speaks in this way. Coriolanus, in his
retort, equates his prejudices, defiantly and unilaterally, with the
voice of reason:

> I'll give my reasons,
> More worthier than their voices. [III. i. 118.]

His certainty is at once his strength and his weakness; for the refusal
to yield, which may be proper to authority, is impossibly confused
in his reaction to crossing with the inability to understand. Returning
to the dangerous question of the distribution of corn to the populace,
he argues bluntly that those who 'ne'er did service', who only rallied

Q

unwillingly to the cause of Rome at a moment of supreme need, when 'the navel of the state was touch'd', have no reason to protest when their superiors take from them what was, at best, 'a frank donation'. To offer concessions to this 'bosom multiplied', allowing them to *digest* as their right what has been offered in gracious 'courtesy', is to lead the rebellious elements among the people to ascribe to weakness concessions which need never have been granted. It will be said,

> We did request it.
> We are the greater poll, and in true fear
> They gave us our demands. [III. i. 132.]

To open the way to this situation is to 'break ope the locks o' the senate' and to bring in what the speaker, with a last touch of concentrated vigour, calls 'the crows to peck the eagles'.

Of all this, it need only be said that the voice of passion is turning a reasonable and cogent argument into a mockery. The facts may be as Coriolanus states them; but to assert them thus, and at this moment, is to invite disaster. Menenius and Brutus unite in agreeing that more than enough has been said; but their interruptions, far from leading to a return to reason, make this most unmanageable of heroes even more determined to force upon his unwilling hearers the unpalatable truth. 'Take more', he cries, like one who has an unpleasant but wholesome medicine to administer, and denounces the consequences of 'this double worship' in terms which make it clear that the distinction between right and wrong is impossibly clear to his vehement and blinkered mind. The situation in Rome is one in which

> one part does disdain with cause, the other
> Insult without all reason; [III. i. 142.]

where 'purpose', which requires a focus of authority, is lacking, 'nothing is done to purpose'. Those who 'love the fundamental part of state', which is housed in the patricians, and who have good reason to 'doubt the change on't' must be ready – and here the argument, for all its powerful expression, is more directly backed by a strain of personal impulsiveness – to assert their preference for 'a noble life before a long', or, in a direct return to the prevailing line of bodily imagery, 'to jump a body with a dangerous physic' and thereby avoid the death that will be 'sure without it'. As passionate disdain reinforces natural conviction, the gathering flood of rhetoric ranges over a superb field of comparisons, from the notion of plucking out ruthlessly the 'multitudinous tongue' of the populace to that which spurns all vacillation as the shame of those who know no better than to lick 'the sweet which is their poison'. Those of the

speaker's own allegiance who fail to follow the logic of his argument
to its plain conclusion are scathingly rebuked for their defection:

Your dishonour
Mangles true judgement and bereaves the state
Of the integrity which should become't. [III. i. 156.]

The intention of such to do good is vitiated by the absence of true
'power' to achieve it and irreparably compromised by an ignoble
and pusillanimous surrender to 'the ill which doth control't'.

The attitude which inspires this diatribe finally removes all
chance of compromise. The tragedy of Coriolanus is brought upon
him, not by views wrongly held – for they are rationally defensible
and, indeed, to a Jacobean mind, highly cogent – but by the in-
transigent obstinacy which drives him to unbalanced and im-
moderate conclusions. The representatives of the people, taking up,
from their own standpoint, a conservative position, denounce him as
a 'traitorous innovator'; his reply dismisses them contemptuously as
'bald tribunes', admitted, in an unhappy surrender to expediency,
'When not what's meet but what must be, was law', to their unneces-
sary office. Here at least, in his call upon his friends to take advantage
of 'a better hour' to 'throw their powder i' the dust', Coriolanus
overreaches himself. It is no part of the exercise of true authority to
overthrow institutions which, given their existence, should be defended for the common good. Under the pressure of mutual
unreason, threat is answered by threat, force by the appeal to force;
the tribunes demand the arrest of the new consul as a traitor to the
state and its established institutions. The central public issue is thus
joined, and what follows will be of necessity a descent into chaos and
civil strife.

Coriolanus meets the order for his arrest by dismissing Sicinius
contemptuously as 'old goat' and 'rotten thing', and by an open
threat:

I shall shake thy bones
Out of thy garments. [III. i. 178.]

Summoned by their leaders the mob intervene, and Menenius' plea
for 'more respect' is drowned in the rising clash of opposed passions.
'Confusion's near', he exclaims, 'out of breath', and again, but to no
effect: 'This is the way to kindle, not to quench'. It is left to a senator
to point openly to the threat of anarchy. The effect of Sicinius'
order and, we may add, of Coriolanus' arrogance, will be 'to unbuild
the city, and to lay all flat'. The argument, put forward to support
the patrician claim to authority, is as one-sided as the retort by
which Sicinius counters it, 'What is the city but the people?', a

proposition to which the crowd offer enthusiastic support. The threat
to Rome, which exceeds, on a balanced view, any partial interpretation of the facts, is finally brought home by Cominius' warning:

> That is the way to lay the city flat,
> To bring the roof to the foundation;
> And bury all which yet distinctly ranges
> In heaps and piles of ruin. [III. i. 203.]

To this plea for a necessary 'distinction' in social functions, the
nearest approach to a detached statement so far made, the tribunes
reply that it is their authority, and so a constituted organ of the
state, that has been called into question; the choice which their
enemies have forced upon them is one between victory and annihilation:

> Or let us stand to our authority,
> Or let us lose it. [III. i. 207.]

The rising clash of contrary wills and interests, beautifully reflected
in the dramatic construction, culminates finally in the movement
to bear the hero to the Tarpeian rock, and

> from thence
> Into destruction cast him. [III. i. 212.]

The 'destruction' which this wild determination envisages is more
than that of an arrogant and irreconcilable enemy. From this
moment to the end of the scene, the rock will stand as a symbol, not
only of the end towards which Coriolanus' own passions are inexorably driving him, but of the will of Roman society to achieve its
own ruin.

Standing against this rising tide of chaos, Menenius makes a last
plea for 'temperance'. His 'prudent helps', however, are brushed
aside by Brutus as 'cold ways',

> very poisonous
> Where the disease is violent, [III. i. 220.]

and Coriolanus is left with only his sword to defend him from the
enemies he has himself created. As he draws it, Menenius urges him
to take advantage of the lull won by this display of force to retire
from the scene. 'All will be naught else', he argues with prudent
realism; but the hero's supporters have by now lost any vestige of
concern for the common good. 'We have as many friends as enemies',
Cominius asserts, and Menenius' plea 'Shall it be put to that?'
falls on deaf ears. Coriolanus, reiterating his contempt for foes whom

he regards as 'not Romans' but as barbarians, 'litter'd in the very porch of the Capitol', insists on an appeal to force –

> On fair ground
> I could beat forty of them – [III. i. 241.]

which amounts to a caricature of martial valour; and upon this irresponsible gesture Menenius comments with an irony: –

> I could myself
> Take up a brace o' the best of them; yea, the two tribunes –
> [III. i. 242.]

to which the sporting image[1] lends a distinctive and appropriate colour.

Gradually and momentarily, indeed, some sense of reality asserts itself and, for so long, the tendency of the scene moves against the hero's primary reactions. Menenius and Cominius, aware that the odds are 'beyond arithmetic', recognize that

> manhood is called foolery, when it stands
> Against a falling fabric. [III. i. 245.]

The popular indignation, faced by open defiance, must end, like a rage of 'interrupted waters', by carrying before it the very structure of society. Under these circumstances, Menenius proposes to set his 'old wits' against those who, as he contemptuously insinuates, 'have little' wit to boast of. The value of his intervention is limited by the element of confessed opportunism which underlies it; his intention is to 'patch', for the moment and 'with cloth of any colour', the damage which has been done and which threatens the order he holds dear with inconceivable ruin. That this attitude will not suffice, in the face of contrary forces each determined to contemplate destruction, to restore Roman society to a healthy and organic unity events will very soon show.

Having torn the unwilling Coriolanus from the scene of conflict, Menenius admits the weaknesses by which his heroic stature is limited:

> His nature is too noble for the world;
> He would not flatter Neptune for his trident,
> Or Jove for's power to thunder. [III. i. 254.]

Whether this is 'nobility' or obstinacy, the sign of an incapacity to

[1] Compare, for the idea, Scarus in *Antony and Cleopatra*:

> Let us score their backs
> And snatch 'em up, as we take hares, behind:
> 'Tis sport to maul a runner. [IV. vii. 12.]

come to terms with life, is a question which the entire action insistently poses; indeed Menenius, whose judgements are limited to the values of his own class, is not qualified to give it an impartial answer. Here, at all events, he stresses a real failing, the hero's inability to control the elementary motions of passion to which his nature continually impels him:

His heart's his mouth:
What his breast forges, that his tongue must vent. [III. i. 256.]

We have seen this account repeatedly endorsed in Coriolanus' own actions. When anger moves him, all normal considerations are thrust aside, at times to ends of heroism on the field of battle, at others to be replaced by expressions of blind obstinacy and headstrong folly. In either case, emotion must 'vent' its own excess, explosively and imperiously, into action.

The plea for moderation to which this reading of the facts leads is still based, of course, upon expediency. When Menenius protests 'Could he not speak 'em fair?', it is a tactical error and not a failure in sympathy or understanding that he deplores. There are abundant signs, however, that the time for moderation of this kind has passed. Menenius' own true feelings are revealed when he says of the people 'I would they were in Tiber!'; and Brutus and Sicinius, when they return, appeal to the rigour of the law against one whose declared desire it is to be 'every man himself'. They are supported in their move towards the rock by the citizens whose 'mouths' they are and whom they regard, in a phrase which grimly anticipates the vengeance they are seeking, as their 'hands'.

Against the approaching disaster Menenius enters a last plea for moderation. He is met by Brutus' blunt refusal to recognize Coriolanus as consul; but he is able to advance his request that Rome should not, 'like an unnatural dam', devour her own 'deserved children', and to Sicinius' retort that the hero must be regarded as a disease to be cut away for the health of the social body he replies by advancing a characteristic compromise:

O, he's a limb that has but a disease;
Mortal, to cut it off; to cure it, easy. [III. i. 294.]

The argument would only have substance if Coriolanus' character, or the ambition of his enemies, were such as to give it a minimum of support, and if the speaker himself were truly convinced of the need for the 'cure' he advocates. In fact, none of these conditions is operative. The arguments which Menenius has advanced to gain precious time Sicinius rejects as 'clean kam'; and when the patrician appeals to the services rendered to the city by one whom he admits to be 'a gangrened foot' in the body politic, Brutus forces the surgical comparison to a ruthless conclusion:

> Pursue him to his house, and pluck him thence;
> Lest his infection, being of catching nature,
> Spread further. [III. i. 307.]

The fact is that both parties to this sterile conflict are by now self-dedicated to destruction.

For the moment, however, resolution stands on either side at a precarious point of balance. Menenius is able to counter the ferocious determination of his enemies by insinuating that, in cold reason, they may yet come to regret what has been perpetrated in 'tiger-footed rage'; moreover, as he points out, the hero has powerful friends whose reaction may lead to an outburst of 'parties' which would end, in the crowning disaster of civil strife, by the sacking of 'great Rome with Romans'. The new Consul is to be excused as a man 'bred i' the wars', ill-schooled in 'bolted language'; as such,

> meal and bran together
> He throws without distinction. [III. i. 320.]

When, finally, he undertakes to produce a reasonable Coriolanus to answer the charges brought against him, he has the support of the senators and obtains the unwilling acquiescence of Sicinius who sees this concession, however, as a temporary device to gain time before finally compassing the enemy's ruin. To this dangerous course Menenius accedes in the certainty that, unless the hero can be brought to reason, 'what is worst will follow'.

Side by side with this public crisis, which focuses upon his person all the discordant elements which compose it, the play has consistently kept before us the conflicts by which Coriolanus' own nature is shaken. Beneath his excessive reaction to the situations in which he finds himself lie personal incongruities which political unwisdom cannot sufficiently explain. These are now related to their intimate causes when the hero, before finally confronting his enemies, turns to his mother for confirmation of the resolution he has taken upon himself (III. ii) and finds, where he most needs support, only an incomprehensible betrayal. Obsessed by the need to maintain consistency in his own eyes, he rejects all thought of conciliation. 'Let them pull all about mine ears', he cries, in a kind of sinister dedication to self-destruction; let 'ten hills' be piled upon the Tarpeian rock,

> That the precipitation might down stretch
> Below the beam of sight. [III. ii. 4.]

Beneath this inflated rhetoric the determination still to 'be thus', unbreakably self-consistent, seems to be as strong as ever; but there are already signs that it represents rather hysteria, the concealment from himself of inner weakness, than the strength it so fanatically asserts. When his patrician companion agrees that this determination is 'noble', his puzzled comment begins to reveal the shaky foundations upon which it rests:

> I muse my mother
> Does not approve me further. [III. ii. 7.]

This same mother has instilled into him the sense of patrician superiority by which he now stands. From her he has learnt to see the people as 'woollen vessels',

> things created
> To buy and sell with groats, to show bare heads
> In congregations, to yawn, be still and wonder,
> When one but of my ordinance stood up
> To speak of peace or war. [III. ii. 9.]

She has, in fact, been responsible for the values and attitudes which have inspired his life; to her, therefore, at this moment of supreme crisis he naturally turns to bolster up a confidence which he feels, albeit obscurely, to be crumbling beneath him.

The entry of Volumnia, thus significantly prefaced, opens a decisive interchange. Coriolanus initiates it by reproving her for having wished him 'milder' and so, in a sense very real to him, 'false' to his own nature. Her reply is the opposite of that for which he looks to her. It amounts to an appeal to expediency, in which, as she indirectly confesses, her ambitions for him play an important part:

> I would have had you put your power well on,
> Before you had worn it out. [III. ii. 17.]

In this spirit, far from confirming him in his obstinacy, she reproves him for having revealed his intentions before his enemies 'lacked the power' to cross him effectively. Thus divided by considerations of expediency, mother and son are still united in their attitude to the people. His 'let them hang' is echoed by her ominous rejoinder, 'Ay, and burn too';[1] but the contrast between this shared resentment and the unpalatable course of action she now proceeds to urge upon him dominates the exchange which follows.

[1] This is the first reference to the idea of 'burning' which will come to be almost obsessively related to Coriolanus' revenge as he approaches Rome in the closing scenes of the play. The point is well made by A. C. Bradley in his lecture on the play (*Oxford Lectures on Poetry*, London, 1909).

As a first step, Menenius enters to lend Volumnia the support of his own worldly experience. He reproves Coriolanus for having been 'too rough' and stresses the danger of civil war; the alternative to moderation is to see the city 'cleave in the midst, and perish'. To this Volumnia adds her decisive plea, the voice, she says, of a heart 'as little apt' as his to temporize, but proceeding from a mind that, unlike his own,

> leads my use of anger
> To better vantage. [III. ii. 30.]

Her son receives these counsels as a man puzzled, adrift in his moral bearings; how can the idea that he should 'use' his primary impulses to attain calculated ends be comprehensible to him? His question 'What must I do?' is in effect a plea for orientation, a confession of helplessness. When Menenius, with a frankness that borders on brutality, points him back to the tribunes the blow to his self-respect is intolerably plain:

> For them! I cannot do it to the gods;
> Must I then do't to them? [III. ii. 38.]

This is a hero who, having thus far sought from his 'gods' the confirmation of his own simplicities, finds himself moving in a world too subtle, too indirect for his understanding: a world, moreover, to which even his mother, upon whose teaching his self-respect has so far rested, seems ready to abandon him.

It is she, indeed, who now strikes the decisive blow at his prized consistency by calling him 'too absolute' – as if he could be so in his own esteem – and by wrapping her counsel in what must strike him as a deep moral ambiguity:

> therein you can never be too noble,
> But when extremities speak. [III. ii. 40.]

That nobility can ever be in excess, that 'extremities' exist which can bend it to the force of external circumstance, is a notion that Volumnia's own teaching has made inconceivable for her son. To question this teaching now, in relation to the very populace he has learnt from her to despise, is to shatter the foundations of his self-respect. She, of all people, cannot without inflicting irrevocable harm tell him that

> Honour and policy, like unsever'd friends,
> I' the war do grow together, [III. ii. 42.]

and urge him to use both indifferently to attain the ends which she has willed upon his unprepared and incomprehending simplicity.

Not only, however, does she do precisely this, but, having done so, she goes on to develop the argument with a flexibility which her son must find foreign to all that she stands for in his mind. In war, she urges, it is in accordance with 'honour' to seem 'the same you are not' and to shape 'policy' accordingly; why then should it be 'less or worse' to do precisely this in an emergency of peace? From this opening, which he can only receive in shame-faced embarrassment – 'Tush, tush!' – and with a bewilderment which marks his initial sense of betrayal ('Why force you this?'), she goes on to urge him to dissimulation:

> now it lies on you to speak
> To the people; not by your own instruction,
> Nor by the matter which your heart prompts you,
> But with such words that are but roted in
> Your tongue, though but bastards and syllables
> Of no allowance to your bosom's truth. [III. ii. 52.]

The wording of this advice is calculated to bring home to Coriolanus the moral monstrosity, as it must seem to him, which it implies. To tell such a man that he must speak, not from the 'heart', according to the promptings of that 'honour' which is life to him, but according to the dictates of expediency is to run counter to the self-respect, the narrow but absorbing sense of fitness, for which he has been taught to live; and, by a crowning irony, it is the mother from whom he derived these values and to whom he has looked for support from childhood, that has struck the blow which now almost visibly shatters him. Most shocking of all, perhaps, is the assumption that dissembling is an acceptable and even necessary part of the warrior's noble occupation:

> Now, this no more dishonours you at all
> Than to take in a town with gentle words,
> Which else would put you to your fortune and
> The hazard of much blood. [III. ii. 58.]

The one-sidedness, the artificial simplicity, of the hero's attitude to his martial profession could hardly be more devastatingly exposed.

Scarcely less grave is the revelation of the motives which have determined this advice. These must seem to him barely compatible with the notions of integrity and honour under the guise of which pride of family and caste have presented themselves to him since childhood. Volumnia's appeal is finally to friendship, to what we might call, in modern terms, class solidarity; but it implies a denial of the values upon which these narrow but absorbing realities have hitherto rested and upon which his nature, equally narrow and self-absorbed, has been built. As she puts it:

> I would dissemble with my nature, where
> My fortunes and my friends at stake required
> I should do so in honour. [III. ii. 62.]

The invitation to 'dissemble', not merely with the world, but with his own nature, is precisely one which the hero cannot, after a life-time based on the negation of such a possibility, accept. It amounts to a denial of all simple ethical values, and more precisely of those which he is fitted to understand. The notions of 'honour' and 'dissembling', hitherto so clearly separated in his mind, are now presented to him as intolerably mingled; virtue and friendship, far from being the foundations upon which his cherished integrity can rest, have now become pointers to disorientation and inner doubt.

Still bearing the brunt of an argument which Menenius supports with his 'Noble lady!' – an exclamation in which the adjective begins to sound equivocal, and in which anxiety and suspense play their part – Volumnia goes on to depict most vividly the piece of play-acting which she is urging upon her son. The manner of her doing this can only add to his shame. His 'bonnet' is to be stretched out in supplication, his knee to be seen 'bussing the stones': and all this in the service of what he must see, however she may seek to disguise it, as an ignoble act of persuasion:

> for in such business
> Action is eloquence, and the eyes of the ignorant
> More learned than the ears. [III. ii. 75.]

Still more ignominiously, the 'waving' of his head must correct the impulse of the 'stout heart', which is to become

> humble as the ripest mulberry
> That will not hold the handling. [III. ii. 79.]

Worst of all, the hero is to prostitute his soldiership, declaring himself the servant of the people he is to woo and exhibiting himself as tongue-tied and unapt of speech:

> being bred in broils,
> Hast not the soft way which, thou dost confess,
> Were fit for thee to use, as they to claim,
> In asking their good loves. [III. ii. 81.]

By the end of this harangue, in which his mother urges upon him an act of submission at once ostentatious and false, Coriolanus is a hero shattered in his inner integrity, exposed to the play of forces which can have for him no intimate reality.

His friends, however, agree in urging upon him the necessity and the simplicity of what he has to do. Menenius characteristically recognizes the generosity of the very people whom he treats, even at this moment, with contempt –

> For they have pardons, being ask'd, as free
> As words to little purpose – [III. ii. 88.]

and Volumnia, in her conclusion, bends him finally to the yoke she has so incongruously fashioned. 'Go, and be ruled', she says, with a return to the authority which he has always craved from her, and in the following recognition of his true nature –

> I know thou hadst rather
> Follow thine enemy in a fiery gulf
> Than flatter him in a bower – [III. ii. 90.]

the moral violence which she has done to him is, with a certain implied cynicism, recognized for what it is.

Cominius' tidings from the forum underline the force of these arguments. 'All's in anger', and only if Caius Marcius is ready to 'frame his spirit' to 'fair speech' can a general disaster be averted. Once more, Volumnia's intervention is decisive: 'He must and will'. Thus pressed from all sides, the hero submits. The speech which confirms his surrender opens with a typically self-conscious display of the nobility for which he has lived and which he is being asked to sacrifice. 'Must I go show them my unbarb'd sconce? Must I?', he asks, with what amounts to a plea to those around him to reverse their demand upon him, and adds,

> With my base tongue, give to my noble heart
> A lie, that it must bear? [III. ii. 100.]

At this moment, in which he is agreeing to renounce it, the idea of 'nobility' for which he has lived haunts the speaker's mind. In giving his assent – 'Well, I will do't' – he insists that he is being forced by circumstances, that were there but this single plot to lose,

> This mould of Marcius, they to dust should grind it,
> And throw't against the wind; [III. ii. 102.]

the force of 'grind to dust', with its sense of hard and relentless pressure, answers to the tense act of the will which he is so unnaturally imposing upon himself. The speech, indeed, balances this new determination with a suggestion that he will never be able to carry through the purpose he has taken upon himself, that he is being obliged to take up

> a part, which never
> I shall discharge to the life. [III. ii. 105.]

Once again, however, the play of external pressures is decisive. Cominius offers to 'prompt' him in his unfamiliar role, and Volumnia adds the unique appeal of her maternity:

> I prithee now, sweet son, as thou hast said
> My praises made thee first a soldier, so,
> To have my praise for this, perform a part
> Thou hast not done before. [III. ii. 107.]

Her responsibility in thus manœuvring her son into an equivocal position is of decisive importance for the future development of his tragedy. We shall have cause to remember the pressure she is now putting upon him when they meet for the last time to decide the fate of Rome.

Coriolanus, as he finally accedes, whips himself into an evocation of the ridiculous, which will eventually produce its counter-effect in wildly impulsive action:

> Away, my disposition, and possess me
> Some harlot's spirit! [III. ii. 111.]

The effect of what he is agreeing to do is, in his own mind, to deny his manhood and prized integrity. His 'throat of war' which formerly 'quired with my drum' is now to become a pipe 'small as an eunuch', to decline ignominiously to a voice described as 'virgin', suitable only for lulling infants to sleep. Thus incensed, the outraged indignation passes on to evoke 'the smiles of knaves' and 'schoolboy's tears', by which he sees himself surrounded, and the whole graphic series of images is rounded off by a supreme picture of indignity:

> a beggar's tongue
> Make motion through my lips, and my arm'd knees,
> Who bow'd but in my stirrup, bend like his
> That hath receiv'd an alms! [III. ii. 117.]

The entire passage, with its sense of unnatural rigidity stooping to an ignoble submission, leads to a last desperate refusal to contemplate dishonour, to sacrifice his self-respect and

> surcease to honour mine own truth,
> And by my body's action teach my mind
> A most inherent baseness. [III. ii. 121.]

In the poignant reference to 'my own truth' the nature of the hero's sacrifice is most vividly portrayed. For the last time before he returns to the forum, he seeks to restore his integrity, to shore up the fragments of that 'nobility' which, as it seems to his bewildered mind, all around him are determined he shall betray.

This last reaction, however, is based by now on illusion, represents the striking in compensation of an attitude by one who has finally lost his bearings. The last word rests, as always, with Volumnia, who intervenes to say that it has become her own 'dishonour', not to incite her son to shame, but to have been obliged to urge upon him a course of action to which filial duty should have sufficiently prompted him. Coriolanus is accused of showing pride under the guise of 'dangerous stoutness'; his valour he inherited from her, but this 'pride' she declares to be his alone. Thus upbraided, threatened with desertion by the power which has so far sustained his being, Coriolanus can only return, like a faithful but bewildered hound, to his mother's heel. 'I am going to the market-place': the simple phrase conveys a complete collapse of the preceding show of energy. It is followed, in a mood between the pathetic and the absurd, by the plea 'Chide me no more'. It is in the last resort because he is unprepared by education and temperament for the situation which faces him that the hero finds himself cornered between empty defiance and inconceivable surrender. To the latter choice, ruefully and without comprehension, he now submits himself. In bitter anticipation of his coming behaviour: –

> I'll mountebank their loves,
> Cog their hearts from them, and come home beloved
> Of all the trades in Rome – [III. ii. 132.]

he feels himself, as it were, contemplating the sacrifice of his male integrity. It is supremely ironic that Volumnia, having achieved her purpose by tying up her son in doubt and self-distrust, should claim at the last to leave him free: 'Do thy will'. In fact, his will is for his friends and, above all, for her to dispose of. As he leaves for his ordeal, with the words 'honour' and 'mildly' ringing inarticulate and clashing changes in his stunned thought, we know that they have prevailed. The consequences of their victory for Rome and for himself will emerge in the remaining course of the tragedy.

Whilst Coriolanus has been thus forcing himself to this unnatural submission, the mood of his enemies has hardened against him. The tribunes have been busy (III. iii) organizing the assembled people to play their part; when the time comes, they are to contribute their 'voices', not ceasing from their 'din confused' until they have enforced the execution of what their leaders 'chance to sentence'. In making these sinister preparations, the tribunes show how much they rely upon the weaknesses of their enemy. He has been accustomed

> Ever to conquer and to have his worth
> Of contradiction; [III. iii. 26.]

once his reason has been 'chaf'd', confused by the anger which crossing of any kind rouses in him, he will not again be 'rein'd to temperance'. At such moments, he will utter what is in his heart, and to this his enemies may reasonably look, in Brutus' savage phrase, 'to break his neck'. In the coming struggle, no holds will be barred. It is to be a battle for survival, which will be carried to its conclusion even if the precious unity of the city is thereby to be shattered by civil strife.

Into this ominous situation Coriolanus makes his entrance, with Menenius and the senators urging 'calm' upon him in anxious prevision of what may occur. Replying to this advice, he lays stress upon the humiliation which is being forced upon him; he comes, he says, less as a warrior than

> as an ostler, that for the poorest piece
> Will bear the knave by the volume. [III. iii. 32.]

In this spirit, he accepts, albeit briefly, the demands of the tribunes in accordance with the lesson he has learnt: 'I am content'. The relief with which his friends underline this gesture – 'Lo, citizens, he says he is content' – is a measure of their uneasiness; and Menenius seeks to back this ungracious concession by that excessive concentration on the hero's wounds which, as we have seen, is particularly calculated to rankle in his thoughts and which will end by producing the very reaction he fears. Coriolanus, indeed, at once dismisses the gashes thus debased to a spectacle as 'scars to move laughter only'; we know enough of him by now to see in this diffidence the prelude to an outburst of repudiation. Menenius, however, devoid – as we must surely feel at this point – of either shame or a sense of propriety, goes on to excuse the hero for his 'rougher accents', in terms which prompt even Cominius to an uneasy 'Well, well, no more!', in an effort to steer the whole unseemly episode towards a decent close.

Already, however, it is too late for this to be possible. Coriolanus' true nature, reacting against the shame which he has been brooding over in embittered silence, begins to find issue in threats. His next query is notably more aggressive in tone. 'What is the matter', he cries,

> That being pass'd for consul with full voice,
> I am so dishonour'd that the very hour
> You take it off again? [III. iii. 58.]

This is the voice of one who feels the need to return at any cost to the secure foundations of his self-respect. To the tribunes this new attitude comes as the chance for which they have been waiting, and they reply that he is there 'to answer, not to accuse'. For a last brief moment, Coriolanus resumes, albeit with difficulty, the docility that has been so painfully instilled into him.

This state of affairs cannot, of its nature, last. The tribunes, who feel the initiative passing to them, have no interest in a peaceful solution. They charge their enemy with having sought for himself 'power tyrannical' and with having constituted himself into 'a traitor to the people'. The immediate effect is to leave him speechless. 'How, traitor!',[1] he exclaims; and then once more the tide of emotion overflows its self-imposed dams and the speaker, obscurely aware that he has been manœuvred into self-betrayal, expresses his open reaction in a sinister evocation of fire and destruction. 'The fires i' the lowest hell fold in the people!'; the image, with its implied acceptance of civil strife, looks forward for the first time to the avenging power which will soon seek to cover its confusion by threatening the city with ruin and devastation.

Having thus committed himself beyond possible repair, Coriolanus feels his treasured self-respect returning to him. He is able to give himself the satisfaction of answering the 'injurious' tribunes in

<blockquote>
a voice as free
As I do pray the gods. [III. iii. 72.]
</blockquote>

This illusory recovery, however, leads only to the clash which will finally ruin him. Against the rising uproar from the people – 'To the rock, to the rock with him!' – Sicinius presses for a sentence of death, which Brutus more politically, but not more generously, seeks to mitigate by recalling the hero's past service to Rome. Coriolanus is now in no mood to accept praise from one whom he despises and repudiates. As Menenius appeals desperately to the only force that might conceivably hold him in check – 'Is this the promise that you made your mother?' – he declares his readiness to accept rather death than the humiliation which surrender would imply:

<blockquote>
I would not buy
Their mercy at the price of one fair word. [III. iii. 88.]
</blockquote>

Confronted by this defiance, Sicinius finally promulgates the sentence of banishment behind which, as symbol of headstrong ruin and perverse resolution, lies the shadow of the abyss:

---

[1] The accusation of treachery will be repeated at the end of the play, and will evoke the same tongue-tied response. See V. v, and p. 286 below.

> in the power of us the tribunes, we
> Even from this instant, banish him our city,
> In peril of precipitation
> From off the rock Tarpeian. [III. iii. 98.]

The claim of the tribunes to exclusive power is pushed at this point to disastrous conclusions. Justice is affirmed by their representatives in the name of the people, of a part at the expense of the whole. Upon the ominous image of the Tarpeian rock is imposed, we may feel, that of the Gadarene swine rushing headlong to disaster.

The last efforts of Cominius and Menenius to impose a return to moderation are brushed aside by the rising pressure from every quarter. In their repeated cries 'It shall be so', the Roman people in effect will their own doom; and, against their outcry, Coriolanus, released at last from the obligation to contain himself, gives vent to a flood of vituperation. 'Common cry of ours': 'reek o' the rotten fens',

> whose loves I prize
> As the dead carcasses of unburied men,
> That do corrupt my air; [III. iii. 119.]

the tide of invective asserts itself against Cominius' last effort to evoke, in terms in which intimate feeling forces its way through the iron bonds which this tragedy habitually imposes upon it, the positive values of the patrician family ideal:

> I do love
> My country's good with a respect more tender,
> More holy and profound, than mine own life,
> My dear wife's estimate, her womb's increase,
> And treasure of my loins. [III. iii. 109.]

Against this attempt to identify intimate and public attachments Coriolanus, whose tragedy rests equally upon a family foundation, accepts his banishment by uttering a bitter curse against the city in whose service his life has been spent:

> Have the power still
> To banish your defenders; till at length
> Your ignorance, which finds not till it feels,
> Making not reservation of yourselves,
> Still your own foes, deliver you as most
> Abated captives to some nation
> That won you without blows. [III. iii. 125.]

The curse thus spoken in hate and personal resentment confirms the tragedy which the hero has brought upon himself. As a gesture

258 of Shakespeare: The Roman Plays

against nature, it is the equivalent in public terms of Lear's denunciation of the daughters who turned unnaturally against him.[1] As in the earlier play, tragedy follows from setting passion above reason, from the choice of the part at the expense of the whole; and if external perversity imposes the choice, it is accepted in a spirit of answering perversity to the ruin of hero and city alike. 'Despising' the world which formerly applauded him Coriolanus turns his back upon the foundations of his personal integrity, becomes a shattered figure dedicated to a revenge which is not the less unnatural because the city upon which it is visited has brought it upon itself. 'There is a world elsewhere', he cries in a last gesture of defiance; exactly what that world is, the last stages of his tragedy will show.

IV

The expulsion of Coriolanus from Rome marks the opening of an indeterminate stage, answering to his own position, in the development of the tragic action. Adrift on a sea of chaos, his first instinct is once more to turn for moral support to the mother whose 'precepts' have raised him, in his own esteem, above 'the lot of common men'. In her return to consistency, he sees mirrored the possibility of his own. 'Resume', he pleads, recalling how unaccountably she failed him at their last meeting,

> that spirit, when you were wont to say,
> If you had been the wife of Hercules,
> Six of his labours you'ld have done, and saved
> Your husband so much sweat. [IV. i. 16.]

In the absence of more solid ground for comfort, the appeal is backed by an assertion of stoic fatalism –

> 'Tis fond to wail inevitable strokes,
> As 'tis to laugh at 'em – [IV. i. 26.][2]

and leads to the striking of a heroic attitude for their common benefit:

> My mother, you wot well
> My hazards still have been your solace: and
> Believe't not lightly – though I go alone,
> Like to a lonely dragon, that his fen

[1] *King Lear*. II. iv.

[2] For something of the spirit of this, compare Edgar in *King Lear*:
> The lamentable change is from the best;
> The worst returns to laughter. [IV. i. 5.]

Makes fear'd and talk'd of more than seen – your son
Will or exceed the common, or be caught
With cautelous baits and practice. [IV. i. 27.]

The expression of this farewell answers to an emotional state of some
complexity. Coriolanus is attempting to see the unknown dangers
which await him in the light of his own past; they are further
challenges, 'hazards' which he will offer, as he has been accustomed
to do, for the 'solace' of his formidable mother. The assertion of
continuity, however, is made in a new situation, which nothing in
his past experience has prepared him to meet. 'Alone', severed
henceforth from all that has supported or sustained him, he seeks
refuge in romantic self-transformation; if he now needs to see himself as a 'lonely dragon', 'fear'd' and 'talk'd of' in the future as in the
past, it is because he feels himself out of depth in the world which
awaits him and will no longer be able to lean upon the support for
which his nature craves. Beyond the rhetoric and the poetry, hope
and fear balance one another inconclusively in his mind: hope that
he will continue to be true to the heroic image he has formed for
himself and thereby 'exceed the common', stand out from the normal
run of mankind; fear that this consistency may be tested, not by
exposure to the open hazards which he has been brought up to face
and overcome, but by more insidious perils which proceed from his
own nature and which he senses himself, at this decisive crisis in his
fortunes, particularly ill-fitted to resist.

Volumnia, indeed, is not deceived as to her son's true situation.
'Whither wilt thou go?' she asks, and begs him to

determine on some course,
More than a wild expousture to each chance
That starts i' the way before thee. [IV. i. 35.]

This appeal to a sense of reality moves Coriolanus, not least, perhaps,
because it touches upon his own uncertainty. The tongue-tied
intensity of his exclamation – 'O, the gods!' – stands out from the
more fluent rhetoric that has gone before. The moment of doubt, if it
exists, is at once covered by further assertion; describing himself as
'yet unbruis'd' by fortune, he faces the future with a show of spirit:

While I remain above the ground, you shall
Hear from me still, and never of me aught
But what is like me formerly. [IV. i. 51.]

His own career will lend a distinctive irony to these professions,
leading him to seek the ruin of his fellow-countrymen and to achieve

his own; but this craving for consistency, this projection into the unknown future of a confidence derived from his heroic past, will lend to his manifest ruin the force of personal tragedy.

Coriolanus' next appearance will bring him face to face with Aufidius under circumstances that neither can have foreseen. Their meeting is preceded, not accidentally, by the curious episode (IV. iii) which brings together a Volscian spy and a Roman for a brief encounter on the highway. The meeting, with its suggestion of cynicism and confused loyalties, has its own significance for what is to follow. The Roman admits frankly that his city is threatened by 'strange insurrections'. He also foresees, without apparent regret, the retribution which is from now on increasingly reflected in imagery of consuming fire; for if he can report that the 'main blaze' of internal strife in the city has been quenched by Coriolanus' banishment, the threat of its aggravated return 'lies glowing . . . and is almost mature for the violent breaking-out'. He also has views on the implications of this situation for Rome's chief enemy; as one who subscribes readily to the idea, born of worldly experience and expressed with a certain cynical satisfaction, that 'the fittest time to corrupt a man's wife is when she's fallen out with her husband', he has no difficulty in believing that 'your *noble* Tullus Aufidius' (the implications of the adjective are not, in the context, unequivocal) 'will appear well' in the wars, 'his great opposer being now in no request of his country'. The effect of the exchange is to suggest that the fortunes of Romans and Volscians are involved, like those of their respective champions, in a common and finally ironic destiny; as much is implied by these two observers who, meeting as natural enemies, yet proceed happily to celebrate the chance which has brought them together. 'I am most fortunate', as the Volscian puts it, 'thus accidentally to encounter you; you have ended my business, and I will merrily accompany you home'. Over supper the Roman will lightheartedly inform his new acquaintance of 'most strange things' concerning his own city, 'all tending to the good of their adversaries'. There could hardly be a more appropriate introduction to the strange encounter which immediately follows.

Coriolanus, when we next find him in Antium (IV. iv), shows himself aware of the equivocal situation which his presence there implies. In the world into which circumstances have so unaccountably thrust him, every reversal of loyalty is conceivable. Sworn friends, whose 'double bosoms *seem* to wear one heart', who appear to 'twin' in 'love unseparable', may find themselves opposed 'on the dissension of a doit', whilst rivals such as Aufidius and himself, who formerly lived for one another's overthrow, will now,

by some chance,
Some trick not worth an egg, [IV. iv. 20.][1]

be brought together to 'interjoin their issues'. His unnatural determination is only balanced by the uncertainty of his reception; for
Aufidius may either slay him, and so do 'fair justice' upon his enemy,
or accept his unnatural offer of service. The entire action is marked
from this point by the web of contradictions which, proceeding from
the hero's own decision, can only end by involving him in
destruction.

These contradictions are mirrored in the terms in which Coriolanus
now addresses himself to his rival (IV. v). Here, perhaps more than
elsewhere, the study of the words and turns of phrase by which
Shakespeare has modified North's text, which he follows closely at
this point,[2] is revealing. Arrogance, with a touch of enigmatic
bitterness, marks his preliminary self-discovery to the Volscian
servants. Having cut himself off from Rome, exiled himself to what
he describes bitterly as 'the city of kites and crows', he recognizes
that he has made himself acceptable to none:

I have deserved no better entertainment,
In being Coriolanus. [IV. v. 10.]

The sense of his untenable position leads him, as though in compensation, to assume an attitude of defiance. Stressing the 'hurt and
mischief' which he has done to the Volscians he rises, as though foreseeing his enemy's reaction, to a proud assertion of the painful service,

The extreme dangers, and the drops of blood
Shed for my thankless country; [IV. v. 74.]

all this, he insists, gained for him in Rome the surname which must
be most galling to those to whom he now offers his services. These
glories, however, belong to the past. In the present, 'only that name
survives'; the rest has been erased by the 'cruelty and envy' of his
own people, added to the betrayal of the 'dastard nobles' who have

suffer'd me by the voice of slaves to be
Whoop'd out of Rome. [IV. v. 83.]

In its tense and passionate concentration, the hero's declaration

---

[1] Compare, for the phrase, Hamlet's
. . . all that fortune, death and danger done,
Even for an egg-shell. [*Hamlet* IV. iv. 52.]

[2] North's text for this speech may be conveniently found in Kenneth Muir op.
cit. p. 220–21.

hovers between outraged nobility and resentment, the personal 'spite' which has moved him to a resolution which he knows to be indefensible in order to be 'full quit of these my banishers'.

With his mind thus relieved of the load of personal animus which weighs upon it, Coriolanus passes to his main purpose: an appeal, at once eloquent and characteristically naïve, to his life-long enemy to 'make my misery serve thy turn'. It is appropriate that this proposal, dedicated to negation and destruction, should turn, before it ends, into the voice of 'spleen', taking refuge from its own vanity in an empty caricature of purpose:

> I will fight
> Against my canker'd country with the spleen
> Of all the under fiends. [IV. v. 96.]

Whatever voice speaks here, it is not that of heroism or firm consistency. The true spirit of his resolution is contained in Coriolanus' final admission that, if his offer is not accepted, he is 'longer to live most weary'; moved by the sense of vanity which, from now on, dogs his career, he offers his throat to be cut by his rival, even as, with a remnant of his native pride, he stresses yet again the harm he has done to the enemy into whose hands he is now delivering himself.

If Coriolanus thus shows himself lost in a world of ill-considered perplexities, Aufidius' reply – his most considerable utterance in the play – is notably and, in view of his normal attitudes, strangely romantic in tone:

> Let me twine
> Mine arms about that body, where against
> My grained ash an hundred times hath broke,
> And scarr'd the moon with splinters: here I clip
> The anvil of my sword, and do contest
> As hotly and as nobly with thy love
> As ever in ambitious strength I did
> Contend against thy valour. Know thou first,
> I loved the maid I married; never man
> Sigh'd truer breath; but that I see thee here,
> Thou noble thing! more dances my rapt heart
> Than when I first my wedded mistress saw
> Bestride my threshold. [IV. v. 112.]

It seems curious at first sight that Aufidius, habitually moved by envy and emulation, should give fine expression to the ecstatic values of war at the very moment when Coriolanus is finally and irrevocably renouncing them. The inconsistency, however, is true to the tragic conception, in which contradiction plays an essential part.

Aufidius, who welcomes his former enemy so generously, will not on that account be the less ready to take advantage of his weakness. Heroism, which his rival has always recognized, and consuming jealousy live together in his nature: in much the same way, Coriolanus himself is divided between heroic integrity and an intimate sense of failure. Shakespeare's sense of human complexity, never more clearly manifest than in his estimate of public motives, confers upon this decisive meeting a distinctive note of tragic irony.

The later stages of Aufidius' welcome, indeed, notably modify the opening lyricism. The romantic values of war are replaced by an emphasis on tough physical rivalry –

> I had purpose
> Once more to hew thy target from thy brawn – [IV. v. 125.]

and by the recalling of a dream in which he has seen himself closely involved with his rival, 'Unbuckling helms, fisting each other's throat', engrossed by the clash of armed bodies in ruthless conflict. After this transition, the speech ends on a combination of offered friendship and careful calculation. Aufidius confers upon Coriolanus the leadership of his own 'revenges', not simply out of deference to his soldiership, but because he is 'best experienced' to know 'his country's strength and weakness' and so to bring about its ruin. Upon these conditions he declares himself ready to greet his one-time opponent as 'more a friend than e'er an enemy'; but there is an undertone in the rounding-off of his welcoming gesture 'Yet, Marcius, that was much' – which suggests that this strange coincidence, though acceptable while it serves the turn of the moment, must not be expected to last.

Aufidius' servants, indeed, have few illusions in this respect. They have seen their general astonishingly 'make a mistress' of his greater rival and 'turn up the white o' the eye', not without a suggestion of hypocrisy, 'to his discourse'. What he stands to gain by so doing is, in their view, another matter. 'Cut i' the middle, and but one half of what he was yesterday', the greater part of his reputation has passed to his enemy. Coriolanus, at all events, has been set brutally in motion against his own countrymen: 'He'll go, he says, and sowle the porter of Rome gates by the ears; he will mow down all before him, and leave his passage poll'd'. To the servants, whom the issues at stake fail to move to any intimate concern, this state of things is an acceptable prelude to a 'stirring world'; for war, in their view, 'exceeds peace, as far as day doth night', being 'spritely, waking, audible, and full of vent', where the contrary state is 'a very apoplexy, lethargy, mull'd, deaf, sleepy, insensible', 'a getter of more bastard children than war's a destroyer of men'. In this position, the last word rests, naturally enough, with the open cynicism implied in the servant's terse observation, 'I hope to see Romans as cheap as Volscians'. There could be no better summary of the spirit of disillusioned realism which, throughout this play, so disconcertingly lends its distinctive irony to the development of the tragic theme.

Whilst Coriolanus is thus completing his reconciliation with his enemy, the tribunes in Rome bask complacently in the shadow of a comfortable peace: the peace, indeed, upon which Aufidius' servants have just passed their incisive comments. 'His remedies are tame i' the present peace', says Sicinius of the banished Consul; adding, not without truth, that his friends would have preferred to see their city less fortunate:

> Here do we make his friends
> Blush that the world goes well; who rather had,
> Though they themselves did suffer by't, behold
> Dissentious numbers pestering streets than see
> Our tradesmen singing in their shops and going
> About their functions friendly. [IV. vi. 4.]

The balance of judgement is, as ever, admirably maintained. The tribune, for all his complacency, touches on the real limitations of patrician patriotism; he can also point to the true advantages of social peace. The friendliness of the tradesmen 'singing' as they go about their legitimate affairs points to a reality outside the narrow outlook of those who despise them; equally, however, in recognizing this reality, it fails to take into account the flimsy foundations upon which peace itself rests and the menace which is already gathering beyond the city walls.

To Menenius, meanwhile, grown 'most tired' and unusually deferential, the tribunes turn to savour the fruits of their victory. 'Your Coriolanus is not much miss'd', 'the commonwealth doth stand', they point out complacently; and Menenius is bound to admit that they seem to be in the right. The citizens, for their part, salute their leaders with obsequious deference, which is received with a mixture of satisfaction and contempt:

> This is a happier and more comely time
> Than when these fellows ran about the streets,
> Crying confusion. [IV. vi. 27.]

The absent Coriolanus is dismissed as 'a worthy officer i' the war', but 'insolent' and 'ambitious past all thinking': judgements which carry their share of truth, but spoken in a mood of satisfaction which takes the wish for the reality and thereby invites retribution.

This exchange of comfortable unrealities is interrupted by the ominous news of Aufidius' advance. Menenius greets it with barely concealed pleasure, Brutus with a characteristic gesture of cruelty towards the bearer: 'Go see this rumourer whipp'd'. The patrician, visibly growing in satisfaction as his enemies waver, ironically urges caution, 'lest you shall chance to whip your information', whilst his rival clings to the convenient belief that such unwelcome news 'cannot be', 'is not possible'. Both are overtaken by the further tidings that Marcius has joined Aufidius; and yet a third messenger confirms his approach in consuming 'fire' and destruction. Finally, as the news spread, Cominius appears, to support Menenius in up-braiding the tribunes ('O, you have made good work!') and to stress the imperturbable power and cruelty of the hero's advance:

> He is their god: he leads them like a thing
> Made by some other deity than nature,
> That shapes men better; and they follow him,
> Against us brats, with no less confidence
> Than boys pursuing summer butterflies,
> Or butchers killing flies. [IV. vi. 91.]

The warrior who formerly, in Cominius' great eulogy,[1] bestrode the field like an inhuman engine of destruction is now concentrated upon his avenging passion, transformed into a 'thing' fashioned 'by some other deity than nature', without either the weakness or the compassion proper to his human state. This evocation of ruthless energy is full of varied implication for the hero's approaching tragedy. To be 'other than nature', which Coriolanus is now assuming to be a condition of strength, will turn out to be a sign of weakness. The avenging power which is implacably moving upon Rome will prove to be riven by inconsistencies, to be rather less than more than the impersonal and consuming force it claims to be; but in the meantime, thus fashioned to his own simplified and self-justifying image of himself, the former hero proceeds upon the path he has chosen and his advance against those who are, without his leadership, no more than helpless 'brats' recalls the irresponsible cruelty of children towards butterflies[2] or the action of 'butchers killing flies'.

Menenius receives these tidings with an irrepressibly bitter satis-faction. 'You and your apron-men', he says, 'have made good work', sacrificing Rome to woo 'the breath of garlic-eaters'. The only hope of salvation lies in the avenger's mercy; but who can hope for this after the treatment which Rome herself has meted out to her former hero? 'If he could burn us all into one coal', he concludes, taking up

[1] II. ii. See pp. 233-4 above.
[2] Compare Volumnia in I. iii. See p. 220 above.

yet again the image of consuming fire which now concentrates the impression of the wrath to come, 'We have deserved it'. Paralysed by fear, the citizens can only seek to dissociate themselves from their leaders. 'When I said, banish him, I said, 'twas pity': 'though we willingly consented to his banishment, yet it was against our will'.[1] Sicinius, in a last effort to muster up failing courage, accuses the patricians of desiring the ruin of their own city:

> These are a side that would be glad to have
> This true which they so seem to fear; [IV. vi. 152.]

but those who follow him have by now lost their former confidence at the test of reality. 'I ever said we were i' the wrong when we banished him', their spokesman pleads, wise after the event; and indeed the tribunes themselves now fear the worst, as Brutus implies when he says

> would half my wealth
> Would buy this for a lie! [IV. vi. 161.]

Under the threat of approaching retribution, Roman society is ready to disintegrate once more into faction and mutual reproach.

In the Volscian camp, meanwhile, the presence of the traditional enemy constitutes, scarcely less ominously, a disturbing influence. Aufidius, feeling his reputation shadowed by this uncomfortable association, is nonetheless bound to accept the indignity he has brought upon himself:

> I cannot help it now,
> Unless, by using means, I lame the foot
> Of our design. [IV. vii. 6.]

The choice of cunning as a guide in life brings with it its own form of servitude. Without Coriolanus, the Volscians cannot hope to prevail over Rome; with him, their situation cannot be clear or easy. The hero's own character exasperates this sense of discomfort. He bears himself 'more proudlier' than his rival had supposed possible, though this, on reflection, was only to be expected:

> his nature
> In that's no changeling; and I must excuse
> What cannot be amended. [IV. vii. 10.]

Neither is for the moment in a position to dispense with the other; but when the time comes for a clash which, as Aufidius foresees,

---

[1] Compare, in II. iii. 4, the Third Citizen's reflection on democracy: 'We have power in ourselves to do it, but it is a power that we have no power to do'.

must either 'break his neck or hazard mine', the Volscian already hints that he holds cards of his own in reserve.

These depend, in the last analysis, upon his insight into Coriolanus' own nature. Reflecting on his rival's strange situation, he recognizes the nobility which will make him to his own city

> As is the osprey to the fish, who takes it
> By sovereignty of nature. [IV. vii. 34.]

This unwilling tribute stands out against the harsh and twisted grain of the general argument; but, as Aufidius goes on to consider the various stages which have brought Coriolanus to this turning-point in his fortunes, the outline of his enemy's tragedy assumes a sinister shape in his keen, resentful mind. Having begun as 'a noble servant' to Rome, he soon showed himself unable 'to carry his honours even', to accept serenely the distinctions which his prowess brought him. Even in his moments of most assured triumph, there has been in his nature a visible flaw – call it 'pride' or 'defect of judgement' – which has made him impossibly and unilaterally resolved

> Not to be other than one thing, not moving
> From the casque to the cushion, but commanding peace
> Even with the same austerity and garb
> As he controll'd the war. [IV. vii. 42.]

To this iron inflexibility Aufidius looks for the 'spice of madness' which will destroy him. 'One fire drives out one fire, one nail one nail'; when the hero has served his turn, he will be left in the isolation he has brought upon himself and so at the mercy of his enemy.

For the moment, however, the advance of Coriolanus is marked by a sense of iron consistency. This sense covers an illusion, is fostered by himself to cover weakness; but, until this becomes apparent, it stands out menacingly against a Rome ever more helpless and divided as retribution approaches. Cominius, we learn (V. i), has failed to obtain mercy by 'kneeing' his path to the conqueror who appeared before him as the embodiment of an impersonal force implacably concentrated on the vision of avenging fire:

> He was a kind of nothing, titleless,
> Till he had forg'd himself a name o' the fire
> Of burning Rome. [V. i. 13.]

In relation to this purpose, former loyalties and friendships have become, in the hero's mind, so much indifferent straw in a pile of 'musty chaff':

> he said, 'twas folly,
> For one poor grain or two, to leave unburnt,
> And still to nose the offence. [V. i. 26.]

To Menenius, the image offers an opportunity to rebuke the tribunes once more for their irresponsible behaviour;[1] but they are long past defending themselves and cling to their last hope as they beg him to use his privileged position to plead for the city in its extremity.

Menenius accepts the mission with some hope of success. His arguments to explain away Cominius' failure are very much in character. The hero, he suggests, had met the Roman embassy on an empty stomach:

> The veins unfill'd our blood is cold, and then
> We pout upon the morning, are unapt
> To give or to forgive; but, when we have stuff'd
> These pipes and these conveyances of our blood
> With wine and feeding, we have suppler souls
> Than in our priestlike fasts. [V. i. 52.]

The argument comes appropriately enough from the elderly epicurean who advances it; but to Cominius, who has just seen Coriolanus, it fails to carry conviction. His rejoinder brings a little closer the pervasive image of consuming fire:

> I tell you, he does sit in gold, his eye
> Red as 'twould burn Rome; and his injury
> The gaoler to his pity. [V. i. 64.]

Obsessed by this vision, Cominius can see no hope in an appeal to humanity; but in spite of his pessimism and in anticipation of the decisive meeting to come, he allows himself to consider what may be achieved, as a last resort, by the hero's 'noble mother and his wife'.

First, however, Menenius has to try his hand in vain. The Volscian sentries greet him (V. ii) with blunt forecasts of failure:

> You'll see your Rome embraced with fire, before
> You'll speak with Coriolanus. [V. ii. 7.]

The appeal to friendship is not less tartly met. How can a Roman, one of those who has 'push'd out' the defender of the city, 'think to front his revenges with the easy groans of old women, the virginal palms of your daughters, or with the palsied intercession of such a decayed dotard as you seem to be'? In the stern climate of the moment such hope seems remote indeed, and the sentry returns to

---

[1] You are the musty chaff, and you are smelt
Above the moon; we must be burnt for you. [V. i. 31.]

the implacable evocation of 'the intended fire your city is ready to flame in', to end by dismissing bitingly the 'weak breath' which Menenius seeks to oppose to the approaching fury.

As Coriolanus makes his entry, Menenius affects to treat the sentry with contempt; then, true to his sentimental vein, he makes his appeal as from 'thy old father' to his child: 'O my son, my son! thou art preparing fire for us; look thee, here's water to quench it'. Only at this point, we may note, is this hero, whom his mother has so conspicuously dominated, related to any notion of a father. The appeal falls on deaf ears. True to the impersonality he has imposed upon himself, Coriolanus dismisses his former friend and mentor – for Aufidius' benefit as much as for his own – with a blunt, laconic 'Away!'. In support of this attitude he stresses, in words that will soon bring their appropriate retribution, his renunciation of natural ties. 'Wife, mother, child, I know not!', he affirms, and follows the assertion with an unconscious declaration of the ignominy to which he has sunk:

> My affairs
> Are servanted to others: though I owe
> My revenge properly, my remission lies
> In Volscian breasts. [V. ii. 88.]

He clings, in other words, to the idea of revenge as 'proper', dependant on his own determination; but, for the rest, his will is 'servanted' to those whose purposes can never coincide with his honour.

Thus involved in contradiction, Coriolanus can only seek to cover the uneasiness at his heart by a show of resolute ruthlessness:

> Mine ears against your suits are stronger than
> Your gates against my force. [V. ii. 94.]

'Force', as always, is set against natural feeling, and in the gap which separates these opposites lies the hero's ruin. Already, almost in spite of himself, he hands a letter to Menenius – 'for I loved thee' – and then, sensing that the gesture may be held to imply weakness, turns to Aufidius with a show of firmness:

> This man, Aufidius,
> Was my beloved in Rome; yet thou behold'st. [V. ii. 98.]

Aufidius' comment – 'You keep a constant temper' – is carefully non-committal; what else, it suggests, can Coriolanus do, having surrendered his freedom of action to his enemies? To Menenius, meanwhile, the rejection comes as a bitter blow, and under the weight of it he turns away towards Rome: 'He that hath a will to die by himself fears it not from another: let your general do his worst'.

Against this observation, the reflection of a lonely and disillusioned old age, the Volscian sentries set their own arrogant confidence in a Coriolanus who appears to them, on the eve of his decisive test, the 'rock', 'the oak not to be windshaken'.

The final confrontation between the hero and his family (V. iii) reveals the unreality upon which this confidence is founded. It is beyond doubt one of Shakespeare's most moving and eloquent creations. As the culminating point in a long and consistent development, we cannot fail to respond to the tragedy of the hero's dilemma; but it would be falsifying the dramatic intention not to give proper weight at the same time to the irony which is equally a distinctive feature of the situation. Mother and son, brought together for the last time, are obliged by the circumstances of their meeting to face the disconcerting reality of their relationship. Coriolanus, who has learnt from Volumnia to place supreme value upon military glory and personal honour, finds himself passionately dedicated to an ignoble and unnatural revenge; and she, who has moulded him from childhood to the image of her own intense and narrow consistency, is faced with the prospect of seeing all that she holds most dear destroyed, in the name of that consistency, by a monster of her own creation. This disaster she averts by her eloquent appeal to natural ties and loyalties; but, precisely because these intimate bonds have been imperfectly or one-sidedly mirrored in their own relationship, the return to peace and harmony in public life is paid for, still appropriately, by her son's downfall.

The scene opens – ironically enough in view of what is to follow – with Coriolanus displaying his firmness for the benefit of his new allies: 'You must report to the Volscian lords how plainly I have borne this business'. From now on, he declares,

> fresh embassies and suits,
> Nor from the state nor private friends, hereafter
> Will I lend ear to; [V. iii. 17.]

but the declaration is immediately followed by the shouts which greet the approach of Volumnia and, with her, of his final confrontation with himself and his situation. His reaction to the interruption, uttered even before he knows its cause, strikingly reflects the precarious nature of his resolve:

> What shout is this?
> Shall I be tempted to infringe my vow
> In the same time 'tis made? I will not. [V. iii. 19.]

There could be no clearer anticipation of all that is to come. The self-appointed man of steel is about to be revealed in his true frailty,

confronted with the humanity he has so obstinately sought to deny;
though it is his tragedy that this necessary return to the foundations
of his moral being can only be accomplished in the process of breaking a nature which is indisposed to bow before reality.

All this is a significant prelude to the entry of the suppliants.
Coriolanus' greeting of them, like the words he has just spoken, is
wrapped in contradiction. His first utterance is a spontaneous recognition of natural duty. His welcome to 'my wife' is followed, as the
memory of filial devotion returns to flood his being, by an act of
reverence to

> the honoured mould
> Wherein this trunk was fram'd; [V. iii. 22.]

and the double apostrophe leads, naturally and intimately, to an
affectionate greeting for 'the grandson to her blood'. To these
words, however, which reveal so much more than he can now afford
to show, he adds, immediately and as though to cover himself, an
emphatic repudiation of normal affection. 'All bond and privilege
of nature, break!', he cries, almost in desperation. Let 'obstinacy'
prevail over natural emotion, absolve him from all normal conceptions
of duty. The stress lies, as his tragic situation imposes, on the rejection
of nature. To be stiffly 'obstinate' is to be 'virtuous', because the
speaker's dedication to his unnatural purpose demands it; even
those 'dove's eyes' which could, under other circumstances, make
gods 'forsworn' – and the poignancy of the phrase is already charged
with the pressure of rejected emotions – must not now prevail upon
him to set aside the purpose upon which he has so unnaturally staked
his entire being.

This self-imposed rigidity, however, is already accompanied by
signs of weakening purpose. For all his show of firmness, Coriolanus
goes on to a notable admission:

> I melt, and am not
> Of stronger earth than others. [V. iii. 28.]

To see his mother bowed before him in supplication is, he adds in a
tone of shocked bewilderment,

> As if Olympus to a molehill should
> In supplication nod; [V. iii. 30.]

for to look up in veneration to her, and through her to the values
upon which his conception of his own 'nobility' has always rested,
has been his deepest source of inspiration. Deprived of this support,
cast upon a world which he finds it impossible to understand or
accept, his own purposes have become grotesque, inhuman, and

unnatural; and the time has come for 'nature' to reassert herself, even at the cost of his ruin. The presence of his son, implying a further intercession which 'Great nature cries, "Deny not"', points compulsively in the same direction.

Having admitted so much, and for himself so dangerously, Coriolanus takes refuge in further emphatic denials of instinct and family alike. The speech ends, less in the assertion of determined purpose at which it aims, than in a confession of intimate puzzlement:

> Let the Volsces
> Plough Rome, and harrow Italy: I'll never
> Be such a gosling to obey instinct, but stand,
> As if a man were author of himself
> And knew no other kin. [V. iii. 33.]

The strange conclusion is indeed revealing. Coriolanus, seeks, by sheer emphasis of assertion, to return to the simplicity of purpose which his being craves. Let the Volscians, whom he has so often defeated in his country's service, 'plough Rome' and bring Italy to ruin. These monstrous ends, the denial of everything for which he has so far lived, have become natural and acceptable (or so he would like to force himself to believe) in the situation which has been imposed upon him. To 'obey instinct', by accepting the validity of the intimate emotion he has just allowed himself to reveal, is – so he seeks to believe – to confess himself a 'gosling', incapable of asserting integrity of will in his new situation. Self-depreciation here is a cover for the doubt and inner contradiction which, once admitted, must involve him in disaster. To smother the powerful voice of 'instinct' Coriolanus needs to postulate the impossible, to assert that a man may be 'author of himself' and know 'no other kin'. The effect is to make him a renegade, not only to his city and to the family which has bred him, but – in a sense deeper than he can yet fully understand – to his own being.

When he ceases to speak, enough has been said to show where the hero's resolution will be vulnerable. As though to play upon his weakness, his wife now breaks her habitual silence with the most direct of pleas to 'my lord and husband'; and, in a further effort to escape from himself, Coriolanus recognizes the force of the blow even as he makes to turn it aside. 'These eyes', he says, 'are not the same I wore in Rome'. If they are not so, it is because he is no longer the man he was; and because the remnants of his former self still exist beneath the mask of his perverse consistency it is not long before his true feelings compel expression. The first indication of what is to come is a recognition of the clumsiness with which, like a 'dull actor' who has forgotten the lines assigned to him, he moves towards the exposure of his 'full disgrace'. The admission leads naturally to a more personal expression of the emotions which, do what he will to smother them, remain so close to his heart. 'Best of my flesh', he salutes his wife with rare and intimate intensity, and goes on to beg forgiveness for the 'tyranny' which his attitude towards her implies; but, once feeling has thus forced its way to the surface, he makes yet again to cover it, pleads to be allowed to maintain the fiction he has chosen to present to the world:

> do not say,
> For that, 'Forgive our Romans'. [V. iii. 43.]

The plea, however, is already advanced in the name of a lost cause, and the emotion he seeks to repudiate finds issue, immediately, in a further lyrical outburst which gains enormously by contrast with Virgilia's habitual reticence and with his own assertions of iron sufficiency:

> O, a kiss
> Long as my exile, sweet as my revenge!
> Now, by the jealous queen of heaven, that kiss
> I carried from thee, dear, and my true lip
> Hath virgin'd it e'er since. [V. iii. 44.]

Beneath the depth of feeling, the sense of a return, through emotions so long and so perversely excluded, to the foundations of the speaker's being, there lies a further revelation of character. The emphasis on virgin purity, so intense and beautiful in its expression, answers to an essential simplicity of nature: the simplicity which underlies, on its more positive side, the code of martial 'honour' for which he has lived and which he cannot, without involving himself in ruin, sever from its intimate inspiration. Because the simplicity is true, dramatically convincing in its presentation, Coriolanus' downfall must affect us as truly tragic; because his own perverse choices lead him irrevocably to deny it, a pitiless element of irony shadows his end.

Even closer to Coriolanus' dilemma are the words which follow. Recalling the presence, before him and in supplication, of the mother who has dominated his life, he repudiates his own resolution as so much idle 'prating', reproaches himself for having left her so long 'unsaluted'. The gesture of natural submission at once imposes itself:

> sink, my knee, i' the earth;
> Of thy deep duty more impression show
> Than that of common sons. [V. iii. 50.]

There could be no better comment on the determination, so recently

s

asserted, to show himself 'author' of his own decisions, autonomous, released from the ties of nature. As the hero's knee bends, a frame of tense and self-imposed rigidity bows to the reality it has sought to evade, even while it seeks, in a vestige of obstinate pride, to assert its devotion in terms more absolute than those afforded to 'common sons'. The emphasis cannot conceal the reality of the transformation which is taking place before our eyes. Nature, so long and so vainly denied, is beginning to reassert herself. The way is open for Volumnia to press her plea and to compass, through her very success, the downfall which her son's choices have from the first implied.

Her initial words are a recall to the ties he has so unnaturally sought to repudiate. 'Stand up, *blest*': the simple word of affection balances perfectly the situation which has obliged her to humiliate her pride, to kneel on the hard earth, 'with no softer cushion than the flint', in protest against her son's determination. She has been forced, in effect, 'unproperly' to 'show duty',

> as mistaken all this while
> Between the child and parent. [V. iii. 55.]

The reproof is charged with implications which, poignant as they are on the personal level, transcend the immediate dramatic situation, relating it to a statement of universal principle. Repeatedly in Shakespeare's later plays,[1] the concept of reconciliation finds dramatic expression when the child kneels before its parents to receive the grace of blessing. Here, in reversal of this relationship, it is the mother who kneels; but the affront thus offered to nature is so shaking, so contrary to the permanent demands of life, that it suffices to overcome the son's rigidity and to bring him back to his place in the order he has offended. Coriolanus' answer to her gesture of supplication is, in effect, a return to the essence of their relationship. 'Your knee to me? to your corrected son?'; his sense of an unnatural inversion of pieties is strong enough to reflect itself, as the full implication of his decisions begins to come home to him, in an eloquent evocation of cosmic chaos:

> Then let the pebbles on the hungry beach
> Fillip the stars; then let the mutinous winds
> Strike the proud cedars 'gainst the fiery sun,
> Murdering impossibility, to make
> What cannot be, slight work. [V. iii. 58.]

In the tension of its heightened rhetoric, this amounts to an admission that the resolution Coriolanus has taken upon himself is contrary to nature and therefore, in the long run, must fail to assert itself,

[1] See my book *Shakespeare: The Last Phase* (London, 1954).

'cannot be'. Volumnia is not slow to realize her advantage. She drives it home by affirming the reality of the bond which unites them in language at once simple and charged with feeling. 'Thou art *my* warrior', she says, with what is in effect a proud affirmation of her ascendancy, and adds, stressing the intimacy of a bond before which all lesser loyalties must bow in recognition, the single, decisive phrase 'I holp to frame thee'.

In further support of this assault upon the neglected foundations of his being, she now brings forward Virgilia. His wife's presence draws from Coriolanus an outburst in which purity is once more evoked in the splendid and characteristic lyricism of his lost simplicities. He salutes in her 'the noble sister of Publicola', 'the moon of Rome',

> chaste as the icicle
> That's curded by the frost from purest snow
> And hangs on Dian's temple. [V. iii. 65.]

The words, in their intense and concentrated emotion, throw light upon the speaker's own nature, illuminate the tensions which will finally undo his declared determination. This is, on its intimate side, the ideal which has made him what he is, which he cannot, without doing violence to his nature, repudiate. To round off her plea, it only remains for Volumnia to bring forward his son, a 'poor epitome' of himself, with the prayer that he may come in time to inherit his father's true nobility, the image which belongs to family, friends, and city, not that which is now so unnaturally turned against all three. Coriolanus' response to this last appeal, his prayer that the 'god of soldiers' may fill his son's thoughts with 'nobleness', and so make him stand out 'like a great sea-mark', 'invulnerable' to the shame which he senses in himself, reflects a hero who is seeking, albeit obscurely, through his son some measure of compensation for his own ignominy.

Volumnia, as she feels her natural authority thus reasserting itself, causes the boy to kneel in support of her embassy. 'Your knee, sirrah': the terse command is admirably in character, and through the gesture which it imposes the presentation of her case is made complete:

> Even he, your wife, this lady, and myself
> Are suitors to you. [V. iii. 77.]

Coriolanus is now left to choose between alternatives which lead either way to ruin. Aware that in proposing to act as 'author of himself', he has in fact undertaken to attempt the impossible, he seeks once more, but in terms curiously lame, empty of inner conviction, to arm himself against the crisis he foresees:

> The thing I have forsworn to grant may never
> Be held by you denials. [V. iii. 80.]

The statement amounts to a plea to those before him to refrain from
undermining his resolution, to leave him the consistency to which, as
it slips from him, he feels the need somehow to cling:

> Do not bid me
> Dismiss my soldiers . . .
> . . . tell me not
> Wherein I seem unnatural. [V. iii. 81, 83.]

Nothing could indicate more clearly the extent of his mother's victory
in this strange, unnatural contest of wills. Coriolanus is, in effect,
horrified to find where his own choices have led him. Moved by this
horror he begs, in a last desperate attempt to escape the consequences which he now sees unfolding themselves before him, to be
allowed to cling to the fiction of firm resolve which has become
associated in his mind, as the one remaining constant in a world of
shattered certainties, with the determination to exact revenge:

> desire not
> To allay my rages and revenges with
> Your colder reasons. [V. iii. 84.]

The certainties, however, have become by this time illusions, sur-
vivals from the wreckage of his integrity. In seeking to dismiss as
'colder reasons' the considerations which are now forcing themselves
so inexorably upon him, and in the effort to cling to his passionate
'rages and revenges' as somehow guaranteeing his moral consistency, Coriolanus comes very close to recognizing the tragic split
which, deriving from the obscure intensities which have at once
shaped and flawed his heroic stature, is now visibly widening in his
perplexed and shattered conscience.

Volumnia, in reply, lays the burden of choice squarely and, as it
must seem to him, ruthlessly upon her son. 'We will ask', she says,

> That, if you fail in our requests, the blame
> May hang upon your hardness. [V. iii. 90.]

Thus confronted with his responsibility, Coriolanus seeks refuge for
the last time in evasion, in an empty show of the confidence he can
no longer feel:

> Aufidius, and you Volscians, mark; for we'll
> Hear nought from Rome in private; [V. iii. 92.]

by so doing, far from recovering the certainty he has lost, he invites the presence of hostile witnesses to his collapse. The studied remoteness of his final gesture to the suppliants – 'Your request' – cannot conceal the fact that he has overstepped the limits of safety, that his mind already harbours a recognition of his need to capitulate. The positions in this tense clash of wills are by now reversed, leading inevitably to the avenger's collapse and to the triumph of those who came to beg his mercy. Volumnia, fully aware of the advantage which her motherhood has placed in her hands, is ready to concentrate all the emotional resources at her command upon a supreme appeal to which nothing in her son's nature can suggest an effective answer.

Her opening line of attack still rests upon pathos, stresses the sorrowful condition of the suppliants, deprived respectively of a father, a husband, and a son, reduced to the misery which their 'raiment' and 'state of bodies' betoken. The reversal of nature which this situation visibly reveals remains the foundation of her plea. The sight of him, which should have made their eyes 'flow with joy, hearts dance with comforts', seems to have led in fact only to an unnatural grief, '*Constrains* them weep and shake with fear and sorrow'; the simple intensity of phrase at this point, so true and rhythmically appropriate in contrast to the cumulative oratory in which it is embedded, is in itself a triumph of dramatic expression. Emotion, deprived of its natural fulfilment, appeals to the pent-up feelings which the hero, silent and on guard against his own nature, is still trying, clumsily and impossibly, to keep under control. Thus prepared, the way is open for the final and supremely effective presentation of a picture which involves the reversal of every spontaneous, natural value in Coriolanus' proposed course of action. 'Mother, wife, and child' must be ready to see 'the son, the husband, and the father' engaged, most monstrously, in

tearing
His country's bowels out. [V. iii. 102.]

The ruthless brutality of the phrase, the culmination of so many that have gone before, makes a most striking foil to the appeal to filial tenderness upon which the argument rests.

By his choice, indeed, Coriolanus has imposed upon those closest to him an intolerable decision. 'Bound' to pray for their country's well-being, and yet 'bound' equally to desire the victory of their own kin (the reiteration of the phrase 'wherein we are bound' is wonderfully effective) the suppliants must either betray Rome, 'our dear nurse', or else, in the hero's own person, abandon 'our comfort in the country'. The unnatural alternative – and it is Volumnia's aim, by stressing its intolerable nature, to bring it to resolution – is presented in terms of Coriolanus' own possible futures. He must either be led prisoner by the defenders of his native city (and the emphasis is on 'manacles', on the iron constraint which must, in this event, answer to his new status as 'a foreign miscreant') or else, by another beautifully conceived and characteristic effect, find grotesque fulfilment when he is in a position to

> Triumphantly tread on thy country's ruin;

in the latter event, his victory will be the supremely unnatural one which can only lead him to

> bear the palm for having bravely shed
> Thy wife and children's blood. [V. iii. 117.]

Faced by the alternatives thus bestowed upon her by her son (and yet could it not be argued that her own nature, by imposing itself immoderately upon him, has in some sense conceived this destiny?), Volumnia announces her readiness to take her 'fortune' into her own hands. If he cannot rise above himself to show the 'noble grace' of a true hero, so using his power as to reconcile 'both parts' rather than 'to seek the end of one',

> thou shalt no sooner
> March to assault thy country than to tread –
> Trust to't, thou shalt not – on thy mother's womb,
> That brought thee to this world. [V. iii. 122.]

No image of horror could be better calculated to strike at Coriolanus' deepest emotions, and to destroy his declared inflexibility. By the end of this speech, his remaining faith in himself has been undermined, the sapping by his own act of the deepest foundations of his being brought home to him. The defiance of the boy, to whom his father should look in nature to keep his name 'living to time', but who now joins in repudiating him –

> A' shall not tread on me;
> I'll run away till I am bigger, but then I'll fight – [V. iii. 127.]

emphasizes the reality of his situation with intolerable effect.

Shattered by this cumulative assault, Coriolanus visibly retreats. 'I have sat too long', he says, and adds the revealing admission,

> Not of a woman's tenderness to be,
> Requires nor child nor woman's face to see. [V. iii. 129.]

He confesses, in other words, to natural emotion, whilst making the gesture of evading it. Volumnia has now reached the point when she can effectively call upon reason to widen the breach that her appeal to filial instinct has opened. To save the Romans from destruction, she argues, need not be to turn against his new friends; the 'honour' he has pledged to them is not, properly conceived, at stake in his decision. The stated object of her plea is reconciliation, its end a peace for which he will be blest by both parties to this sterile conflict. To sack Rome, on the other hand, is to leave behind him an epitaph of scorn, which will run thus:

> 'The man was noble,
> But with his last attempt he wip'd it out,
> Destroy'd his country; and his name remains
> To the ensuing age abhorr'd'. [V. iii. 145.]

The appeal is to the values of honour and *nobility* which the hero has derived from his mother, upon which his faith in his integrity has been founded, and which she is now using, with profound irony, to undermine his false, impossible consistency. Addressing him, with a last touch of intimacy – 'Speak to me, son' – as one who, following her precepts, has 'so affected the fine strains of honour' as to 'imitate the graces of the gods', she now urges upon him a course for which nothing in her own education of him has prepared him. He, who formerly, not without a touch of grotesque exaggeration, aspired 'To tear with thunder the wide cheeks o' the air', must now mould himself to clemency, must so comport himself as

> to charge thy sulphur with a bolt
> That should but rive an oak. [V. iii. 152.]

The new plea is made in the name of the divine prerogative of mercy; unfortunately, coming from the mother who has for so long exalted his ruthlessness as a warlike virtue, it amounts at this stage to an invitation to reverse a decision upon which his entire course of life has been, however impossibly, founded, and so to destroy the belief in himself which she has always required of him. For a 'noble man' to persist in the unnatural pursuit of his revenge is not, indeed, 'honourable'. Of this dishonour the presence before him of his mother, kneeling in supplication, is tangible proof; yet – we must add – the irony which colours the tragic situation and makes its disastrous resolution inevitable stems from the fact that everything in their previous relationship has made the change of purpose which she now exacts from him inconceivable.

Having made her point, Volumnia returns to the emotional ground of her appeal, calling upon Virgilia – 'He cares not for your weeping' – and on the boy to support her. 'No man in the world' is more 'bound' to his mother; and yet, she suggests with supremely galling intention, even this he, of all men, seems to have forgotten:

> yet here he lets me prate
> Like one i' the stocks. [V. iii. 159.]

Her love, again, is contrasted most effectively, through a typically homely image, with the supremely unnatural fact of his indifference:

> Thou hast never in thy life
> Show'd thy dear mother any courtesy. [V. iii. 160.]

That this should be said of Coriolanus is a supreme stroke of irony, to which the brusque domestic endearment which follows adds its own effect:

> When she, poor hen, fond of no second brood,
> Has cluck'd thee to the wars, and safely home,
> Loaden with honour. [V. iii. 162.]

The mother's *possession* of her son's emotional being, now about to assert itself triumphantly in imposing his surrender to her incomprehensibly changed demands upon him, could hardly be more effectively stated.

It has become, indeed, Volumnia's intention to force Coriolanus to make the choice which, intolerable as it is, is the only one open to him. The dilemma, as she represents it, is brought home to him with irresistible logic. Either her request is 'unjust', which neither reason nor natural feeling can show, or he is himself unnatural:

> if it be not so,
> Thou art not honest, and the gods will plague thee,
> That thou restrain'st from me the duty which
> To a mother's part belongs. [V. iii. 165.]

Embarrassed and visibly weakening, but still incompletely understanding his situation, Coriolanus turns away. At her behest, her companions kneel, accusing him of showing more 'pride' than 'pity' to his own kin. Repulsed, they will return to Rome to 'die among our neighbours'; but, before they go, and with the boy once more reinforcing their plea (though Volumnia must know by now that her son's silence betokens surrender), she prepares to leave him with a final and supremely galling accusation of dishonour:

> This fellow had a Volscian to his mother;
> His wife is in Corioli, and his child
> Like him by chance. [V. iii. 178.]

The final implication of his son's bastardy is perhaps, for Coriolanus, the most telling blow of all. As Volumnia, her work done, returns to silence, the background is still that of a city soon to be 'afire', which –

when the moment for its destruction comes – will give her motive to denounce him for the last time.

Coriolanus is left 'silent', holding his mother by the hand and contemplating the sorry spectacle of his shattered integrity. When at last he speaks, the effect is overwhelming in its recognition of disaster. 'O mother, mother!', he exclaims, 'What have you done?' The question comes from one bewildered, conscious not of a true resolution to his conflicting loyalties, but of obscurely threatening deities who look down upon an 'unnatural scene' and 'laugh' at what they see. The sardonic note which has throughout lent the scene a distinctive quality finds issue at this point in a vision of life, as it presents itself to the hero, finally desolate and meaningless. Coriolanus no longer knows where in reality he stands. In bowing to his mother, he is returning to the foundation of his emotional being; but her triumph, though 'happy' to the city of their common devotion, must be to himself 'most dangerous', even 'mortal'. The movement of the verse admirably reflects his inner uncertainty. Left only with the prospect of accepting the fate which he no longer feels any motive to avoid ('let it come'), he turns to Aufidius, who has contemplated the entire exchange in silence, with a pathetic admission of failure:

> though I cannot make true wars,
> I'll frame convenient peace. [V. iii. 190.]

The irony implied in the confession, coming from Coriolanus, that he, who has lived for martial glory, to whom peace has so often seemed an intolerable interruption of the serious business of life, cannot wage 'good wars', but can only hope to make 'convenient peace', is shattering indeed. He follows it with an attempt, strangely lame and halting, to justify himself in the eyes of his new friends:

> Now, good Aufidius,
> Were you in my stead, would you have heard
> A mother less? or granted less, Aufidius? [V. iii. 191.]

The return to nature is accompanied by a plea for moral support, pathetically addressed to those who can have no further use for him. Aufidius, as we might expect, receives it non-committally: 'I was moved withal'. Already it is clear that the world of external realities will not so easily adapt itself to meet the hero in his new attitude of bewildered frailty, or allow him to evade the consequences of his own choices. From now on, Coriolanus moves in a moral limbo from which death alone can release him.

The end of this great scene is appropriately muted into silence. Coriolanus makes an attempt to recapture that superiority to emotion which he has so often claimed as a virtue:

> it is no little thing to make
> Mine eyes to sweat compassion; [V. iii. 195.]

but we must feel by now that the 'compassion' which suited the victorious warrior has become a sign of weakness in the divided vestige of former greatness now before us. His situation is, on any count, intolerable. Having agreed to make peace with Rome, his recent past prevents him from returning there; and so he must turn back with an Aufidius who is now ready to discard him to meet the fate which he has brought upon his own head. The last broken apostrophe: 'O mother! wife!' shows a man groping among the ruin of the intimate feelings so recently, and to such bitter ends, revived in him: a man at sea in his moral judgements and in the world of public realities. Aufidius, content to remain ominously in the background, is ready to exploit the contradiction between 'mercy' and 'honour' in his enemy, whom he still contemplates with the eye of envy: 'out of that', he comments, reflecting on his foreseen advantage,

> I'll work
> Myself a former fortune, [V. iii. 201.]

achieving by guile the supremacy that has so long evaded him in the open field. The tragedy is ready to move rapidly to its inevitable conclusion.

v

As a result of Coriolanus' decision Rome passes (V. iv) from the depth of despair to deliverance. The transition is most effectively compressed into a tense and economical dramatic statement. Menenius' application to the hero of the image of the 'corner-stone' of the Capitol, spoken before the news of Volumnia's success has reached the city, answers to the hard inflexibility which has so recently impressed him in their meeting:

> The tartness of his face sours ripe grapes: when he walks, he moves like an engine, and the ground shrinks before his treading; he is able to pierce a corslet with his eye; talks like a knell, and his hum is a battery. He sits in his state, as a thing made for Alexander. . . He wants nothing of a god but eternity and a heaven to throne in. [V. iv. 19.]

The emphasis rests on bitter and inflexible determination, upon the machine ruthlessly and inhumanly dedicated to ends of destruction.

When Menenius sums up his impression by saying that, except for 'eternity', Coriolanus lacks none of the attributes of divinity, Sicinius – speaking for once profoundly – adds by way of comment, 'Yes, mercy, if you report him truly', only to find confirmation in Menenius' rejoinder: 'there is no more mercy in him than there is milk in a male tiger'. The inhumanity to which Coriolanus has dedicated himself is never more graphically indicated. It is also stressed, however, that the city has brought these calamities upon itself. By banishing their hero, the Romans have failed in respect to their own values; and now that he has returned – in yet another ruthless image – 'to break their necks',[1] the gods who have inspired these values show that 'they respect not us'.

There follows the report that the crowd has turned on the tribunes, whose lives hang in the balance. Then, by a reversal as speedy as it is effective, Rome learns what we already know, that 'the ladies have prevailed', and a contrasted mood of 'merriment', of relief from tension, is set in motion. The new spirit makes itself felt in a poetic transformation, which bursts the iron bonds that have so far re-strained imagination in the public scenes of the play. The messenger is as certain of the truth of his tidings of peace as he is that 'the sun is fire', and he follows up his assertion with a most graphic picture of the returning tide:

Ne'er through an arch so hurried the blown tide – [V. iv. 51.]

as the 'recomforted' swarmed in jubilation through the city gates. The trumpets sound, the drums beat in joyful relief. 'All together', as the stage direction has it,

> The trumpets, sackbuts, psalteries, and fifes,
> Tabors and cymbals and the shouting Romans
> Make the sun dance. [V. iv. 53.]

The effect, by contrast with the preceding weight of menace, is overwhelming, for all the economy of means with which it is achieved. Even the tribunes, whose discomfiture is brought home to them for the last time by Menenius, share the universal relief, 'help the joy'; Volumnia is hailed as 'our patroness, the life of Rome', the 'tribes' are called together to 'praise the gods', 'triumphant fires' are lit in rejoicing and flowers strewn in acclamation before the city's saviours. The meaningless 'noise' that formerly dictated Marcius' banishment by the mob is now to be 'unshouted', as if it had never

---

[1] Compare I. iii. 50.
> He'll beat Aufidius' head below his knee,
> And tread upon his neck,
Quoted on p. 220 above.

been, and the scene which opened under the shadow of imminent doom ends on a swelling note of 'welcome'.

The restoration of peace, however, though it restores Roman society to sane unity and produces these manifestations of life and joy, is powerless to ward off the hero's own fate. Having cut himself off from the natural sources of his strength, his tragedy remains to be sealed. As the last scene (V.v) opens, Aufidius has returned to Corioli to press home his advantage before his rival's return. He describes himself as a man

> by his own alms *empoison'd*,
> And with his charity slain; [V. v. 11.]

the reference to poison, not the first put into his mouth,[1] answers to the bitterness of his moral state. The conspirators around him further exasperate this resentment by hinting at the 'danger' that will shortly threaten him if his rival is not destroyed. They must, however, still proceed as they 'do find the people', whose uncertain reaction only the course of events can determine; for the mob will

> remain uncertain whilst
> 'Twixt you there's difference; but the fall of either
> Makes the survivor heir of all. [V. v. 17.]

The duplicity of Aufidius in this delicate situation is confirmed by his talk of a 'pretext' to strike at his rival, and by the assertion that this pretext can be made to admit of 'a good construction'. Envy and resentment still predominate in his embittered heart:

> I raised him, and I pawn'd
> Mine honour for his truth; [V. v. 21.]

the accusation that Coriolanus has 'water'd his new plants with dews of flattery', so to 'seduce' his friends, is typically and ominously double-edged. Even his rival's pliancy he now interprets as trickery:

> He bow'd his nature, never known before
> But to be rough, unswayable, and free. [V. v. 25.]

What most hurts Aufidius is less the sense of betrayal than the fact that, after having received his former enemy in order to destroy Rome, he has himself come to be regarded as a secondary figure in the common enterprise:

[1] Compare
> My valour's poison'd
> With only suffering stain by him. [I. x. 17.]

at the last
I seem'd his follower, not partner, and
He waged me with his countenance, as if
I had been mercenary. [V. v. 38.]

A stain of mixed motives, egoism and love of power issuing in
treachery and mistrust, spreads through these exchanges; even the
conspirators who surround Aufidius are moved to indignation by the
loss of the expected spoils of Rome. Aufidius' final comment is at
once a declaration of the cynicism which has throughout shadowed
his martial reputation and an exposure of Coriolanus' real weakness:

At a few drops of women's rheum, which are
As cheap as lies, he sold the blood and labour
Of our great action; [V. v. 46.]

only through the fall of the hated rival who has now played into his
hands can Aufidius hope to 'renew' himself in his wounded self-
esteem.

The return of Coriolanus is announced, in contrast with the stealth
and secrecy which has surrounded that of Aufidius, by the blaze of
music and public acclamation, 'splitting the air with noise'. That the
hated Roman has thus been able to impress his own people is,
indeed, one of Aufidius' keenest sources of resentment. Beneath the
rejoicing, however, Coriolanus' position is false, finally untenable;
as one of the conspirators puts it, the 'noise' which acclaims him
comes from those whom an unprejudiced eye must regard as 'patient
fools', 'whose children he hath slain' and who now

their base throats tear
With giving him glory. [V. v. 53.]

'Glory', 'noise': like so much in the earlier part of this tragedy its
conclusion is wrapped in the scepticism of its attitude to public
eminence. It is also in accordance with this attitude that Aufidius
and his associates should decide that Coriolanus is to be killed before
he can speak, thus burying his dangerous 'reasons' with his 'body'.
We learn, finally, on the entry of the lords of the city, that Aufidius
has prepared the ground by advance letters setting his accusations
before the Volscian senate. The net of intrigue is tightly drawn
round a hero who, in his self-imposed isolation, is already lost.

Thus surrounded on every side by hostility and plotting, Coriolanus at last makes his entry. He seems, most typically, unaware that
recent events have changed his relationship to his unnatural allies.
Only thus can we account for the extraordinary naïvety of his
opening salutation:

> I am return'd your soldier;
> No more infected with my country's love
> Than when I parted hence, but still subsisting
> Under your great command. [V. v. 71.]

We may feel, beneath this assumption of confidence, a determination to affirm what the speaker himself knows, in his heart, to be no longer true; that he, of all men, should have come to consider patriotism as an 'infection' is sufficiently revealing. Seeking to justify himself at all costs, he goes on to boast that he has brought 'shame' to his own city; but at this point Aufidius, brushing aside this unbelievably clumsy attempt to obtain approval, bluntly accuses him of being a 'traitor'. The charge is near enough to the truth to rankle, and Coriolanus meets it with a return to the tongue-tied arrogance which has always marked his moments of crisis and unwilling self-revelation. 'Traitor! how now!', 'Hear'st thou, Mars!'; from this moment, all shadow of reasoning abandons his confused and harassed thoughts.

In contrast to this inarticulate reaction, Aufidius' savage comments strike home with an unanswerable irony:

> dost thou think
> I'll grace thee with that robbery, thy stol'n name
> Coriolanus, in Corioli? [V. v. 88.]

Marcius, in his enemy's bitter and scornful accusation, has betrayed 'for certain drops of salt' the cause to which he has sold his integrity; and it is finally absurd that, isolated and exposed by his own choice, he should cling to an illusion of firmness. In Aufidius' accusation, we should note the characteristic tautness, the sharp friction of textures, which gives life to the allegation that his rival has broken his 'oath and resolution' like 'a twist of rotten silk'. The charge, vivid, keen, and supremely biting in its effect, is finally driven home by a stabbing reference to the hero's adolescent dependence:

> at his nurse's tears
> He whin'd and roar'd away your victory,
> That pages blush'd at him, and men of heart
> Look'd wondering at each other. [V. v. 97.]

The fact that Aufidius' own motives are far from direct or clear cannot take from the effect of his words as a reflection of the extent of his rival's tragic failure.

Coriolanus himself, indeed, clearly feels by now the impossible nature of his position. When Aufidius ends by dismissing him as a 'boy of tears' he is driven beyond stammering to a last outburst of indignation in which feeling and incongruity are blended. The accusation, and the contempt which goes with it, run through his mind until death, and he reacts to them with threats and empty scoldings. His heart, 'too great for what contains it'[1], dwells on the word 'boy' with an insistence that covers an intimation of failure which all his indignation cannot finally allay:

> 'tis the first time that ever
> I was forced to scold. [V. v. 105.]

The 'scolding' takes the form of a verbal counter-attack on Aufidius, this 'cur' 'who wears my stripes impress'd upon him', who 'must bear my beating to his grave'. This degeneration of a heroic attitude into empty vituperation covers a final sense of inadequacy. Moved beyond all measure of reason, Coriolanus proceeds to ram his past victories most inopportunely down the throats of those he formerly defeated, and dwells in livid rage on the insult implied in Aufidius' dismissal of himself as 'Boy!'.[2] We must feel, together with the attempted recovery of spirit in one who has allowed his nature to be caught in self-destroying contradictions, the sense that a measure of truth underlies the contemptuous description.

Aufidius, at all events, does not hesitate to take full advantage of his rival's clumsiness 'Why, noble lord!', he exclaims,

> Will you be put in mind of his blind fortune,
> Which was your shame, by this unholy braggart,
> Fore your own eyes and ears? [V. v. 118.]

At this, the conspirators and the Volscian people combine in what is, after all, an act of retribution. Not for nothing has the man before them killed 'my son', 'my daughter', 'my cousin', 'my father'. The plea uttered by one Volscian lord in favour of Coriolanus' nobility, though also valid:

> The man is noble, and his fame folds in
> This orb o' the earth – [V. v. 126.]

falls on deaf ears. To the last the hero's thoughts are fixed on the insult offered him, and on the simplicities of revenge:

> O, that I had him
> With six Aufidiuses, or more, his tribe,
> To use my lawful sword! [V. v. 129.]

[1] Compare Antony on Julius Caesar's death: 'then burst his mighty heart' [*Julius Caesar* III. ii. 191.]

[2] The implications of the word 'Boy!' have been well brought out by Wyndham Lewis in *The Lion and the Fox* (London, 1927).

The tone of contempt contrasts strikingly, and most revealingly, with
the preceding gesture of arrogant nobility:

> If you have writ your annals true, 'tis there,
> That, like an eagle in a dove-cot, I
> Flutter'd your Volscians in Corioli;
> Alone I did it. [V. v. 114.]

'Alone': perhaps here, in the turning into an heroic virtue of what is
in fact a weakness, the isolation from his fellow-men which birth and
prejudice have combined to impose upon him, lies in great part the
key to Coriolanus' tragedy. Both the scolding and the lost dignity
represent some aspects of the truth about this strangely divided,
inopportune hero; and since these aspects do not harmonize, since
he cannot now hope to recover the shattered simplicity which he
abjured with his duty to his city, the tide of vengeance flows over
him with the repeated clamour of 'kill', and Aufidius, in a last gesture
of gratuitous brutality, 'stands on his body' in triumph.

The deed once accomplished and the destruction of heroism complete, the last exchanges of the tragedy fall to a lull, a tardy reaction
against the preceding violence. 'Hold!', call the lords, too late
aghast at what they have accomplished. 'Thou has done a deed
whereat valour will weep', says one of them reproachfully to
Aufidius, and his companion, after a plea for the remnants of dignity
– 'tread not upon him' – calls upon all to be 'quiet', to contemplate
in horrified silence what base rivalry and twisted passion have between them accomplished. Aufidius insists that he has been justified
in cutting off the danger which Coriolanus, now safely dead, must
always in life have presented to the Volscian state; and, though we
know that this is far from a complete or honest statement of his own
motives, he is in part excused by the dispassionate comment of one
of his supporters:

> His own impatience
> Takes from Aufidius a great part of blame. [V. v. 146.]

'Let's make the best of it': on this note of disillusioned conformity,
and on a brief elegiac excursion – in which, however, the bitter
memory of the dead hero's enmity to the Volscians is stressed for the
last time[1] – the play ends.

---

[1]   Though in this city he
Hath widow'd and unchilded many a one,
Which to this hour bewail the injury,
Yet shall he have a noble memory. [V. v. 152.]